MICROSOFT® EXCEL
SMALL BUSINESS CONSULTANT

WINDOWS™ VERSION

MICROSOFT® EXCEL

SMALL BUSINESS CONSULTANT

WINDOWS™ VERSION

STEPHEN L. NELSON

PUBLISHED BY
Microsoft Press
A Division of Microsoft Corporation
One Microsoft Way
Redmond, Washington 98052-6399

Copyright © 1990 by Stephen L. Nelson

All rights reserved. No part of the contents of this book
may be reproduced or transmitted in any form or by any means
without the written permission of the publisher.

Library of Congress Cataloging-in-Publication Data
Nelson, Stephen L., 1959–
    Microsoft Excel small business consultant / Stephen L. Nelson.
       p.   cm.
    ISBN 1-55615-274-4 : $39.95
    1. Microsoft Excel (Computer program)   2. Business--Data
processing.   3. Small business--Data processing.   4. Electronic
spreadsheets.   I. Title.
HF5548.4.M523N454   1990
650'.028'55369--dc20   89-13944
                                                                                           CIP

Printed and bound in the United States of America.

1 2 3 4 5 6 7 8 9 MLML 4 3 2 1 0

Distributed to the book trade in Canada by General Publishing Company, Ltd.

Distributed to the book trade outside the United States and Canada by Penguin Books Ltd.

Penguin Books Ltd., Harmondsworth, Middlesex, England
Penguin Books Australia Ltd., Ringwood, Victoria, Australia
Penguin Books N.Z. Ltd., 182–190 Wairau Road, Auckland 10, New Zealand

British Cataloging in Publication Data available

COMPAQ DESKPRO 386® is a registered trademark of Compaq Computer Corporation. Hercules® is a registered trademark of Hercules Computer Technology. AT®, IBM®, and Personal System/2® are registered trademarks of International Business Machines Corporation. Microsoft® and MS-DOS® are registered trademarks and Windows™ is a trademark of Microsoft Corporation.

This book and the accompanying software are provided "as is" without warranty of any kind as to content, performance, results, or suitability. Warranties of any kind whatsoever, including those for fitness for a particular purpose, are expressly excluded. Neither Microsoft Press nor anyone else who has been involved in the creation or production of the book and accompanying software shall be liable for any direct, indirect, consequential, or incidental damages (including without limitation damages for loss of business profits and the like) arising out of the use of the book and accompanying software even if Microsoft Press has been advised of the possibility of such damages.

CONTENTS

1   An Introduction   1

2   Asset Depreciation Templates   9

3   Debt Amortization Templates   61

4   Future Value Templates   103

5   Cost Center Template   133

6   Sales and Cost of Sales Template   143

7   Profit Volume and Break-Even Analysis Template   163

8   Cash Flow Forecast and Analysis Template   199

9   Financial Statements with Ratios Template   245

Appendix: Auditing and Documenting Your Financial Spreadsheets   301

Index   306

1

An Introduction

The 17 Microsoft Excel spreadsheet templates included on the accompanying disks and described in this book are intended to serve as a toolkit that can save you time when you're building financial models, no matter how simple or complex. Using any or all of the templates can free you from many of the time-consuming steps of building good financial spreadsheets. Without the burden of creating financial spreadsheets from scratch, you can focus on the other aspects of computer-based business modeling: developing robust, solid inputs to your models; running your models; examining and assessing the outputs; and making better business decisions and recommendations, which is the ultimate goal of creating financial models.

WHAT THIS PRODUCT CONTAINS

The Microsoft Excel Small Business Consultant product contains this book and a 360 KB 5¼-inch disk. The disk holds the entire template collection. See the back cover of this book if you'd like to order a 720 KB 3½-inch disk that contains the same templates.

What's on the Disk

The disk includes five asset depreciation templates, four debt amortization templates, three future value templates, a cost center template, a sales and cost of sales template, a profit volume analysis template, a cash flow forecast and analysis template, and a financial statement with ratios template.

Asset depreciation templates Each of the five depreciation templates (STRAIGHT.XLS, DECLIN'G.XLS, SUMYEARS.XLS, ANNUITY.XLS, and ACTIVITY.XLS) uses a different depreciation method: straight-line, declining balance, sum-of-the-years'-digits, annuity/sinking fund, and activity. Each template calculates an asset's depreciation expense, accumulated depreciation, and net book value for each period in the schedule. Chapter 2 of this book describes the depreciation templates.

Debt amortization templates The four amortization templates (FIXRATE.XLS, VARIRATE.XLS, FIXDUE.XLS, and VARIDUE.XLS) consist of a schedule for fixed interest rate, ordinary annuity debt; a schedule for variable interest rate, ordinary annuity debt; a schedule for fixed rate, annuity due debt; and a schedule for variable rate, annuity due debt. Both ordinary annuity templates assume that you make debt service payments at the end of the payment period, a payment method sometimes also called payments in arrears. Both annuity due templates assume that you make debt service payments at the beginning of the payment period, a method sometimes also called payments in advance. Chapter 3 describes these templates.

Future value templates The three future value templates (FVDPOSIT.XLS, FVORDANN.XLS, and FVANNDUE.XLS) consist of a template to calculate the future value of an initial, onetime deposit; a template to calculate the future value of a series of equal payments made at the end of each payment period; and a template to calculate the future value of a series of equal payments made at the beginning of each payment period. Each template also lets you solve for any one of the four variables: future value, initial deposit or payment amount, interest rate, or number of periods. Chapter 4 describes these templates.

Cost center template The simple cost center template (COSTSRPT.XLS) uses standard cost or expense classifications and should prove satisfactory for simple planning and budgeting. (Cost center schedules are also called expense summaries.) For complex models, it can serve as a starting point. Chapter 5 describes the template.

Sales and cost of sales template

The sales and cost of sales template (SALESRPT.XLS) calculates sales, costs of goods sold, other variable sales costs, and gross margins. Businesses that produce or purchase inventory also can use the template to calculate inventory balances in units and inventory balances in dollars using a weighted average costing method. Chapter 6 describes the template.

Profit volume and break-even analysis template

The profit volume and break-even template (PROFTVOL.XLS) calculates costs and profits at different revenue volumes. The extensive and powerful charting abilities of Microsoft Excel can make your financial models easy to interpret and effective in communicating the results to other decision makers, particularly those not knowledgeable about finance and accounting. The template also provides data to two charts (COSTPROF.XLC and BREAKEVN.XLC) that are included on the templates disks. COSTPROF.XLC, an area chart, shows the revenues, costs, and profits over the range of volumes for which the template calculates revenues, costs, and profits. BREAKEVN.XLC, a line chart, shows the total revenues plotted against the total costs, with the intersection of these two lines identifying the break-even point. Chapter 7 describes the template and the two charts.

Cash flow forecast and analysis template

The cash flow forecasting and analysis template (CASHFLOW.XLS) forecasts asset or investment cash flows and applies standard financial measures of profitability and liquidity to the cash flows such as internal and adjusted rates of return, net present values, and payback period calculations. Chapter 8 describes the template.

Financial statement with ratios template

The financial statement with ratios template (FINANCLS.XLS) generates a balance sheet, an income statement, and a cash flow statement. It also calculates standard financial ratios and constructs common size balance sheets and income statements from these statements. Chapter 9 describes the template and also describes how to use an existing set of financial statements either to calculate financial ratios or to construct common size financial statements.

What's in This Book

This book provides documentation and background information to assist you in using the templates on the accompanying disks. The book is organized so that you can turn to the section describing a specific template and get all the information you need to operate that template.

How each chapter of this book is organized

The structure of each chapter and of each discussion of a template within a chapter is the same.

An introductory section describes the template or templates discussed in the chapter, general applications of the template or templates, and a brief description of what the template or templates do.

For each template within a chapter, the section titled "What the Template Contains and Does" explains the likely source of any input variables, the mathematics of any calculations, and the output variables generated by the model. The section titled "Entering Your Own Data" describes the steps you take to enter new data into the template and to access the results. The section titled "Customizing the Template" describes the steps required to complete several standard modifications to the template. The section titled "Linking This Template to Other Spreadsheets" introduces an example link and then details the steps to complete the link. (Linking refers to Microsoft Excel's ability to reference cells in other spreadsheets. In this way, you can build small spreadsheets that are easy to create, maintain, and enhance, linking them together to run large, sophisticated models.)

Other features of this book

To complement the templates and enhance their usefulness as building blocks for constructing your own business models, the appendix of this book discusses using Microsoft Excel's built-in auditing and documenting features. The powerful auditing and documenting features of Microsoft Excel strengthen the construction of your models, minimize model errors, and support and strengthen your customization of the templates.

WHAT YOU NEED

As mentioned at the beginning of this chapter, the collection of templates on the accompanying disks is intended to serve as a toolkit. And as with a real toolkit, you should know some basics before you attempt to use the tools.

Finance and Accounting Knowledge

Chapters 2 through 9 provide short primers on the fundamental modeling activity performed by each template. For example, Chapter 2 outlines the logic and mechanics of asset depreciation and Chapter 8 outlines the forecasting methods used and the logic and mechanics of the profitability and liquidity measures applied by the cash flow forecasting and analysis template. However, you should know the basics of finance and accounting before using these templates, particularly the more complex templates, such as the cash flow forecasting and analysis template and the financial statement with ratios template. In general, to use a template, you need a strong grasp of the model's inputs, the model's mechanics and mathematics, and the model's outputs. For example, to use the straight-line depreciation template in Chapter 2, you need to understand how to develop the original cost of an asset, the salvage value, and the estimated life. You also must be familiar with the process by which the straight-line depreciation calculations are made. And you need to understand the significance and applications of the calculated results of the model, such as the period depreciation expense, the accumulated depreciation, and the net book value. If you find that the finance or accounting theory of a particular template is still unclear after reading those sections of the chapter that describe the template, I suggest reading a basic finance and accounting book, such as *Introduction to Financial Management* by Charles W. Haley and Lawrence D. Schall (McGraw-Hill, 1988) or *Intermediate Accounting* by Donald E. Kieso and Jerry J. Weygandt (John Wiley and Sons, 1988).

Microsoft Excel Skills

This book assumes that you are familiar with the operation of spreadsheets and with the operation of Microsoft Excel. The instructions for using a template are not at a detailed, keystroke level. They assume

Microsoft Excel Small Business Consultant

that you know how to start Microsoft Excel, retrieve files, enter numbers into cells, print files, and save files. The instructions for modifying or customizing the templates assume that you know how to enter and edit formulas; cut, copy, and paste portions of the document; unprotect and protect documents; and use the formatting commands. If you have not yet acquired this level of proficiency with Microsoft Excel, you might want to work through the financial and business chapters in the *Microsoft Excel Sampler* that you received in your Microsoft Excel package. For specific, detailed information on Microsoft Excel commands and functions, consult the *Microsoft Excel Reference Guide, Microsoft Excel Functions and Macros,* or a book about Microsoft Excel, such as *Running Microsoft Excel* by The Cobb Group: Douglas Cobb and Judy Mynhier (Microsoft Press, 1988).

A System That Can Run Microsoft Excel

To use the templates, you need only the minimum hardware configuration required for Microsoft Excel:

- An IBM Personal System/2, IBM PC AT, COMPAQ DESKPRO 386, or a machine that is compatible with one of these.

- 640 KB of memory to run any individual template. (In general, the performance of Microsoft Excel improves as you add memory because more of the program is able to reside in memory. For more information on memory management and related issues, consult the memory management topic in the *Microsoft Excel Reference Guide*.)

- An IBM VGA, IBM EGA, Hercules Graphics Card, or other graphics card compatible with Microsoft Windows/286 or Microsoft Windows/386.

- A hard disk.

- MS-DOS 3.0 or later.

- A 5¼-inch floppy-disk drive (or a 3½-inch floppy-disk drive if you choose to order the 3½-inch disk).

HOW TO USE THE TEMPLATES

To begin using any of the templates:

1. Make a backup of the templates disk. If you need information on copying the contents of one disk to another disk, see the operating system manual that came with your computer.

2. Put the original templates disk in a safe place.

3. Put a write-protect tab on the backup templates disk you created. This prevents you from accidentally saving a modified template onto the backup templates disk by using the same filename as the original template, thereby overwriting the original, which provided the foundation for the spreadsheet.

4. Use your backup as the source disk from which you load templates. You can also create a directory or subdirectory on your hard disk and copy the templates there. If you copy the templates to your hard disk, open the files as read-only so that you do not accidentally overwrite the original template.

5. Turn to the chapter of this book that discusses the template you want to use. Review the primer section of the chapter and follow the instructions for using the template.

2

Asset Depreciation Templates

Financial accounting standards and tax accounting laws require that you depreciate an asset in the process of calculating profits. Methods and conventions for doing this vary depending on the asset, the industry, and the party to whom profits are reported. The purpose, however, remains the same: to allocate the cost of the asset over the years it will be used.

The five asset depreciation templates, described in this chapter, automate the preparation of asset depreciation schedules and provide foundations for customizing depreciation schedules. These templates (and the depreciation convention each uses) are:

- STRAIGHT.XLS (straight-line)
- DECLIN'G.XLS (declining balance)
- SUMYEARS.XLS (sum-of-the-years'-digits)
- ANNUITY.XLS (annuity or sinking fund)
- ACTIVITY.XLS (activity)

This chapter shows you how to use these five templates, print them, modify them, and link them with subsidiary spreadsheets.

ASSET DEPRECIATION: A SHORT PRIMER

Asset depreciation answers the question, "How much does the asset cost per period?" To answer that question, you need to: know the cost of the asset, estimate the number of periods in the asset's useful life, project any salvage value the asset will have at the end of its useful life, and choose a depreciation method. For example, suppose your business purchases a delivery truck for $10,000, uses it for five years, and then sells it for $2,000. Using the simplest depreciation method, straight-line depreciation, you calculate the cost of the truck over the five years as the $10,000 original cost less the $2,000 salvage value for a result of $8,000. Now divide the $8,000 by the five years of useful life. The result—$1,600—is the depreciation expense.

Straight-line depreciation is the most popular method because it's easy to apply and intuitive. The other methods—declining balance, sum-of-the-years'-digits, annuity/sinking fund, and activity—simply allocate the asset cost over the asset's useful life in different ways.

The declining balance depreciation method expenses more of the cost of the asset in the early periods of an asset's estimated life than in the later periods. It does so using the following formula:

(Declining Balance Percentage)*(Net Book Value)/(Estimated Life)

For example, suppose you want to recalculate the first year's depreciation expense for the delivery truck using 200 percent declining balance depreciation. The declining balance percentage is 200 percent. The net book value, because no depreciation has occurred, is $10,000. The estimated life is five years. Accordingly, you calculate the first year's depreciation expense as:

200%*($10,000/5 years)

or $4,000.

The declining balance percentage is always greater than 100 percent. Accordingly, the formula accelerates the depreciation of an asset. Often, federal and state income tax laws determine usage of the declining balance depreciation method. Tax laws allow declining balance depreciation for many types of assets and specify a variety of declining balance percentages to be used, including 125, 150, 175, and 200 percent, depending on which year you acquire and begin using an asset. Generally, the tax law in effect when you buy and begin using an asset determines the types of assets for which you can use the declining balance method, as well as the declining balance percentage.

The sum-of-the-years'-digits depreciation method, like the declining balance method, also expenses more of the cost of an asset in the early periods of an asset's estimated life than in the later periods. It does so using the following formula:

(Periods Left in Estimated Life)/(Sum of the Periods' Digits)*(Original Cost–Salvage Value)

For example, suppose you want to recalculate the first year's depreciation expense for the delivery truck using the sum-of-the-years'-digits method. The periods left in the estimated life, because the asset is still new, is five years. The sum of the periods' (or years') digits is 1+2+3+4+5, or 15. The original cost less the salvage value is $10,000–$2,000, or $8,000. Accordingly, you calculate the first year's depreciation expense as:

(5/15)*$8,000

or $2,667.

Because the fraction becomes smaller in each succeeding period, the amount of depreciation expensed each year becomes smaller.

The annuity and sinking fund depreciation methods are mechanically identical, so this toolkit supplies the same template for both. Both of these methods expense less of the cost of an asset in the early periods of an asset's life than in the later periods, so they are roughly the opposite of the declining balance and sum-of-the-years'-digits methods in this regard. The annuity and sinking fund methods also include in their depreciation expenses a specified return on the investment. Generally, the annuity and sinking fund methods violate the Generally Accepted Accounting Principles (GAAP). (Generally Accepted Accounting Principles are the rules and methods that certified public accountants, with help from business and the government, develop and use for financial accounting. Usually, when people refer to Generally Accepted Accounting Principles, they mean the pronouncements of the Financial Accounting Standards Board, an independent professional group.) Because they are contrary to GAAP and because they are complex, these methods are rarely used in practice except in heavily regulated industries such as public utilities in which rate-setting agencies often specify returns on investment. The annuity and sinking fund depreciation methods use the following formula to calculate depreciation expenses:

(Original Cost−(Present Value of the Salvage Value))/(Present Value Factor of an Ordinary Annuity for n Periods at i%)

where n equals the estimated life, and i equals the specified return on investment.

For example, suppose you want to recalculate the first year's depreciation expense for the delivery truck using the annuity or sinking fund method. Also suppose that you are assured a 10 percent return on assets by a state regulatory agency. The 10 percent is the specified return on investment. The original cost is $10,000. The estimated life is five years. The present value of the salvage value is calculated as follows: For each year in the asset's estimated life, the $2,000 salvage value is divided by the sum of 1 plus the specified return on investment, or $(1+10\%)^5$, or $1,241.84. You can calculate the present value of an ordinary annuity for 10 periods using a 10 percent discount rate using the PV function as follows:

=PV(.10,5,1)

for a result of 3.7908. Accordingly, you calculate the depreciation expense as:

($10,000–$1,241.84)/3.7908

or $2,310.37.

This depreciation amount also includes assumed investment revenue of 10 percent on the asset cost of $10,000, or $1,000, meaning the actual amount of the asset being expensed in this period is $2,310.37 minus $1,000, or $1,310.37. As the net book value of the asset becomes smaller over its useful life, the assumed investment revenue becomes smaller. Consequently, the $2,310.37 of depreciation represents less assumed investment revenue and more actual asset being expensed. The assumed investment revenue amounts to the assumed return on assets allowed by the regulatory agency.

The activity method depreciates an asset as it's used, instead of as time passes, by calibrating the estimated life of an asset in units of use. It does so by using the following formula:

(Period Units of Use/Estimated Life in Units of Use)
*(Original Cost–Salvage Value)

For example, suppose you want to recalculate the first year's depreciation expense for the delivery truck using the activity depreciation method. If a delivery truck lasts for 100,000 miles and you anticipate driving the truck 30,000 miles the first year, you calculate the first year's depreciation expense as:

30,000/100,000*($10,000–$2,000)

or $2,400.

In general, financial accounting standards and the tax laws guide you in determining asset cost, useful life, and salvage value and in selecting a depreciation method. Accordingly, if you're building a depreciation schedule to use for tax accounting, your best resources are the publications of the Internal Revenue Service and your tax adviser. Alternatively, if you're building a depreciation schedule to use for financial accounting, your best resources are the publications of the Financial Accounting Standards Board and your certified public accountant.

> **HINT:** Be consistent in the financial measurement periods you use in depreciating assets. If you're building a monthly forecast, calculate depreciation expenses on a monthly basis and enter the useful life in months. Alternatively, if you're building a quarterly or yearly forecast, calculate your depreciation expenses on a quarterly or yearly basis and enter the estimated life of the asset in quarters or years.

STRAIGHT-LINE DEPRECIATION TEMPLATE (STRAIGHT.XLS)

You can use the straight-line depreciation template (STRAIGHT.XLS), shown in Figure 2-1, to construct depreciation schedules with the straight-line method. The straight-line method expenses the original cost of an asset in equal increments over the useful life of the asset. In general, you use this template if you're calculating depreciation for income tax purposes and the tax laws require the straight-line method. You can also use this template if you're calculating depreciation for financial accounting and you feel that the allocation of costs matches economic reality.

Given three parameters—original cost, salvage value, and estimated life—this template calculates the period depreciation, the accumulated depreciation, and the net book value for each period of the forecasting horizon. You need this information to calculate business profits and losses, to report asset balances on the balance sheet, and to calculate any gains or losses on the disposal of assets.

What the Template Contains and Does

The two parts to the straight-line template are the Straight-Line Depreciation Calculation Inputs box in the range B2:C6 and the Straight-Line Depreciation Schedule, starting with the title in row 8.

2: Asset Depreciation Templates

Straight-Line Depreciation Calculation Inputs	
Original Cost	$150,000
Salvage Value	$25,000
Estimated Life	18

Straight-Line Depreciation Schedule			
Period	Period Depreciation	Accumulated Depreciation	Net Book Value
1	$6,944	$6,944	$143,056
2	$6,944	13,889	136,111
3	$6,944	20,833	129,167
4	$6,944	27,778	122,222
5	$6,944	34,722	115,278
6	$6,944	41,667	108,333
7	$6,944	48,611	101,389
8	$6,944	55,556	94,444
9	$6,944	62,500	87,500
10	$6,944	69,444	80,556
11	$6,944	76,389	73,611
12	$6,944	83,333	66,667
13	$6,944	90,278	59,722
14	$6,944	97,222	52,778
15	$6,944	104,167	45,833
16	$6,944	111,111	38,889
17	$6,944	118,056	31,944
18	$6,944	125,000	25,000
19	$0	125,000	25,000
20	$0	125,000	25,000

Figure 2-1. *The straight-line depreciation template, showing depreciation for an asset with an original cost of $150,000, a salvage value of $25,000, and an estimated life of 18 periods.*

Straight-Line Depreciation Calculation Inputs

The calculation inputs are Original Cost, Salvage Value, and Estimated Life. These are the only three variables you enter, and, unless you turn off cell protection, the three cells containing these values are the only cells within the spreadsheet into which you can enter data.

Most often, the tax accounting laws or financial accounting standards that apply to your modeling assumptions determine the method you use to calculate these variables. Therefore, it would be difficult for me

15

to give specific instructions on how you should come up with these inputs. In general, the Original Cost value should be the cost of acquiring and placing into service the asset that you are depreciating. This amount might include the asset purchase price, sales tax, shipping insurance costs, freight charges, and installation costs. The Salvage Value figure is the residual value of the asset at the end of its estimated useful life. The Estimated Life value is the number of periods during which the asset works for the purpose intended. The useful life of an asset is also called its economic life. For tax accounting purposes, the useful life and salvage value sometimes are defined by tax law. For financial accounting purposes, previous experience with an asset might provide historical data for estimating the useful life.

For convenience and good documentation within the template, cell C4 contains the original cost and is named Original_Cost, cell C5 contains the salvage value and is named Salvage_Value, and cell C6 contains the estimated life and is named Estimated_Life. The formulas within the Straight-Line Depreciation Schedule use these cell names rather than the cell addresses.

Straight-Line Depreciation Schedule

The Straight-Line Depreciation Schedule has four columns: Period, Period Depreciation, Accumulated Depreciation, and Net Book Value.

Period. The period identifier simply numbers the time periods over which you're depreciating the asset. If you're using the template for accounting and bookkeeping, use a number of periods that is equal to or greater than the estimated life of the asset. However, if you're using the template as a building block for a financial projection, you'll probably want the number of periods in your depreciation schedule to correspond to the number of periods in the other schedules that make up your financial forecasting model.

The first period identifier is stored in cell B11 as the integer 1. Periods that follow are stored as the previous period plus 1. For example, the formula for the second period is:

```
=B11+1
```

The formula for the third period is:

    =B12+1

and so on.

Period Depreciation. Period depreciation is the depreciation expense for the current period. If you're using the template for depreciable assets accounting, the Period Depreciation expense is the debit component of a depreciation journal entry and ultimately shows up in the profit and loss statement. If you're using the template as part of a financial forecast, you can include the Period Depreciation expense from other expenses in the profit and loss forecast. Additionally, any income tax effect of this noncash expense ripples through the cash flow statement.

Because the asset is expensed equally in each period in straight-line depreciation, the basic Period Depreciation formula used in the first period is incorporated in the formula for each period of the forecasting horizon:

    =SLN(Original_Cost,Salvage_Value,Estimated_Life)

The formula for subsequent periods is modified to prevent an asset from being depreciated below its salvage value and to deal with an estimated life expressed as a noninteger. Starting in the second period, the basic formula is enclosed in a MIN statement, which selects the smaller of two amounts: the straight-line depreciation expense or the amount yet to be depreciated. For example, the Period Depreciation formula for the second period is:

    =MIN(SLN(Original_Cost,Salvage_Value,Estimated_Life),
    E11−Salvage_Value)

The E11−Salvage_Value portion of the formula calculates the amount yet to be depreciated. In subsequent periods, this part of the formula uses the Net Book Value amount from the previous period.

Accumulated Depreciation. If you're using the template for depreciable assets accounting, the incremental increase in accumulated depreciation is the credit component of a depreciation journal entry and ultimately shows up on the balance sheet as an adjustment to the asset's carrying cost. If you're using the template as part of a financial forecast, you can include the accumulated depreciation from the original cost of the asset in the balance sheet forecast to show the asset's net book value. Alternatively, you might simply use the Net Book Value amount calculated by this schedule.

The formula for the accumulated depreciation balance in the first period is:

=SUM(C$11:C11)

The second-period formula is:

=SUM(C$11:C12)

and so on.

Net Book Value. The net book value is the asset's carrying cost and is the amount that you report either individually or with other assets' net book values on any historical or pro forma balance sheets.

For each period, the Net Book Value amount is the Original Cost amount less any accumulated depreciation. The formula for the first period is:

=Original_Cost−D11

The second-period formula is:

=Original_Cost−D12

and so on.

Entering Your Own Data

To enter your own data in the straight-line depreciation template, follow these steps:

1. Load the file named STRAIGHT.XLS from the templates disk. The template initially contains the default inputs shown in Figure 2-1.
2. In cell C4, enter the original cost of acquiring an asset and placing it into service.
3. In cell C5, enter the salvage value of the asset or group of assets.
4. In cell C6, enter the estimated life of the asset (or the average life, if you're using group or composite depreciation).
5. Save your changes by saving the spreadsheet and giving it a new filename. Save it on the disk on which you plan to store the rest of the financial model you're constructing or on which you plan to store the rest of the depreciable assets accounting information.
6. Print the spreadsheet.

Customizing the Template

You can use the straight-line template for a wide variety of depreciation schedules. However, you might want to change the template so that it more precisely meets your requirements. For example, you can add text that describes the asset or identifies the supporting documentation for the schedule. You can also increase or decrease the number of periods.

Before you change anything on the straight-line depreciation template other than the calculation inputs, unprotect the document.

Increasing the number of periods

To increase the number of periods, follow these steps:

1. Remove the border from the last row of the depreciation schedule.
2. Copy the current last row of the schedule, the row for Period 20, down as needed. (You'll probably want either as many rows in the schedule as there are forecasting periods in your overall model or as many rows as there are accounting periods in the asset's estimated life.)

3. Replace the border at the bottom of the depreciation schedule.

4. Reinstate cell protection as needed.

Decreasing the number of periods

To decrease the number of periods, follow these steps:

1. Delete any unneeded rows from the bottom of the schedule.

2. Add a border at the new bottom of the depreciation schedule.

3. Reinstate cell protection as needed.

DECLINING BALANCE DEPRECIATION TEMPLATE (DECLIN'G.XLS)

You can use the declining balance template (DECLIN'G.XLS), shown in Figure 2-2, to construct depreciation schedules with the declining balance method. In general, you use this template if you've selected or been counseled by your tax adviser to use a declining balance convention, such as Accelerated Cost Recovery System (ACRS) or modified Accelerated Cost Recovery System (MACRS), for tax accounting. You can also use this template if you're calculating depreciation for financial accounting and you feel that the allocation of costs matches economic reality.

Given four parameters—original cost, salvage value, estimated life, and the decline percentage—this template calculates the depreciation expense, the accumulated depreciation, and the net book value for each period of the forecasting horizon.

The schedule also calculates the excess depreciation expense taken as a result of using the declining balance method, because this excess might be subject to special tax treatment either on a current basis or at disposal. To calculate the excess, this template incorporates a straight-line depreciation schedule.

Finally, this template incorporates a schedule that uses the declining balance depreciation method over the first periods of an asset's estimated life but switches to the straight-line depreciation convention when that method maximizes the expense charged. This last schedule

2: Asset Depreciation Templates

Declining Balance Depreciation Calculation Inputs	
Original Cost	$150,000
Salvage Value	$25,000
Estimated Life	18
Decline Percent	175%

Declining Balance Depreciation Schedule			
Period	Depreciation	Accumulated Depreciation	Net Book Value
1	$14,583	$14,583	$135,417
2	13,166	27,749	122,251
3	11,886	39,634	110,366
4	10,730	50,364	99,636
5	9,687	60,051	89,949
6	8,745	68,796	81,204
7	7,895	76,691	73,309
8	7,127	83,818	66,182
9	6,434	90,253	59,747
10	5,809	96,061	53,939
11	5,244	101,305	48,695
12	4,734	106,040	43,960
13	4,274	110,314	39,686
14	3,858	114,172	35,828
15	3,483	117,655	32,345
16	3,145	120,800	29,200
17	2,839	123,639	26,361
18	1,361	125,000	25,000
19	0	125,000	25,000
20	0	125,000	25,000

Straight-Line Depreciation Schedule			
Period	Depreciation	Accumulated Depreciation	Net Book Value
1	$6,944	$6,944	$143,056
2	6,944	13,889	136,111
3	6,944	20,833	129,167
4	6,944	27,778	122,222
5	6,944	34,722	115,278
6	6,944	41,667	108,333
7	6,944	48,611	101,389
8	6,944	55,556	94,444
9	6,944	62,500	87,500
10	6,944	69,444	80,556
11	6,944	76,389	73,611
12	6,944	83,333	66,667
13	6,944	90,278	59,722
14	6,944	97,222	52,778
15	6,944	104,167	45,833
16	6,944	111,111	38,889
17	6,944	118,056	31,944
18	6,944	125,000	25,000
19	$0	125,000	25,000
20	$0	125,000	25,000

Excess Accelerated Depreciation
$7,639
$13,860
$18,801
$22,587
$25,329
$27,130
$28,080
$28,263
$27,753
$26,617
$24,917
$22,706
$20,036
$16,950
$13,489
$9,689
$5,583
$0
$0
$0

Straight-Line Conversion Depreciation Schedule			
Period	Depreciation	Accumulated Depreciation	Net Book Value
1	$14,583	$14,583	$135,417
2	13,166	27,749	122,251
3	11,886	39,634	110,366
4	10,730	50,364	99,636
5	9,687	60,051	89,949
6	8,745	68,796	81,204
7	7,895	76,691	73,309
8	7,127	83,818	66,182
9	6,434	90,253	59,747
10	5,809	96,061	53,939
11	5,244	101,305	48,695
12	4,734	106,040	43,960
13	4,274	110,314	39,686
14	3,858	114,172	35,828
15	3,483	117,655	32,345
16	3,145	120,800	29,200
17	2,839	123,639	26,361
18	1,361	125,000	25,000
19	0	125,000	25,000
20	0	125,000	25,000

Figure 2-2. *The declining balance depreciation template, showing depreciation for an asset with an original cost of $150,000, a salvage value of $25,000, an estimated life of 18 periods, and a declining balance of 175 percent.*

is required because the declining balance depreciation formula does not completely depreciate assets with very low salvage values. Without this feature, an asset might not be completely depreciated over its estimated life.

What the Template Contains and Does

The five parts of the declining balance template are the Declining Balance Depreciation Calculation Inputs box, the Declining Balance Depreciation Schedule, the Straight-Line Depreciation Schedule, the Excess Accelerated Depreciation schedule, and the Straight-Line Conversion Depreciation Schedule.

Declining Balance Depreciation Calculation Inputs

The calculation inputs are Original Cost, Salvage Value, Estimated Life, and Decline Percent. These are the only four variables you enter, and, unless you turn off cell protection, the four cells containing these values are the only cells within the spreadsheet into which you can enter data.

Most often, the tax accounting laws or financial accounting standards that apply to your modeling assumptions determine the method you use to calculate these variables. Therefore, it would be difficult for me to give specific instructions on how you should come up with these input variables. In general, the Original Cost value should be the cost of acquiring and placing into service the asset that you are depreciating. This amount might include the asset purchase price, sales tax, shipping insurance costs, freight charges, and installation costs. The Salvage Value figure is the residual value of the asset at the end of its estimated useful life. The Estimated Life value is the number of periods during which the asset works for the purpose intended. The useful life of an asset is also called the economic life. For tax accounting purposes, the useful life and salvage value sometimes are defined by tax law. For financial accounting purposes, previous experience with an asset might provide historical data for estimating the useful life. The declining balance percentage is usually determined by the income tax laws that apply to the asset being depreciated.

For convenience and good documentation within the template, cell C4 contains the original cost and is named Original_Cost, cell C5 contains the salvage value and is named Salvage_Value, cell C6 contains the estimated life and is named Estimated_Life, and cell C7 contains the declining balance percentage and is named Decline_Percent. The formulas within the schedules use these cell names rather than the cell addresses.

Declining Balance Depreciation Schedule

The Declining Balance Depreciation Schedule has four columns: Period, Period Depreciation, Accumulated Depreciation, and Net Book Value.

Period. The period identifier simply numbers the time periods over which you're depreciating the asset. If you're using the template for accounting and bookkeeping, use a number of periods that is equal to or greater than the estimated life of the asset. However, if you're using the template as a building block for a financial projection, you'll probably want the number of periods in your depreciation schedule to correspond to the number of periods in the other schedules that make up your financial forecasting model.

The first period identifier is stored in cell B12 as the integer 1. Periods that follow are stored as the previous period plus 1. For example, the formula for the second period is:

    =B12+1

The formula for the third period is:

    =B13+1

and so on.

Period Depreciation. If you're using declining balance depreciation over the asset's entire estimated life, period depreciation is the depreciation expense for the current period. If you're using the template for depreciable assets bookkeeping, the Period Depreciation expense is the debit component of a depreciation journal entry and ultimately shows up in the profit and loss statement. If you're using the template as part of a financial forecast, you can add the Period Depreciation expense to other expenses in the profit and loss forecast. Additionally, any income tax effect of this noncash expense ripples through the cash flow statement.

The Period Depreciation formula for the first period in the forecasting horizon is:

=Decline_Percent*Original_Cost/Estimated_Life

In the second period of the forecasting horizon, however, the formula is modified so that it does not depreciate an asset below its salvage value. The Period Depreciation formula for the second period is:

=MIN(Decline_Percent*(Original_Cost−D12)/ Estimated_Life,E12−Salvage_Value)

The Original_Cost−D12 portion of the formula, which represents the declining balance to which the percentage is applied, is the net book value for the asset at the end of the previous period. The formula component Decline_Percent*(Original_Cost−D12)/Estimated_Life is the depreciation expense calculated according to the declining balance calculation method. The formula component E12−Salvage_Value is the amount necessary to fully depreciate the asset. By taking the minimum of these two amounts, the schedule never depreciates an asset below its salvage value. Additionally, when an asset is fully depreciated, no more period depreciation expense is charged.

Accumulated Depreciation. If you're using the template for depreciable assets accounting, the incremental increase in accumulated depreciation is the credit component of a depreciation journal entry and ultimately shows up on the balance sheet as an adjustment to the asset's carrying cost. If you're using the template as part of a financial forecast, you can deduct the accumulated depreciation from the original cost of the asset in the balance sheet forecast to show the asset's net book value. Alternatively, you might simply use the Net Book Value amount calculated by this schedule.

The formula for the Accumulated Depreciation balance in the first period is:

=SUM(C$12:C12)

The second-period formula is:

=SUM(C$12:C13)

The third-period formula is:

=SUM(C$12:C14)

and so on.

Net Book Value. The net book value is an asset's carrying cost and is the amount that you report either individually or with other assets' net book values on any historical or pro forma balance sheets.

For each period, the Net Book Value amount is the Original Cost amount less any accumulated depreciation. The first-period net book value formula is:

=Original_Cost–D12

The second-period formula is:

=Original_Cost–D13

The third-period formula is:

=Original_Cost–D14

and so on.

Straight-Line Depreciation Schedule

The Straight-Line Depreciation Schedule has four columns: Period, Period Depreciation, Accumulated Depreciation, and Net Book Value.

Period. The period identifier simply numbers the time periods over which you're depreciating the asset. If you're using the template for accounting and bookkeeping, use a number of periods that is equal to or greater than the estimated life of the asset. However, if you're using the template as a building block for a financial projection, you'll probably want the number of periods in your depreciation schedule to correspond to the number of periods in the other schedules that make up your financial forecasting mode.

The first period identifier is stored in cell G12 as the integer 1. Periods that follow are stored as the previous period plus 1. For example, the formula for the second period is:

```
=G12+1
```

The formula for the third period is:

```
=G13+1
```

and so on.

Period Depreciation. Period depreciation is the depreciation expense for the current period. If you're using the template for depreciable assets accounting, the Period Depreciation expense is the debit component of a depreciation journal entry and ultimately shows up in the profit and loss statement. If you're using the template as part of a financial forecast, you can add the Period Depreciation expense to other expenses in the profit and loss forecast. Additionally, any income tax effect of this noncash expense ripples through the cash flow statement.

Because the asset is expensed equally in each period in straight-line depreciation, the basic Period Depreciation formula used in the first period is incorporated in the formula for each period of the forecasting horizon:

```
=SLN(Original_Cost,Salvage_Value,Estimated_Life)
```

The formula for subsequent periods is modified to prevent an asset from being depreciated below its salvage value. Starting in the second period, the basic formula is enclosed in a MIN statement, which selects the smaller of two amounts: the straight-line depreciation expense or the amount yet to be depreciated. For example, the period depreciation formula for the second period is:

```
=MIN(SLN(Original_Cost,Salvage_Value,
Estimated_Life),J12-Salvage_Value)
```

The J12–Salvage_Value portion of the formula calculates the amount yet to be depreciated. In subsequent periods, this part of the formula uses the Net Book Value amount from the previous period.

Accumulated Depreciation. If you're using the template for depreciable assets accounting, the incremental increase in the Accumulated Depreciation value is the credit component of a depreciation journal entry and ultimately shows up on the balance sheet as an adjustment to the asset's carrying cost. If you're using the template as part of a financial forecast, you can deduct the Accumulated Depreciation amount from the original cost of the asset in the balance sheet forecast to show the asset's net book value. Alternatively, you might simply use the Net Book Value amount calculated by this schedule.

The formula for the Accumulated Depreciation balance in the first period is:

```
=SUM(H$12:H12)
```

The second-period formula is:

```
=SUM(H$12:H13)
```

and so on.

Net Book Value. The net book value is an asset's carrying cost and is the amount that you report either individually or with other assets' net book values on any historical or pro forma balance sheets.

For each period, the Net Book Value amount is the Original Cost amount less any accumulated depreciation. The formula for the first period is:

=Original_Cost–I12

The second-period formula is:

=Original_Cost–I13

and so on.

Excess Accelerated Depreciation The calculated results in the one-column Excess Accelerated Depreciation schedule are simply the difference between net book values calculated using declining balance depreciation and those calculated using straight-line depreciation. In certain situations, this excess accelerated depreciation is accorded special income tax treatment.

There is, however, another reason to use this schedule: When the salvage value of an asset is very low relative to the original cost, the declining balance method might not fully depreciate an asset by the end of its estimated life. This circumstance can result in a negative amount in the excess accelerated schedule. A negative amount means the declining balance method has under-depreciated the asset. The negative result is the amount of missing depreciation and is sometimes expensed as depreciation in the last period of the estimated life.

For example, change the salvage value in the template to $2,500, as shown in Figure 2-3. Note that in cell E29 the net book value in period 18, the last period in the asset's estimated life, is $23,798, even though by this time the asset should be fully depreciated to its salvage value of $2,500. The amount of the missing depreciation is calculated in cell L29 as –21,298, or ($23,798–$2,500).

2: Asset Depreciation Templates

Declining Balance Depreciation Calculation Inputs	
Original Cost	$150,000
Salvage Value	$2,500
Estimated Life	18
Decline Percent	175%

Declining Balance Depreciation Schedule

Period	Depreciation	Accumulated Depreciation	Net Book Value
1	$14,583	$14,583	$135,417
2	13,166	27,749	122,251
3	11,886	39,634	110,366
4	10,730	50,364	99,636
5	9,687	60,051	89,949
6	8,745	68,796	81,204
7	7,895	76,691	73,309
8	7,127	83,818	66,182
9	6,434	90,253	59,747
10	5,809	96,061	53,939
11	5,244	101,305	48,695
12	4,734	106,040	43,960
13	4,274	110,314	39,686
14	3,858	114,172	35,828
15	3,483	117,655	32,345
16	3,145	120,800	29,200
17	2,839	123,639	26,361
18	2,563	126,202	23,798
19	2,314	128,515	21,485
20	2,089	130,604	19,396

Straight-Line Depreciation Schedule

Period	Depreciation	Accumulated Depreciation	Net Book Value
1	$8,194	$8,194	$141,806
2	8,194	16,389	133,611
3	8,194	24,583	125,417
4	8,194	32,778	117,222
5	8,194	40,972	109,028
6	8,194	49,167	100,833
7	8,194	57,361	92,639
8	8,194	65,556	84,444
9	8,194	73,750	76,250
10	8,194	81,944	68,056
11	8,194	90,139	59,861
12	8,194	98,333	51,667
13	8,194	106,528	43,472
14	8,194	114,722	35,278
15	8,194	122,917	27,083
16	8,194	131,111	18,889
17	8,194	139,306	10,694
18	8,194	147,500	2,500
19	$0	147,500	2,500
20	$0	147,500	2,500

Excess Accelerated Depreciation

$6,389
$11,360
$15,051
$17,587
$19,079
$19,630
$19,330
$18,263
$16,503
$14,117
$11,167
$7,706
$3,786
($550)
($5,261)
($10,311)
($15,667)
($21,298)
($18,985)
($16,896)

Straight-Line Conversion Depreciation Schedule

Period	Depreciation	Accumulated Depreciation	Net Book Value
1	$14,583	$14,583	$135,417
2	13,166	27,749	122,251
3	11,886	39,634	110,366
4	10,730	50,364	99,636
5	9,687	60,051	89,949
6	8,745	68,796	81,204
7	7,895	76,691	73,309
8	7,127	83,818	66,182
9	6,434	90,253	59,747
10	6,361	96,613	53,387
11	6,361	102,974	47,026
12	6,361	109,335	40,665
13	6,361	115,696	34,304
14	6,361	122,057	27,943
15	6,361	128,418	21,582
16	6,361	134,778	15,222
17	6,361	141,139	8,861
18	6,361	147,500	2,500
19	0	147,500	2,500
20	0	147,500	2,500

Figure 2-3. *The declining balance template, using a salvage value that is very low relative to the original cost.*

For each period, the Excess Accelerated Depreciation amount is the Accumulated Depreciation amount for the period in the Declining Balance Depreciation Schedule less the Accumulated Depreciation amount for the period in the Straight-Line Depreciation Schedule. The first-period formula is:

=J12–E12

The second-period formula is:

J13–E13

and so on.

Straight-Line Conversion Depreciation Schedule

The Straight-Line Conversion Depreciation Schedule summarizes the calculated results when you switch from a declining balance depreciation method to a straight-line depreciation method at the point in the asset's estimated life when the straight-line calculation method results in a higher period depreciation expense. For example, in Figure 2-3, the Period Depreciation formula switches to the straight-line method in period 10, resulting in a calculated result of $6,361. Using the declining balance method in period 10 would result in $5,809. Switching from the declining balance method to the straight-line method has the advantage of fully depreciating assets with high salvage values and those with low salvage values. Other than this mechanical difference in the calculation of the Period Depreciation expense, the Straight-Line Conversion Depreciation Schedule is essentially the same as the declining balance schedule.

The straight-line conversion depreciation schedule has four columns: Period, Period Depreciation, Accumulated Depreciation, and Net Book Value.

Period. The first period identifier is stored as 1.000001. The trailing decimal digit of insignificance at the millionths place—the sixth decimal place—is necessary so that the remaining estimated life never reaches 0. If it did, as a denominator in the Period Depreciation formula, it would cause a #DIV/0 (division by 0) error value. Identifiers for the periods that follow are stored as the previous period plus 1. For example, the formula for the second period is:

    =N12+1

The formula for the third period is:

    =N13+1

and so on.

Period Depreciation. The first period's expense uses the declining balance method because it results in a larger depreciation expense than the straight-line method, when the declining balance percentage is greater than 100 percent. So this schedule simply refers to the first-period depreciation expense in the declining balance schedule by using the formula:

    =C12

The formula that calculates the second-period depreciation checks for two conditions: First, it checks to determine whether straight-line depreciation results in a higher period depreciation expense for each of the remaining periods; second, it checks to make sure the asset isn't being depreciated below its salvage value. Given these constraints, the formula for the second period is:

    =MIN(IF(C13>(Q12−Salvage_Value)/(Estimated_Life−N12),C13,
    (Q12−Salvage_Value)/(Estimated_Life−N12)),Q12−Salvage_Value)

Cell C13 contains the declining balance depreciation as calculated in the declining balance schedule. The (Q12−Salvage_Value)/(Estimated_Life−N12) portion of the formula calculates the straight-line depreciation expense for the remaining depreciation. The IF statement simply takes the depreciation expense that is greater: using the declining balance method or using the straight-line method. Finally, the MIN statement verifies that the asset isn't being depreciated below its salvage value.

Accumulated Depreciation. The formula for the accumulated depreciation balance in the first period is:

=SUM(O$12:O12)

The second-period formula is:

=SUM(O$12:O13)

and so on.

Net Book Value. For each period, the Net Book Value amount is the Original Cost amount minus any accumulated depreciation. The first-period formula is:

=Original_Cost−P12

The second-period formula is:

=Original_Cost−P13

and so on.

Entering Your Own Data

To enter your own data in the declining balance depreciation template, follow these steps:

1. Load the file named DECLIN'G.XLS from the templates disk. The template initially contains the default inputs shown in Figure 2-2.

2. In cell C4, enter the original cost of acquiring and placing the asset into service. (If you're using group or composite depreciation, enter the total cost of all the assets in the group.)

3. In cell C5, enter the salvage value of the asset or group of assets.

4. In cell C6, enter the estimated life of the asset (or the average life, if you're using group or composite depreciation).

5. In cell C7, enter the declining balance percentage you've selected or have been directed to use by your tax adviser.

6. Save your changes by saving the spreadsheet and giving it a new filename. Save it on the disk on which you plan to store the rest of the financial model you're constructing or on which you plan to store the rest of the depreciable assets accounting information.

7. Print the spreadsheet.

Customizing the Template

You can use the declining balance template for a wide variety of depreciation schedules. However, you might want to change the template so that it more precisely meets your requirements. For example, you can add text that describes the asset or identifies the supporting documentation for the schedule. You can also increase or decrease the number of periods.

Before you change anything on the straight-line depreciation template other than the calculation inputs, unprotect the document.

Increasing the number of periods

To increase the number of periods, follow these steps:

1. Remove the border from the last row of the depreciation schedule.

2. Copy the current last row of the schedule, row 20, down as needed. (You'll probably want either as many rows in the schedule as there are forecasting periods in your overall model or as many rows as there are accounting periods in the asset's estimated life.)

3. Replace the border at the bottom of the depreciation schedule.

4. Reinstate cell protection as needed.

Decreasing the number of periods

To decrease the number of periods, follow these steps:

1. Clear any unneeded rows from the bottom of the schedule.

2. Add a border at the new bottom of the depreciation schedule.

3. Reinstate cell protection as needed.

SUM-OF-THE-YEARS'-DIGITS TEMPLATE (SUMYEARS.XLS)

You can use the sum-of-the-years'-digits template (SUMYEARS.XLS) shown in Figure 2-4 to construct depreciation schedules with the sum-of-the-years'-digits method. In general, you use this template if you've selected or been counseled by your tax adviser to use the sum-of-the-years'-digits convention for tax accounting. You can also use this template if you're calculating depreciation for financial accounting and you feel the allocation of costs matches economic reality.

Given three parameters—original cost, salvage value, and estimated life—this template calculates the period depreciation, the accumulated depreciation, and the net book value for each period of the forecasting horizon.

The schedule also calculates the excess accelerated depreciation taken as a result of using the sum-of-the-years'-digits method, because this amount might be subject to special tax treatment either on a current basis or at disposal. To calculate the excess, this template incorporates a straight-line depreciation schedule.

What the Template Contains and Does

The four parts to the sum-of-the-years'-digits template are the Sum-of-the-Years'-Digits Calculation Inputs box, the Sum-of-the-Years'-Digits Depreciation Schedule, the Straight-Line Depreciation Schedule, and the Excess Accelerated Depreciation schedule.

2: Asset Depreciation Templates

Sum-of-the-Years'-Digits Calculation Inputs	
Original Cost	$150,000
Salvage Value	$25,000
Estimated Life	18

Sum-of-the-Years'-Digits Depreciation Schedule

Period	Period Depreciation	Accumulated Depreciation	Net Book Value
1	$13,158	$13,158	$136,842
2	$12,427	25,585	124,415
3	$11,696	37,281	112,719
4	$10,965	48,246	101,754
5	$10,234	58,480	91,520
6	$9,503	67,982	82,018
7	$8,772	76,754	73,246
8	$8,041	84,795	65,205
9	$7,310	92,105	57,895
10	$6,579	98,684	51,316
11	$5,848	104,532	45,468
12	$5,117	109,649	40,351
13	$4,386	114,035	35,965
14	$3,655	117,690	32,310
15	$2,924	120,614	29,386
16	$2,193	122,807	27,193
17	$1,462	124,269	25,731
18	$731	125,000	25,000
19	$0	125,000	25,000
20	$0	125,000	25,000

Straight-Line Depreciation Schedule

Period	Period Depreciation	Accumulated Depreciation	Net Book Value	Excess Accelerated Depreciation
1	$6,944	$6,944	$143,056	$6,213
2	$6,944	13,889	136,111	$11,696
3	$6,944	20,833	129,167	$16,447
4	$6,944	27,778	122,222	$20,468
5	$6,944	34,722	115,278	$23,757
6	$6,944	41,667	108,333	$26,316
7	$6,944	48,611	101,389	$28,143
8	$6,944	55,556	94,444	$29,240
9	$6,944	62,500	87,500	$29,605
10	$6,944	69,444	80,556	$29,240
11	$6,944	76,389	73,611	$28,143
12	$6,944	83,333	66,667	$26,316
13	$6,944	90,278	59,722	$23,757
14	$6,944	97,222	52,778	$20,468
15	$6,944	104,167	45,833	$16,447
16	$6,944	111,111	38,889	$11,696
17	$6,944	118,056	31,944	$6,213
18	$6,944	125,000	25,000	$0
19	$0	125,000	25,000	$0
20	$0	125,000	25,000	$0

Figure 2-4. *The sum-of-the-years'-digits template, showing depreciation for an asset with an original cost of $150,000, a salvage value of $25,000, and an estimated life of 18 periods.*

Sum-of-the-Years'- The calculation inputs are Original Cost, Salvage Value, and Esti-
Digits Calculation mated Life. These are the only three variables you enter, and, unless
Inputs you turn off cell protection, the three cells containing these values are
the only cells within the spreadsheet into which you can enter data.

Most often, the tax accounting laws or the financial accounting standards that apply to your modeling assumptions determine the method you use to calculate these variables. Therefore, it would be difficult for me to give specific instructions on how you should come up with these input variables. In general, the Original Cost value should be the cost of acquiring and placing into service the asset you are depreciating. This amount might include the asset purchase price, sales tax, shipping insurance costs, freight charges, and installation costs. The Salvage Value figure is the residual value of the asset at the end of its estimated useful life. The Estimated Life value is the number of periods over which the asset provides benefits. The useful life of an asset is also called the economic life. For tax accounting purposes, the estimated life and the salvage value sometimes are defined by tax law. For financial accounting purposes, previous experience with an asset might provide historical data for forecasting the estimated useful life and salvage values.

For convenience and good documentation within the template, cell C4 contains the original cost and is named Original_Cost, cell C5 contains the salvage value and is named Salvage_Value, and cell C6 contains the estimated life and is named Estimated_Life. The formulas within the actual schedule use these cell names rather than the cell addresses.

Sum-of-the-Years'- The Sum-of-the-Years'-Digits Depreciation Schedule has four col-
Digits Depreciation umns: Period, Period Depreciation, Accumulated Depreciation, and
Schedule Net Book Value.

Period. The period identifier simply numbers the time periods over which you're depreciating the asset. If you're using the template for accounting and bookkeeping, use a number of time periods that is equal to or greater than the estimated life of the asset. However, if you're using the template as a building block for a financial projection, you'll probably want the number of periods in your depreciation schedule to correspond to the number of periods in the other schedules that make up your financial forecasting model.

The first period identifier is stored in cell B11 as the integer 1. Periods that follow are stored as the previous period plus 1. For example, the formula for the second period is:

    =B11+1

The formula for the third period is:

    =B12+1

and so on.

Period Depreciation. Period depreciation is the depreciation expense for the current period. If you're using the template for depreciable assets accounting, the Period Depreciation expense is the debit component of a depreciation journal entry and ultimately shows up in the profit and loss statement. If you're using the template as part of a financial forecast, you can add the Period Depreciation expense to other expenses in the profit and loss forecast. Additionally, any income tax effect of this noncash expense ripples through the cash flow statement.

The Period Depreciation formula for the first period in the forecasting horizon is:

    =SYD(Original_Cost,Salvage_Value,Estimated_Life,B11)

The formula for the second period, however, is modified so that the asset is not depreciated below its salvage value. Starting with the second period, the formula to calculate the Period Depreciation expense is enclosed in an IF statement that first verifies that the asset hasn't already been fully depreciated. For the comparison, rounded amounts are used so that trailing digits of insignificance don't affect the test. The formula for the second period is:

=IF(ROUND(Original_Cost–D11,0)=ROUND(Salvage_Value,0),0,SYD(Original_Cost,Salvage_Value,Estimated_Life,B12)

The Original_Cost–D11 portion is the Net Book Value amount at the end of the previous period. B12 contains the period identifier for the expense that is calculated. In subsequent periods, these parts of the formula change so that the formula always uses the Net Book Value amount from the previous period and the period identifier from the current period.

Accumulated Depreciation. If you're using the template for depreciable assets accounting, the incremental increase in the Accumulated Depreciation amount is the credit component of a depreciation journal entry and ultimately shows up on the balance sheet as an adjustment to the asset's carrying cost. If you're using the template as part of a financial forecast, you can deduct the Accumulated Depreciation amount from the original cost of the asset in the balance sheet forecast to show the asset's net book value. Alternatively, you might simply use the Net Book Value amount calculated by this schedule.

The formula for the Accumulated Depreciation balance in the first period is:

=SUM(C$11:C11)

The formula for the second period is:

=SUM(C$11:C12)

The formula for the third period is:

=SUM(C$11:C13)

and so on.

Net Book Value. The net book value is the asset's carrying cost and is the amount that you report either individually or with other assets' net book values on any historical or pro forma balance sheets.

For each period, the Net Book Value amount is the Original Cost amount less any accumulated depreciation. The formula for the first period is:

=Original_Cost–D11

The second-period formula is:

=Original_Cost–D12

The third-period formula is:

=Original_Cost–D13

and so on.

Straight-Line Depreciation Schedule

The Straight-Line Depreciation Schedule has four columns: Period, Period Depreciation, Accumulated Depreciation, and Net Book Value.

Period. The period identifier simply numbers the time periods over which you're depreciating the asset. If you're using the template for accounting and bookkeeping, use a number of time periods that is equal to or greater than the estimated life of the asset. However, if you're using the template as a building block for a financial projection, you'll probably want the number of periods in your depreciation schedule to correspond to the number of periods in the other schedules that make up your financial forecasting model.

The first period is stored as the integer 1. Periods that follow are stored as the previous period plus 1. For example, the formula for the second period is:

=G11+1

The formula for the third period is:

```
=G12+1
```

and so on.

Period Depreciation. Period depreciation is the depreciation expense for the current period. If you're using the template for depreciable assets accounting, the Period Depreciation expense is the debit component of a depreciation journal entry and ultimately shows up in the profit and loss statement. If you're using the template as part of a financial forecast, you can add the Period Depreciation expense to other expenses in the profit and loss forecast. Additionally, any income tax effect of this noncash expense ripples through the cash flow statement.

Because the asset is expensed equally in each period in straight-line depreciation, the basic Period Depreciation formula used in the first period is incorporated in the formula for each period of the forecasting horizon:

```
=SLN(Original_Cost,Salvage_Value,Estimated_Life)
```

The formula for subsequent periods is modified to prevent an asset from being depreciated below its salvage value. Starting in the second period, the basic formula is enclosed in a MIN statement, which selects the smaller of two amounts: the straight-line depreciation expense or the amount yet to be depreciated. For example, the period expense formula for the second period is:

```
=MIN(SLN(Original_Cost,Salvage_Value,
Estimated_Life),J11-Salvage_Value)
```

The J11-Salvage_Value portion calculates the amount yet to be depreciated. In subsequent periods, this part of the formula uses the Net Book Value amount from the previous period.

Accumulated Depreciation. If you're using the template for depreciable assets accounting, the incremental increase in the Accumulated Depreciation amount is the credit component of a depreciation journal entry and ultimately shows up on the balance sheet as an adjustment to the asset's carrying cost. If you're using the template as part of a financial forecast, you can deduct the accumulated depreciation from the original cost of the asset in the balance sheet forecast to show the asset's net book value. Alternatively, you might simply use the Net Book Value amount calculated by this schedule.

The formula for the Accumulated Depreciation balance in the first period is:

=SUM(H$11:H11)

The second-period formula is:

=SUM(H$11:H12)

and so on.

Net Book Value. The net book value is the asset's carrying cost and is the amount that you report either individually or with other assets' net book values on any historical or pro forma balance sheets.

For each period, the Net Book Value amount is the Original Cost amount less any accumulated depreciation. The formula for the first period is:

=Original_Cost−I11

The second-period formula is:

=Original_Cost−I12

and so on.

Excess Accelerated Depreciation

In certain situations, excess accelerated depreciation is accorded special income tax treatment. The calculated results in the one-column Excess Accelerated Depreciation schedule are simply the difference between the Net Book Value amount for each period calculated in the Sum-of-the-Years'-Digits Depreciation Schedule and the Net Book Value amount calculated in the Straight-Line Depreciation Schedule. The first-period formula is:

=J11–E11

The second-period formula is:

=J12–E12

and so on.

Entering Your Own Data

To enter your own data in the sum-of-the-years'-digits template, follow these steps:

1. Load the file named SUMYEARS.XLS from the templates disk. The template initially contains the default inputs shown in Figure 2-3.

2. In cell C4, enter the original cost of acquiring and placing the asset into service. (If you're using group or composite depreciation, enter the total cost of all the assets in the group.)

3. In cell C5, enter the salvage value of the asset or group of assets.

4. In cell C6, enter the estimated life of the asset.

> **HINT:** When you're using sum-of-the-years'-digits depreciation, express the estimated life in integer format. Accordingly, if you're depreciating an asset over 2½ years, instead of entering the estimated life as 2.5 (years), enter the estimated life as 30 (months).

5. Save your changes by saving the spreadsheet and giving it a new filename. Save it on the disk on which you plan to store the rest of the financial model you're constructing or on which you plan to store the rest of the depreciable assets accounting information.

6. Print the spreadsheet.

Customizing the Template

You can use the sum-of-the-years'-digits template for a wide variety of depreciation schedules. However, you might want to change the template so that it more precisely meets your requirements. For example, you can add text that describes the asset or identifies the supporting documentation for the schedule. You can also increase or decrease the number of periods.

Before you change anything on the sum-of-the-years'-digits template other than the input parameters, unprotect the document.

Increasing the number of periods

To increase the number of periods, follow these steps:

1. Remove the border from the last row of the depreciation schedule.

2. Copy the current last row of the schedule, row 20, down as needed. (You'll probably want either as many rows in the schedule as there are forecasting periods in your overall model or as many rows as there are accounting periods in the asset's estimated life.)

3. Replace the border at the bottom of the depreciation schedule.

4. Reinstate cell protection as needed.

Decreasing the number of periods

To decrease the number of periods, follow these steps:

1. Delete any unneeded rows from the bottom of the schedule.

2. Add a border at the new bottom of the depreciation schedule.

3. Reinstate cell protection as needed.

ANNUITY OR SINKING FUND DEPRECIATION TEMPLATE (ANNUITY.XLS)

You can use the annuity or sinking fund template (ANNUITY.XLS), shown in Figure 2-5, to construct depreciation schedules with the annuity or sinking fund depreciation methods. The annuity and sinking fund depreciation methods include, as part of the depreciation expense, a return on the asset being depreciated. In general, this method violates the Generally Accepted Accounting Principles, and, for this reason, you are unlikely to need this template. However, public

Annuity or Sinking Fund Depreciation Calculation Inputs	
Original Cost	$150,000
Salvage Value	$25,000
Estimated Life	15
Specified Return	10%

Annuity or Sinking Fund Depreciation Schedule				
Period	Period Depreciation	Investment Revenue	Accumulated Depreciation	Net Book Value
1	$18,934	$15,000	$3,934	$146,066
2	18,934	14,607	8,262	141,738
3	18,934	14,174	13,022	136,978
4	18,934	13,698	18,259	131,741
5	18,934	13,174	24,019	125,981
6	18,934	12,598	30,355	119,645
7	18,934	11,965	37,325	112,675
8	18,934	11,268	44,991	105,009
9	18,934	10,501	53,425	96,575
10	18,934	9,658	62,701	87,299
11	18,934	8,730	72,906	77,094
12	18,934	7,709	84,131	65,869
13	18,934	6,587	96,478	53,522
14	18,934	5,352	110,060	39,940
15	18,934	3,994	125,000	25,000
16	0	0	125,000	25,000
17	0	0	125,000	25,000
18	0	0	125,000	25,000
19	0	0	125,000	25,000
20	0	0	125,000	25,000

Figure 2-5. *The annuity or sinking fund depreciation template, showing depreciation for an asset with an original cost of $150,000, a salvage value of $25,000, an estimated life of 15 periods, and a specified return of 10 percent.*

utilities sometimes use these methods for calculating depreciation expenses—a practice that's defensible because the rate-setting process might almost guarantee specific returns on investment. In general, you can use this template if management feels that the rate setting virtually assures a specific return on assets and the annuity or sinking fund method has been selected and approved by management, appropriate regulatory agencies, and your external auditors.

Given four parameters—original cost, salvage value, the estimated useful life, and the specified return on investment—this schedule calculates the period depreciation, the accumulated depreciation, the imputed, or assumed, investment revenue, and the net book value for each period of the forecasting horizon. You need this information to calculate business profits and losses, to report asset balances on the balance sheet, and to calculate any gains or losses on the disposal of assets.

What the Template Contains and Does

The two parts to the annuity or sinking fund template are the Annuity or Sinking Fund Depreciation Calculation Inputs box and the Annuity or Sinking Fund Depreciation schedule.

Annuity or Sinking Fund Depreciation Calculation Inputs

The calculation inputs are Original Cost, Salvage Value, Estimated Life, and Specified Return. These are the only four variables you enter, and, unless you turn off cell protection, the four cells containing these values are the only cells within the spreadsheet into which you can enter data.

Most often, the financial accounting standards and rate-setting regulations that apply to your modeling assumptions determine the method you use to calculate these variables. Therefore, it would be difficult for me to give specific instructions on how you should come up with these input variables. In general, the Original Cost value should be the cost of acquiring and placing into service the asset that you are depreciating. This amount might include the asset purchase price, sales tax, shipping insurance costs, freight charges, and installation costs. The Salvage Value amount is the residual value of the asset at the end of its estimated useful life. The Specified Return value is the return on investment per period that the rate-setting agency uses to set revenues. The Estimated Life value is the number of periods during which the asset provides benefits. The estimated useful life of an asset is also called the economic life. For rate-setting purposes, the estimated life and the salvage value might be defined by agency regulations. Or previous experience with an asset might provide historical data for estimating these inputs.

For convenience and good documentation within the template, cell C4 contains the original cost and is named Original_Cost, cell C5 contains the salvage value and is named Salvage_Value, cell C6 contains the estimated life and is named Estimated_Life, and cell C7 contains the specified return and is named Specified_Return. The formulas within the actual schedule use these cell names rather than the cell addresses.

Annuity or Sinking Fund Depreciation schedule

The Annuity or Sinking Fund Depreciation schedule has five columns: Period, Period Depreciation, Investment Revenue, Accumulated Depreciation, and Net Book Value.

Period. The period identifier simply numbers the time periods over which you're depreciating the asset. If you're using the template for accounting and bookkeeping, use a number of periods that is equal to or greater than the estimated life of the asset. However, if you're using the template as a building block for a financial projection, you'll probably want the number of periods in your depreciation schedule to correspond to the number of periods in the other schedules that make up your financial forecasting model.

The first period identifier is stored in cell B12 as the integer 1. Periods that follow are stored as the previous period plus 1. For example, the formula for the second period is:

=B12+1

The formula for the third period is:

```
=B13+1
```

and so on.

Period Depreciation. Period depreciation is the depreciation expense for the current period. If you're using the template for depreciable assets accounting, the Period Depreciation expense is the debit component of a depreciation journal entry and ultimately shows up in the profit and loss statement. If you're using the template as part of a financial forecast, you can include the Period Depreciation expense with other expenses in the profit and loss forecast. Additionally, any income tax effect of this noncash expense ripples through the cash flow statement.

The basic Period Depreciation formula is:

```
=−(Original_Cost−(Salvage_Value/
(1+Specified_Return)^Estimated_Life))/
PV(Specified_Return,Estimated_Life,1)
```

The minus sign at the beginning of this formula is necessary because the PV function returns a negative value when all of its arguments are positive.

The formula for the second period, however, is modified so that the asset is not depreciated below its salvage value. Starting with the second period, the formula to calculate the Period Depreciation expense is enclosed in an IF statement that first verifies that the asset hasn't already been fully depreciated. For the comparison, rounded amounts are used so that trailing digits of insignificance don't affect the test. The formula for the second period is:

```
IF(ROUND(Original_Cost−E12,0)=ROUND(Salvage_Value,0),0,
−(Original_Cost−(Salvage_Value/
(1+Specified_Return)^Estimated_Life))/
PV(Specified_Return,Estimated_Life,1))
```

Investment Revenue. Investment revenue is the assumed investment return on the asset. If you're using the template for depreciable assets accounting and have selected the annuity depreciation method, the investment revenue for a period is credited to an investment revenue account and ultimately shows up in the profit and loss statement. If you're using the template for depreciable assets accounting and have selected the sinking fund depreciation method, the investment revenue for a period is credited to the depreciation expense account. This results in a net debit to the depreciation expense account equal to the return of the asset principal and the increase in the accumulated depreciation expense for the period. The net depreciation expense ultimately shows up in the profit and loss statement. If you're using the template as part of a financial forecast, you can add the investment revenue to other miscellaneous revenues in the profit and loss forecast.

The first-period Investment Revenue value is the Original Cost value times the Specified Return value. The formula for the first period is:

=Specified_Return*Original_Cost

The formula for the second period, however, is modified so that the previous Net Book Value amount is used and so that investment revenue isn't calculated when the asset is fully depreciated. Starting in the second period, the formula to calculate the Investment Revenue amount is enclosed in an IF statement that first verifies that the asset hasn't already been fully depreciated. For the comparison, rounded amounts are used so that trailing digits of insignificance don't affect the test. The formula for the second period is:

=IF(ROUND(Original_Cost−E12,0)=ROUND(Salvage_Value,0),0,
Specified_Return*(Original_Cost−E12))

The Original_Cost−E12 portion is the Net Book Value amount at the end of the previous period. In subsequent periods, this part of the formula changes so that it always uses the Accumulated Depreciation amount from the previous period.

Accumulated Depreciation. If you're using the template for depreciable assets accounting, the incremental increase in the Accumulated Depreciation amount is the credit component of a depreciation journal entry and ultimately shows up on the balance sheet as an adjustment to the asset's carrying cost. If you're using the template as part of a financial forecast, you can include the Accumulated Depreciation amount with the original cost of the asset in the balance sheet forecast to show the asset's net book value. Alternatively, you might simply use the Net Book Value amount calculated in this schedule.

The first period's Accumulated Depreciation balance is the cumulative return of principal calculated as the cumulative depreciation expense net of the cumulative assumed investment revenue. The formula for the first period is:

=SUM(C$12:C12)−SUM(D$12:D12)

The second-period formula is:

=SUM(C$12:C13)−SUM(D$12:D13)

and so on.

Net Book Value. The net book value is the asset's carrying cost and is the amount that you report either individually or with other assets' net book values on any historical or pro forma balance sheets.

For each period, the Net Book Value amount is the Original Cost amount less any accumulated depreciation. The formula for the first period is:

=Original_Cost−E12

The second-period formula is:

=Original_Cost−E13

and so on.

Entering Your Own Data

To enter your own data in the annuity and sinking fund depreciation template, follow these steps:

1. Load the file named ANNUITY.XLS from the templates disk. The template initially contains the default inputs shown in Figure 2-5.

2. In cell C4, enter the original cost of acquiring and placing an asset into service. (If you're using group or composite depreciation, enter the total cost of all the assets in the group.)

3. In cell C5, enter the salvage value of the asset or group of assets.

4. In cell C6, enter the estimated life of the asset (or the average life if you're using group or composite depreciation).

> **HINT:** For annuity or sinking fund depreciation, you need to express the estimated life in integer format. Accordingly, if you have an asset that you want to depreciate over 2½ years, instead of entering the estimated life as 2.5 (years), enter the estimated life as 30 (months).

5. In cell C7, enter the specified return on investment.

6. Save your changes by saving the spreadsheet and giving it a new filename. Save it on the disk on which you plan to store the rest of the financial model you're constructing or on which you plan to store the rest of the fixed assets accounting information.

7. Print the spreadsheet.

Customizing the Template

You can use the annuity template for either annuity or sinking fund depreciation schedules. However, you might want to change the template so that it more precisely meets your requirements. For example, you can add text that describes the assets or identifies the supporting documentation for the schedule. You can also increase or decrease the number of periods.

2: Asset Depreciation Templates

Before you change anything on the annuity and sinking fund depreciation template other than the calculation inputs, unprotect the document.

Increasing the number of periods

To increase the number of periods, follow these steps:

1. Remove the border from the last row of the depreciation schedule.

2. Copy the current last row of the schedule, row 20, down as needed. (You'll probably want either as many rows in the schedule as there are forecasting periods in your overall model or as many rows as there are accounting periods in the asset's estimated life.)

3. Replace the border at the bottom of the depreciation schedule.

4. Reinstate cell protection as needed.

Decreasing the number of periods

To decrease the number of periods, follow these steps:

1. Delete any unneeded rows from the bottom of the schedule.

2. Add a border at the new bottom of the depreciation schedule.

3. Reinstate cell protection as needed.

ACTIVITY DEPRECIATION TEMPLATE (ACTIVITY.XLS)

You can use the activity depreciation template (ACTIVITY.XLS), shown in Figure 2-6 on the following page, to construct depreciation schedules with the activity method. The activity method is unique among depreciation methods because it expenses the original cost of an asset based on use rather than on time. In general, you use this template if you're calculating depreciation for financial or managerial accounting and you feel that its allocation of costs matches economic reality.

Given the four parameters—original cost, salvage value, estimated useful life (expressed in units of use rather than time), and period units of use—this schedule calculates the depreciation expense, the accumulated depreciation, and the net book value for each period of

Activity Depreciation Calculation Inputs	
Original Cost	$150,000
Salvage Value	$25,000
Estimated Life	5,000

Activity Depreciation Schedule				
Period	Period Units of Use	Period Depreciation	Accumulated Depreciation	Net Book Value
1	300	$7,500	$7,500	$142,500
2	300	$7,500	15,000	135,000
3	400	$10,000	25,000	125,000
4	400	$10,000	35,000	115,000
5	400	$10,000	45,000	105,000
6	500	$12,500	57,500	92,500
7	500	$12,500	70,000	80,000
8	400	$10,000	80,000	70,000
9	400	$10,000	90,000	60,000
10	400	$10,000	100,000	50,000
11	400	$10,000	110,000	40,000
12	400	$10,000	120,000	30,000
13	200	$5,000	125,000	25,000
14	0	$0	125,000	25,000
15	0	$0	125,000	25,000
16	0	$0	125,000	25,000
17	0	$0	125,000	25,000
18	0	$0	125,000	25,000
19	0	$0	125,000	25,000
20	0	$0	125,000	25,000

Figure 2-6. *The activity depreciation template (ACTIVITY.XLS), showing depreciation for an asset with an original cost of $150,000, a salvage value of $25,000, and an estimated life of 5000 units of use.*

the forecasting horizon. You need this information to calculate business profits and losses, to report asset balances on the balance sheet, and to calculate any gains or losses on the disposal of assets.

What the Template Contains and Does

The two parts to the activity template are the Activity Depreciation Calculation Inputs box and the Activity Depreciation Schedule.

2: Asset Depreciation Templates

Activity Depreciation Calculation Inputs

The calculation inputs and the period units of use are the only variables you enter, and, unless you turn off cell protection, these are the only cells into which you can enter data.

Most often, the financial accounting standards or internal managerial accounting conventions that apply to your modeling assumptions determine the method you use to calculate these variables. Therefore, it would be difficult for me to give specific instructions on how you should come up with these input variables. In general, the Original Cost value should be the cost of acquiring and placing into service the asset that you are depreciating. This figure might include the asset purchase price, sales tax, shipping insurance costs, freight charges, and installation costs. The Salvage Value amount is the residual value of the asset at the end of its estimated useful life. The Estimated Life value is the number of units of use the asset will provide. For example, you can express the Estimated Life value in miles for a truck or in hours of operation for a piece of machinery. The estimated useful life of an asset is also called the economic life. For both financial and managerial accounting purposes, previous experience with an asset might provide historical data for estimating the useful life. The period units of use show your estimates of the use of the asset in each of the periods in your forecast.

For convenience and good documentation within the template, cell C4 contains the original cost and is named Original_Cost, cell C5 contains the salvage value and is named Salvage_Value, and cell C6 contains the estimated life and is named Estimated_Life. The formulas within the actual schedule use these cell names rather than the cell addresses.

Activity Depreciation Schedule

The Activity Depreciation Schedule has five columns: Period, Period Units of Use, Period Depreciation, Accumulated Depreciation, and Net Book Value.

Period. The Period identifier simply numbers the time periods over which you're depreciating the asset. If you're using the template as a building block for a financial projection, use the same number of periods in your depreciation schedule as you use in the other schedules that make up your financial forecasting model.

The first-period identifier is stored in cell B11 as the integer 1. Periods that follow are stored as the previous period plus 1. For example, the formula for the second period is:

```
=B11+1
```

The formula for the third period is:

```
=B12+1
```

and so on.

Period Units of Use. Enter either the actual or the forecasted units of use for each period of the forecast.

Period Depreciation. Period depreciation is the depreciation expense for the current period. If you use the template for depreciable assets accounting, the Period Depreciation expense is the debit component of a depreciation journal entry and ultimately shows up in the profit and loss statement. If you use the template as part of a financial forecast, you'll probably add the Period Depreciation expense with other expenses in the profit and loss forecast.

The activity depreciation method expenses a portion of an asset's depreciable cost based on the ratio of that period's units of use to the estimated life, calibrated in units of use. For example, the formula for the first period is:

```
=C11/Estimated_Life*(Original_Cost-Salvage_Value)
```

The formula for subsequent periods is modified to prevent an asset from being depreciated below its salvage value (as might be the case if you accidentally entered more period units of use than the estimated life in units of use). Starting in the second period, the basic formula is enclosed in a MIN statement, which selects the smaller of two amounts: the activity depreciation expense or the amount yet to be depreciated. For example, the period expense formula for the second period is:

```
=MIN(C12/Estimated_Life*(Original_Cost–
Salvage_Value),F11–Salvage_Value)
```

The F11–Salvage_Value portion calculates the amount yet to be depreciated. In subsequent periods, this part of the formula uses the Net Book Value amount from the previous period.

Accumulated Depreciation. If you use the template for depreciable assets accounting, use the incremental increase in accumulated depreciation as the credit component of a depreciation journal entry, and it will ultimately show up on the balance sheet as an adjustment to the asset's original cost. If you use the template as part of a financial forecast, you might deduct the accumulated depreciation from the original cost of the asset on the balance sheet forecast to show the asset's net book value. Alternatively, you can use the Net Book Value amount calculated in this schedule.

The first period's Accumulated Depreciation balance is the first Period Depreciation expense. The formula is:

```
=SUM(D$11:D11)
```

The second-period formula is:

```
=SUM(D$11:D12)
```

and so on.

Net Book Value. Net book value is an asset's original cost minus its accumulated depreciation and is the amount that you would report, either individually or with other assets' net book values, on any historical or pro forma balance sheets.

For each period, the Net Book Value figure is the Original Cost amount less any accumulated depreciation. The formula for the first period is:

=Original_Cost−E11

The second-period formula is:

=Original_Cost−E12

and so on.

Entering Your Own Data

To enter your own data in the activity depreciation template, follow these steps:

1. Load ACTIVITY.XLS from the templates disk. The template initially contains the default inputs shown in Figure 2-6.
2. In cell C4, enter the original cost of acquiring and placing into service an asset.
3. In cell C5, enter the salvage value of the asset.
4. In cell C6, enter the estimated life of the asset, calibrated in units of use.
5. Starting in cell C11, enter the period units of use.

> **HINT:** If you want to fully depreciate the asset, be sure the sum of the period units of use equals the estimated life, calibrated in units of use.

6. Save your changes by saving the spreadsheet and giving it a new filename. Save it on the disk on which you'll be storing the rest of the financial model you're constructing or on which you plan to store the rest of the fixed assets accounting information.
7. Print the spreadsheet.

Customizing the Template

You can use the activity template for a wide variety of depreciation schedules. However, you might want to change the template so that it more precisely meets your requirements. For example, you can add text that describes the asset, describes the units of use that calibrate its estimated life, or identifies the supporting documentation for the schedule. You can also increase or decrease the number of periods.

Before you change anything on the activity depreciation template other than the input parameters, unprotect the document.

Increasing the number of periods

To increase the number of periods, follow these steps:

1. Remove the border from the last row of the depreciation schedule.

2. Copy the current last row of the schedule, the row for Period 20, down as needed. (You'll probably want as many rows in the schedule as there are forecasting periods in your overall model.)

3. Replace the border at the bottom of the depreciation schedule.

4. Reinstate cell protection as needed.

Decreasing the number of periods

To decrease the number of periods, follow these steps:

1. Delete any unneeded rows from the bottom of the schedule.

2. Add a border at the new bottom of the depreciation schedule.

3. Reinstate cell protection as needed.

LINKING THESE TEMPLATES TO OTHER SPREADSHEETS

Although no other templates in this toolkit are designed to provide data to the depreciation templates, you might want to link a depreciation template to a subsidiary spreadsheet.

For example, suppose your firm builds a factory, and you calculate the cost in a schedule of costs called FACTORY.XLS, as shown in Figure 2-7 on the following page. For financial accounting purposes, you depreciate the factory over 20 years on a straight-line basis,

	A	B
1	Costs of New Factory	
2		
3	Building	500000
4	Land	100000
5	Machinery	137500
6	Total Factory Costs	737500

Figure 2-7. *The FACTORY.XLS spreadsheet.*

forecasting a $125,000 salvage value. You use the straight-line depreciation template (STRAIGHT.XLS) to develop a schedule that shows the calculated results of depreciating the factory.

However, rather than simply entering the Original Cost as $737,500, you link this cell to the FACTORY.XLS spreadsheet. Using this approach means that each time you update FACTORY.XLS, your depreciation schedule, via the link, is also updated. To construct such a link with a file named FACTORY.XLS stored in the WINDOWS directory on your hard disk, you'd do the following:

1. Load STRAIGHT.XLS from the templates disk. The template initially contains the default inputs shown in Figure 2-1.

2. In cell C4, enter the original cost of acquiring the factory and placing it into service by entering the formula:

    ='C:\WINDOWS\FACTORY.XLS'!$B$6

   Cell B6 in FACTORY.XLS is the cell that contains the total cost of the factory.

3. In cell C5, enter the salvage value of the factory.

4. In cell C6, enter the estimated life of the factory.

5. Save your changes by creating a new file on the disk on which you plan to store the rest of the financial model you're constructing or on which you plan to store your other depreciable asset accounting records.

6. Print the spreadsheet.

The completed depreciation schedule might look like the one shown in Figure 2-8. The significance of this link is that the value shown in cell C4 ($737,500) isn't a number or formula calculated in this spreadsheet; rather, it is the calculated total cost pulled from FACTORY.XLS.

Straight-Line Depreciation Calculation Inputs	
Original Cost	$737,500
Salvage Value	$25,000
Estimated Life	18

Straight-Line Depreciation Schedule			
Period	Period Depreciation	Accumulated Depreciation	Net Book Value
1	$39,583	$39,583	$697,917
2	$39,583	79,167	658,333
3	$39,583	118,750	618,750
4	$39,583	158,333	579,167
5	$39,583	197,917	539,583
6	$39,583	237,500	500,000
7	$39,583	277,083	460,417
8	$39,583	316,667	420,833
9	$39,583	356,250	381,250
10	$39,583	395,833	341,667
11	$39,583	435,417	302,083
12	$39,583	475,000	262,500
13	$39,583	514,583	222,917
14	$39,583	554,167	183,333
15	$39,583	593,750	143,750
16	$39,583	633,333	104,167
17	$39,583	672,917	64,583
18	$39,583	712,500	25,000
19	$0	712,500	25,000
20	$0	712,500	25,000

Figure 2-8. *The straight-line depreciation template, with the original cost input supplied from another spreadsheet, FACTORY.XLS.*

3

Debt Amortization Templates

Debt amortization schedules ensure that your financial models and accounting records of amortized debt instruments are precise and accurate. Using an amortization schedule lets you track the principal balance, debt service payments, and principal and interest components of the payments on a debt instrument.

The debt amortization templates in this chapter automate the preparation of debt amortization schedules and provide foundations for customizing schedules. These templates (and the amortization conventions they use) are:

- FIXRATE.XLS (fixed interest rate, ordinary annuity)
- VARIRATE.XLS (variable interest rate, ordinary annuity)
- FIXDUE.XLS (fixed interest rate, annuity due)
- VARIDUE.XLS (variable interest rate, annuity due)

This chapter shows you how to use these four templates, print them, modify them, and link them with subsidiary spreadsheets.

AMORTIZING DEBT: A SHORT PRIMER

Debt amortization is the systematic reduction in debt principal made over the term, or life, of the debt through periodic debt service payments. In general, five variables can determine the amortization of a debt: principal, interest rate, amortization term, debt term, and debt service payment. The principal is the amount to be amortized or paid back. The interest rate is the percentage that, when multiplied by the principal at the beginning of the period, calculates the amount of interest. The amortization term is the number of payment periods over which the principal can be completely paid back, given a constant debt service payment. The debt term is the number of time periods over which the debt is outstanding. Although the debt term is generally the same as the amortization term, it can be shorter. In those cases, a balloon payment equal to the unamortized principal is made at the end of the debt term. The debt service payment is the combined principal and interest payment made every period over the debt term.

The timing of a payment—whether it's at the beginning or at the end of the period—also affects the amortization of a debt. Payments made at the end of the period are called payments in arrears, or ordinary annuities. Payments made at the beginning of the period are called payments in advance, or annuities due.

Microsoft Excel's PMT function calculates the payment that, given the interest rate and the principal, completely pays off the debt principal over the amortization term.

The payment is calculated by using the PMT function, which uses the following formulas:

> Payment for an ordinary annuity=Principal/Present Value factor of the ordinary annuity for i and n

> Payment for an annuity due=Principal/Present Value factor of the annuity due for i and n

where i is the period interest rate and n is the number of periods.

All of the variables are defined by the terms of the contract that describes the debt instrument. Accordingly, your best source for determining these variables is the debt contract.

3: Debt Amortization Templates

> **HINT:** Be consistent in the financial measurement time periods you use. If you're building a debt amortization schedule with monthly payments, express your debt and amortization terms in months and use a monthly interest rate. If you're building a debt amortization schedule with quarterly or yearly payments, express your debt and amortization terms in quarters or years and use a quarterly or yearly interest rate.

FIXED RATE, ORDINARY ANNUITY TEMPLATE (FIXRATE.XLS)

You can use the fixed rate, ordinary annuity amortization template (FIXRATE.XLS), shown in Figure 3-1 on the following page, to construct debt amortization schedules for debt instruments with a fixed interest rate and with payments due at the end of the period. The template assumes a balloon payment when regular debt service payments don't completely pay off the outstanding principal by the end of the debt term.

Given four parameters—principal, debt term, amortization term, and interest rate—this template calculates payment amounts, the interest and principal components of each payment, the outstanding principal balance for each period, and any balloon payments necessary to pay off the unamortized principal at the end of the debt term. You need this information to calculate profits and losses, to calculate cash flows, to report asset or liability balances on the balance sheet, and to calculate any gains or losses on the disposal of the asset or the refunding of the liability.

What the Template Contains and Does

The three parts of the fixed rate, ordinary annuity amortization template are the Fixed Interest Rate Amortization Inputs box, the Fixed Interest Rate Amortization Schedule, and the Balloon Payment Schedule.

Fixed Interest Rate Amortization Inputs

The amortization inputs are the only four variables you enter, and, unless you turn off cell protection, the four cells containing these values are the only cells into which you can enter data.

Fixed Interest Rate Amortization Inputs

Principal	$100,000
Debt Term	15
Amortize Term	20
Interest Rate	10.00%

Fixed Interest Rate Amortization Schedule

Period	Total Payment	Interest Component	Principal Component	Principal Balance
1	$11,746	$10,000	$1,746	$98,254
2	11,746	9,825	1,921	96,333
3	11,746	9,633	2,113	94,221
4	11,746	9,422	2,324	91,897
5	11,746	9,190	2,556	89,341
6	11,746	8,934	2,812	86,529
7	11,746	8,653	3,093	83,436
8	11,746	8,344	3,402	80,033
9	11,746	8,003	3,743	76,291
10	11,746	7,629	4,117	72,174
11	11,746	7,217	4,529	67,645
12	11,746	6,765	4,981	62,664
13	11,746	6,266	5,480	57,184
14	11,746	5,718	6,028	51,157
15	11,746	5,116	6,630	44,526
16	0	0	0	0
17	0	0	0	0
18	0	0	0	0
19	0	0	0	0
20	0	0	0	0

Balloon Payment Schedule

Balloon Payment	Full Principal Payment	True Balance
$0	$1,746	$98,254
0	1,921	96,333
0	2,113	94,221
0	2,324	91,897
0	2,556	89,341
0	2,812	86,529
0	3,093	83,436
0	3,402	80,033
0	3,743	76,291
0	4,117	72,174
0	4,529	67,645
0	4,981	62,664
0	5,480	57,184
0	6,028	51,157
44,526	51,157	0
0	0	0
0	0	0
0	0	0
0	0	0
0	0	0

Figure 3-1. *The fixed interest rate, ordinary annuity debt amortization template, showing amortization for a debt of $100,000, amortized over 20 periods but with a balloon payment equal to the outstanding balance at period 15 and an interest rate of 10 percent.*

These variables are defined by the debt contract. In general, the Principal amount is the amount borrowed or loaned at the beginning of the debt term. The Debt Term value is the number of payment periods over which the debt is outstanding. The Amortize Term value is the number of periods over which the calculated payment can fully amortize, or pay off, the principal. The Interest Rate value is the rate per period that, when multiplied by the outstanding balance at the beginning of the payment period, results in the amount of interest expense or interest income for the period. Note that this rate might differ from the rate stated in the debt contract if the compounding period differs from the payment period.

For convenience and good documentation within the template, cell C4 contains the starting debt amount and is named Principal, cell C5 contains the debt term in payment periods and is named Debt_Term, cell C6 contains the amortization term in payment periods and is named Amortize_Term, and cell C7 contains the per-period interest rate and is named Interest_Rate. The formulas within the actual schedules use these cell names rather than the cell addresses.

Fixed Interest Rate Amortization Schedule

The amortization schedule has five columns: Period, Total Payment, Interest Component, Principal Component, and Principal Balance.

Period. The period identifier simply numbers the time periods over which the debt is outstanding and paid down. If you're using the template for accounting, use a number of periods that is equal to or greater than the number of periods over which the debt is outstanding. However, if you're using the template as a building block for a financial projection, you'll probably want the number of periods in your amortization schedule to correspond to the number of periods in the other schedules that make up your financial forecasting model.

The first period identifier is stored in cell B12 as the integer 1. Periods that follow are stored as the previous period plus 1. For example, the formula for the second period is:

```
=B12+1
```

The formula for the third period is:

```
=B13+1
```

and so on.

Total Payment. The total payment is the payment for the current period. If you're using the template for liability bookkeeping, this is the amount you enter as a credit to the cash account. If you're using this template for receivables or investment bookkeeping, this is the amount you enter as a debit to your cash account. If you're using the template as part of a financial forecast and, from your perspective, the debt being amortized represents a liability, you can add the payment amount to other debt service payments in the section of a cash flow forecast that details uses of funds. If you're using the template as part of a financial forecast and, from your perspective, the debt being amortized represents an asset, you can add the payment amount to other debt service payments in the section of a cash flow forecast that details sources of funds.

The Total Payment formula for the first period uses the PMT function, as follows:

```
=-PMT(Interest_Rate,Amortize_Term,Principal)
```

The minus sign to the left of the PMT function is needed because, when the principal amount included is a positive number, the payment calculated is negative. The formula for subsequent periods is modified to display 0 after the debt is paid off. Starting in the second period, the basic formula is enclosed in an IF statement that first verifies that the debt term hasn't already expired. Therefore, in the second period of the forecasting horizon, the Total Payment formula is:

```
=IF(B13<=Debt_Term,-PMT(Interest_Rate,Amortize_Term,Principal),0)
```

B13 contains the period identifier. In subsequent periods, this part of the formula is changed so that the formula always uses the current period identifier.

Interest Component. The interest component is the amount of income or expense accrued over the payment period. If you're using the template for liability bookkeeping, this is the amount you enter as a debit to the interest expense account. If you're using the template for receivables or investment bookkeeping, this is the amount you enter as a credit to the interest income account. If you're using the template for a financial forecast, you can include this amount in either the financing income or financing expense portion of your profit and loss statement.

Each period's Interest Component amount is the previous period's Principal Balance amount times the Interest Rate value. The first-period formula is:

```
=Principal*Interest_Rate
```

The formula for subsequent periods is modified to display 0 after the debt is paid off. Starting in the second period, the basic formula is enclosed in an IF statement that first verifies that the debt term hasn't already expired. Therefore, in the second period of the forecasting horizon, the total payment formula is:

```
=IF(B13<=Debt_Term,F12*Interest_Rate,0)
```

As in the total payment formula, B13 contains the period identifier. F12 contains the ending balance in the previous period. In subsequent periods, these parts of the formula are changed so that the formula always uses the current period identifier and the Principal Balance amount for the previous period.

Principal Component. The principal component is the amount subtracted from the outstanding principal balance when the total payment exceeds the accrued interest. If you're using the template for receivables or investment bookkeeping, this is the amount you enter as a credit to the asset account, reflecting a reduction in the amount owed you. If you're using the template for liability bookkeeping, this is the amount you enter as a debit to the liability account, reflecting a reduction in the amount you owe.

For each period, the Principal Component amount is the Total Payment amount less the Interest Component amount. The first-period formula is:

=C12–D12

The second-period formula is:

=C13–D13

and so on.

Principal Balance. The principal balance is the outstanding balance of the debt at the end of the period. If you're using the template for financial forecasts, this is the amount you include in the balance sheet as either an asset or a liability.

The Principal Balance amount is the previous period's Principal Balance amount minus the Principal Component amount for the current period. The formula for the first period is:

=Principal–E12

The formula for subsequent periods is modified to display 0 for the Principal Balance amount after the debt is paid off. This modification is necessary for those situations in which a balloon payment is paid. Starting in the second period, the basic formula is enclosed in an IF statement that first verifies that the debt term hasn't already expired. Therefore, in the second period of the forecasting horizon, the Principal Balance formula is:

=IF(B13<=Debt_Term,F12–E13,0)

Again, B13 contains the period identifier. F12 contains the ending balance for the previous period. E13 contains the Principal Component amount for the current period. In subsequent periods, these parts of the formula are changed so that the formula always uses the current period identifier, the Principal Balance amount for the previous period, and the Principal Component amount for the current period.

Balloon Payment Schedule

Use the Balloon Payment Schedule when you're working with a debt that contains a balloon payment. The bookkeeping and forecasting methods for balloon payments and principal reductions are the same as the methods for the total payment and principal component described on the amortization schedule.

The Balloon Payment Schedule has three columns: Balloon Payment, Full Principal Payment, and True Balance.

Balloon Payment. The balloon payment is the principal balance outstanding when the debt term ends. The formula for the first period is:

    =IF(B12=Debt_Term,F12,0)

The second-period formula is:

    =IF(B13=Debt_Term,F13,0)

and so on.

Full Principal Payment. The full principal payment for each period is the principal component of the regular payment plus any balloon payment. The schedule uses the Full Principal Payment value as the full principal reduction stemming from regular payments and any balloon payment due. The formula for the first period is:

    =H12+E12

The formula for the second period is:

    =H13+E13

and so on.

True Balance. The true principal balance is the principal balance in the amortization schedule less any balloon payment made. The schedule uses the True Balance value as the principal balance outstanding, because it includes both the principal components of the regular debt service payments and the balloon payment. The formula for the first period is:

=F12–H12

The formula for the second period is:

=F13–H13

and so on.

Entering Your Own Data

To enter your own data in the fixed interest rate, ordinary annuity amortization template, follow these steps:

1. Load FIXRATE.XLS from the templates disk. The template initially contains the default inputs shown in Figure 3-1.
2. In cell C4, enter the starting principal balance of the debt.
3. In cell C5, enter the debt term, in payment periods.
4. In cell C6, enter the amortization term, in payment periods.
5. In cell C7, enter the per period interest rate.
6. Save your changes by saving the spreadsheet and giving it a new filename. Save it on the disk on which you plan to store the financial model you're constructing or on which you plan to store your accounting records.
7. Print the template.

Customizing the Template

You can use the fixed interest rate amortization template without modification for many debt instruments. However, you might want to change the template so that it more closely matches your requirements. For example, you can add text that describes the borrower or lender, the debt contract's other terms, and the supporting documentation for the template. You can also increase or decrease the number of periods. Before you change anything on the template other than the input parameters, unprotect the document.

Increasing the number of periods

To increase the number of periods, follow these steps:

1. Remove the border from the last row of the amortization schedule.

2. Copy the current last row of the amortization schedule down as needed. (You'll probably want either as many rows in the schedule as there are forecasting periods in your overall model or as many rows as there are payment periods in the debt term.)

3. Replace the border at the bottom of the amortization schedule.

4. Reinstate cell protection as needed.

Decreasing the number of periods

To decrease the number of periods, follow these steps:

1. Delete any unneeded rows from the bottom of the schedule.

2. Add a border at the new bottom of the amortization schedule.

3. Reinstate cell protection as needed.

Removing the Balloon Payment Schedule

If the debt you want to track doesn't have a balloon payment, you might want to remove the Balloon Payment Schedule. To do so, follow these steps:

1. Clear all the cells in the balloon payment schedule.

2. Reinstate cell protection as needed.

VARIABLE RATE, ORDINARY ANNUITY TEMPLATE (VARIRATE.XLS)

You can use the variable rate, ordinary annuity amortization template (VARIRATE.XLS), shown in Figure 3-2 on the following page, to construct debt amortization schedules for debt instruments with a variable interest rate and with payments due at the end of each period. The template assumes a balloon payment when regular debt service payments don't completely pay off the outstanding principal by the end of the debt term.

Variable Interest Rate Amortization Inputs	
Principal	$100,000
Debt Term	15
Amortize Term	20

Variable Interest Rate Amortization Schedule

Period	Interest Rate	Total Payment	Interest Component	Principal Component	Principal Balance
1	10.00%	$11,746	$10,000	$1,746	$98,254
2	11.00%	12,534	10,808	1,726	96,528
3	12.00%	13,315	11,583	1,731	94,797
4	13.00%	14,088	12,324	1,764	93,033
5	12.00%	13,340	11,164	2,176	90,857
6	11.00%	12,635	9,994	2,641	88,216
7	10.00%	11,975	8,822	3,153	85,063
8	9.00%	11,362	7,656	3,706	81,357
9	8.00%	10,796	6,509	4,287	77,070
10	8.00%	10,796	6,166	4,630	72,440
11	8.00%	10,796	5,795	5,000	67,439
12	8.00%	10,796	5,395	5,401	62,039
13	8.00%	10,796	4,963	5,833	56,206
14	8.00%	10,796	4,496	6,299	49,907
15	8.00%	10,796	3,993	6,803	43,104
16	8.00%	0	0	0	0
17	8.00%	0	0	0	0
18	8.00%	0	0	0	0
19	8.00%	0	0	0	0
20	8.00%	0	0	0	0

Balloon Payment Schedule

Balloon Payment	Full Principal Payment	True Balance
	$0	$98,254
	0	96,528
	0	94,797
	0	93,033
	0	90,857
	0	88,216
	0	85,063
	0	81,357
	0	77,070
	0	72,440
	0	67,439
	0	62,039
	0	56,206
	0	49,907
43,104	49,907	0
	0	0
	0	0
	0	0
	0	0
	0	0

Figure 3-2. *The variable interest rate, ordinary annuity debt amortization template, showing amortization for a debt of $100,000, amortized over 20 periods but with a balloon payment equal to the outstanding balance at period 15 and with varying interest rates.*

Given four parameters—principal, debt term, amortization term, and period interest rates—this template calculates payment amounts, the interest and principal components of each payment, outstanding principal balances for each period, and any balloon payments necessary to pay off the unamortized principal at the end of the debt term. You need this information to calculate profits and losses, to calculate cash flows, to report asset or liability balances on the balance sheet, and to calculate gains or losses on the disposal of assets and the refunding of liabilities.

What the Template Contains and Does

The three parts of the variable rate, ordinary annuity amortization template are the Variable Interest Rate Amortization Inputs box, the Variable Interest Rate Amortization Schedule, and the Balloon Payment Schedule.

Variable Interest Rate Amortization Inputs

The amortization inputs, along with the Period Interest Rate values in the amortization schedule, are the variables you enter, and, unless you turn off cell protection, these are the only cells into which you can enter data.

These variables are defined by the debt contract. In general, the Principal amount is the amount borrowed or loaned at the beginning of the debt term. The Debt Term value is the number of payment periods over which the debt is outstanding. The Amortize Term value is the number of periods over which the calculated payment can fully amortize, or pay off, the principal.

For convenience and good documentation within the model, cell C4 contains the starting debt amount and is named Principal, cell C5 contains the debt term in payment periods and is named Debt_Term, and cell C6 contains the amortization in payment periods and is named Amortize_Term. The formulas within the actual schedules use these cell names rather than the cell addresses.

Variable Interest Rate Amortization Schedule

The amortization schedule has six columns: Period, Period Interest Rate, Total Payment, Interest Component, Principal Component, and Principal Balance.

Period. The period identifier simply numbers the time periods over which the debt is outstanding and paid down. If you're using the template for accounting, use a number of periods that is equal to or greater than the number of periods over which the debt is outstanding. However, if you're using the template as a building block for a financial projection, you'll probably want the number of periods in your amortization schedule to correspond to the number of periods in the other schedules that make up your financial forecasting model.

The first period identifier is stored in cell B11 as the integer 1. Periods that follow are stored as the previous period plus 1. For example, the formula for the second period is:

```
=B11+1
```

The formula for the third period is:

```
=B12+1
```

and so on.

Period Interest Rate. The period interest rates are the interest rates that, when multiplied by the outstanding balance at the beginning of the payment period, produce the amount of interest expense or interest income for the period. Period interest rates typically are tied to a market-sensitive interest rate index that is based on a widely traded or widely used interest rate, such as the one-year U.S. treasury bill or the one-year London interbank offered rate. You enter either the actual or the forecasted interest rates for each payment period over the debt term in this column.

Total Payment. The total payment is the current period payment. If you're using the template for liability bookkeeping, this is the amount you enter as a credit to the cash account. If you're using this template for receivables or investment bookkeeping, this is the amount you enter as a debit to your cash account. If you're using the template as part of a financial forecast and, from your perspective, the debt being amortized represents a liability, you can add the payment amount to other debt service payments in the section of a cash flow forecast that details uses of funds. If you're using the template as part of a financial forecast and, from your perspective, the debt being amortized represents an asset, you can add the payment amount to other debt service payments in the sources of funds section of a cash flow forecast.

The Total Payment formula for the first period uses the PMT function, as follows:

```
=-PMT(C11,Amortize_Term,Principal)
```

The minus sign to the left of the PMT function is needed because, when the Principal amount is positive, the Total Payment amount is negative. C11 contains the first-period interest rate. In subsequent periods, this part of the formula changes so that the formula always uses the appropriate period's interest rate. However, the formula is modified to display 0 after the debt is paid off. The formula also is modified so that the payment amount that is calculated not only includes the new Period Interest Rate value but also reflects the remaining amortization term and the current Principal Balance amount. Starting in the second period, then, this formula is enclosed in an IF statement that first verifies that the debt term hasn't already expired. In the second period of the forecasting horizon, the Total Payment formula is:

```
=IF(B12<=Debt_Term,-PMT(C12,Amortize_Term-B11,G11),0)
```

B12 contains the period identifier. The Amortize_Term−B11 portion of the formula calculates the remaining amortization term over which the amount in cell G11, the previous period's Principal Balance amount, must be amortized. In subsequent periods, these parts of the formula are changed so that the formula always uses the current period identifier, the remaining amortization term, and the previous period's Principal Balance amount.

Interest Component. The interest component is the amount of income or expense accrued over the payment period. If you're using the template for liability bookkeeping, this is the amount you enter as a debit to the interest expense account. If you're using the template for receivables or investment bookkeeping, this is the amount you enter as a credit to the interest income account. If you're using the template for a financial forecast, you can add this amount in either the financing income or financing expense portion of your profit and loss statement.

Each period's Interest Component value is the Principal Balance amount times the Period Interest Rate value. The formula for the first period is:

```
=Principal*C11
```

However, the formula for subsequent periods is modified to display 0 after the debt is paid off. Starting in the second period, then, the basic formula is enclosed in an IF statement that first verifies that the debt term hasn't already expired. In the second period of the forecasting horizon, the Interest Component formula is:

```
=IF(B12<=Debt_Term,G11*C12,0)
```

Again, B12 contains the period identifier. G11 contains the Principal Balance amount for the previous period. C12 contains the Period Interest Rate value for the current period. In subsequent periods, these parts of the formula are changed so that the formula always uses the current period identifier, the previous period Principal Balance amount, and the current Period Interest Rate value.

Principal Component. The principal component is the amount subtracted from the outstanding principal balance when the total payment exceeds the accrued interest. If you're using the template for receivables or investment bookkeeping, this is the amount you enter as a credit to the asset account, reflecting a reduction in the amount owed you. If you're using the template for liability bookkeeping, this is the amount you enter as a debit to the liability account, reflecting a reduction in the amount you owe.

For each period, the Principal Component value is the Total Payment amount less the Interest Component amount. The formula for the first period is:

    =D11–E11

The second-period formula is:

    =D12–E12

and so on.

Principal Balance. The principal balance is the outstanding balance of the debt at the end of the period. If you're using the template for financial forecasts, this is the amount you include in the balance sheet either as an asset or as a liability.

The Principal Balance amount for each period is the previous period's Principal Balance amount minus the Principal Component amount for the current period. The formula for the first period is:

    =Principal–F11

The formula for subsequent periods is modified to display 0 after the debt is paid off. Starting in the second period, then, the basic formula is enclosed in an IF statement that first verifies that the debt term hasn't already expired. In the second period of the forecasting horizon, the Principal Balance formula is:

    =IF(B12<=Debt_Term,G11–F12,0)

Once again, B12 contains the period identifier. G11 contains the Principal Balance amount for the previous period. F12 contains the Principal Component amount for the current period. In subsequent periods, these parts of the formula are changed so that the formula always uses the current period identifier, the Principal Balance amount for the previous period, and the current Interest Component amount.

Balloon Payment Schedule

Use the Balloon Payment Schedule when you're working with debt that contains a balloon payment. The bookkeeping and forecasting methods for balloon payments and principal reduction are the same as the methods for the total payment and principal component described on the amortization schedule.

The Balloon Payment Schedule has three columns: Balloon Payment, Full Principal Payment, and True Balance.

Balloon Payment. The balloon payment is the principal balance outstanding when the debt term ends. The formula for the first period is:

=IF(B11=Debt_Term,G11,0)

The second-period formula is:

=IF(B12=Debt_Term,G12,0)

and so on.

Full Principal Payment. The full principal payment is the principal component of the regular payment plus any balloon payment. The schedule uses the Full Principal value as the full principal reduction stemming from both regular payments due over the debt term and any balloon payment due during the last payment period of the debt term. The formula for the first period is:

=I11+F11

The formula for the second period is:

=I12+F12

and so on.

True Balance. The true principal balance is the principal balance per the amortization schedule less any balloon payment made. The schedule uses the True Balance value as the principal balance outstanding, including the principal components of both the regular debt service payment and the balloon payment. The first-period formula is:

=G11–I11

The formula for the second period is:

=G12–I12

and so on.

Entering Your Own Data

To enter your own data in the variable interest rate, ordinary annuity amortization template, follow these steps:

1. Load VARIRATE.XLS from the templates disk. The template initially contains the default inputs and period interest rate shown in Figure 3-2.

2. In cell C4, enter the starting principal balance of the debt.

3. In cell C5, enter the debt term, denominated in payment periods.

4. In cell C6, enter the amortization term, denominated in payment periods.

5. In the Period Interest Rate column of the amortization schedule starting in cell C11, enter the period interest rates.

6. Save your changes by saving the spreadsheet and giving it a new filename. Save it on the disk on which you plan to store the financial model you're constructing or on which you plan to store your accounting records.

7. Print the template.

Customizing the Template

You can use the variable interest rate amortization template without modification for many debt instruments. However, you might want to change the template so that it more closely matches your requirements. For example, you can add text that describes the borrower or lender, the debt contract's other terms, the supporting documentation for the template, and assumptions leading to the interest rates forecasted over the debt term. You can also increase or decrease the number of periods.

Before you change anything on the template other than the input parameters, unprotect the document.

Increasing the number of periods

To increase the number of periods, follow these steps:

1. Remove the border from the last row of the amortization schedule.

2. Copy the current last row of the amortization schedule down as needed. (You'll probably want either as many rows in the schedule as there are forecasting periods in your overall model or as many rows as there are payment periods in the debt term.)

3. Replace the border at the bottom of the amortization schedule.

4. Reinstate cell protection as needed.

Decreasing the number of periods

To decrease the number of periods, follow these steps:

1. Delete any unneeded rows from the bottom of the schedule.

2. Add a border at the new bottom of the amortization schedule.

3. Reinstate cell protection as needed.

Removing the Balloon Payment Schedule

If the debt you want to track doesn't have a balloon payment, you might want to remove the Balloon Payment Schedule. To do so, follow these steps:

1. Clear all the cells in the Balloon Payment Schedule.

2. Reinstate cell protection as needed.

3: Debt Amortization Templates

FIXED RATE, ANNUITY DUE TEMPLATE (FIXDUE.XLS)

You can use the fixed rate, annuity due amortization template (FIXDUE.XLS), shown in Figure 3-3 on the following page, to construct debt amortization schedules for debt instruments with a fixed interest rate and payments made at the beginning of the period. The template assumes a balloon payment when regular debt service payments don't completely pay off the outstanding principal by the end of the debt term.

Given the four parameters—principal, debt term, amortization term, and interest rate—this template calculates payment amounts, the interest and principal components of each payment, outstanding principal balances for each period, and any balloon payments necessary to pay off the unamortized principal at the end of the debt term. You need this information to calculate business profits and losses, business cash flows, report asset or liability balances on the balance sheet, and to calculate any gains or losses on the disposal of the asset or the refunding of the liability.

What the Template Contains and Does

The three parts of the fixed rate, annuity due amortization template are the Fixed Interest Rate, Annuity Due Amortization Inputs box; the Fixed Interest Rate, Annuity Due Amortization Schedule; and the Balloon Payment Schedule.

Fixed Interest Rate, Annuity Due Amortization Inputs

The amortization inputs are the only four variables you enter, and, unless you turn off cell protection, the four cells containing these values are the only cells into which you can enter data.

These variables are defined by the debt contract. In general, the Principal amount is the amount borrowed or loaned at the beginning of the debt term. The Debt Term value is the number of payment periods over which the debt is outstanding. The Amortize Term value is the number of periods over which the calculated payment can fully amortize, or pay off, the principal. The Interest Rate value is the interest rate per period that, when multiplied by the outstanding balance at the beginning of the payment period, results in the amount of interest expense or interest income for the period. Note that this rate might differ

Microsoft Excel Small Business Consultant

Fixed Interest Rate, Annuity Due Amortization Inputs	
Principal	$100,000
Debt Term	15
Amortize Term	20
Interest Rate	10.00%

Fixed Interest Rate, Annuity Due Amortization Schedule

Period	Total Payment	Interest Component	Principal Component	Principal Balance
1	$10,678	$0	$10,678	$89,322
2	10,678	8,932	1,746	87,576
3	10,678	8,758	1,921	85,655
4	10,678	8,566	2,113	83,543
5	10,678	8,354	2,324	81,219
6	10,678	8,122	2,556	78,663
7	10,678	7,866	2,812	75,851
8	10,678	7,585	3,093	72,758
9	10,678	7,276	3,402	69,355
10	10,678	6,936	3,743	65,613
11	10,678	6,561	4,117	61,496
12	10,678	6,150	4,529	56,967
13	10,678	5,697	4,981	51,986
14	10,678	5,199	5,480	46,506
15	10,678	4,651	6,028	40,479
16	0	0	0	0
17	0	0	0	0
18	0	0	0	0
19	0	0	0	0
20	0	0	0	0

Balloon Payment Schedule

Balloon Payment	Full Principal Payment	True Balance
$0	$10,678	$89,322
0	1,746	87,576
0	1,921	85,655
0	2,113	83,543
0	2,324	81,219
0	2,556	78,663
0	2,812	75,851
0	3,093	72,758
0	3,402	69,355
0	3,743	65,613
0	4,117	61,496
0	4,529	56,967
0	4,981	51,986
0	5,480	46,506
40,479	46,506	0
0	0	0
0	0	0
0	0	0
0	0	0
0	0	0

Figure 3-3. *The fixed interest rate, annuity due amortization template, showing amortization of a debt of $100,000, amortized over 20 periods but with a balloon payment equal to the outstanding balance at period 15 and an interest rate of 10 percent.*

from the rate stated in the debt contract if the compounding period differs from the payment period.

For convenience and good documentation within the model, cell C4 contains the starting debt amount and is named Principal, cell C5 contains the debt term in payment periods and is named Debt_Term, cell C6 contains the amortization term in payment periods and is named Amortize_Term, and cell C7 contains the per period interest rate and is named Interest_Rate. The formulas within the actual schedule use these cell names rather than the cell addresses.

Fixed Interest Rate, Annuity Due Amortization Schedule

The amortization schedule has five columns: Period, Total Payment, Interest Component, Principal Component, and Principal Balance.

Period. The period identifier simply numbers the time periods over which the debt is outstanding and paid down. If you're using the template for accounting, use a number of periods that is equal to or greater than the number of periods over which the debt is outstanding. However, if you're using the template as a building block for a financial projection, you'll probably want the number of periods in your amortization schedule to correspond to the number of periods in the other schedules that make up your financial forecasting model.

The first-period identifier is stored in cell B12 as the integer 1. Periods that follow are stored as the previous period plus 1. For example, the formula for the second period is:

=B12+1

The formula for the third period is:

=B13+1

and so on.

Total Payment. The total payment is the current period payment. If you're using the template for liability bookkeeping, this is the amount you enter as a credit to the cash account. If you're using this template for receivables or investment bookkeeping, this is the amount you enter as a debit to your cash account. If you're using the template as part of a financial forecast and, from your perspective, the debt being amortized represents a liability, you can add the payment amount to other debt service payments in the section of a cash flow forecast that details uses of funds. If you're using the template as part of a financial forecast and, from your perspective, the debt being amortized represents an asset, the payment amount would probably be added to other debt service payments in the section of a cash flow forecast that details sources of funds.

The Total Payment formula for the first period uses the PMT function, as follows:

```
=-PMT(Interest_Rate,Amortize_Term,Principal,0,1)
```

C11 contains the first period interest rate. The minus sign to the left of the PMT function is needed because, when the Principal Component amount is a positive number, the Total Payment amount that is calculated is negative. In subsequent periods, this part of the formula changes so that the formula always uses the appropriate period's interest rate.

The formula for subsequent periods is also modified to display 0 after the debt is paid off. Starting in the second period, the basic formula is enclosed in an IF statement that first verifies that the debt term hasn't already expired. If it has, the payment amount is zero; the debt has already expired. Therefore, in the second period of the forecasting horizon, the Total Payment formula is:

```
=IF(B13<=Debt_Term,
-PMT(Interest_Rate,Amortize_Term,Principal,0,1),0)
```

B13 contains the period identifier. In subsequent periods, this part of the formula is changed so that it always uses the current period identifier.

Interest Component. The interest component is the amount of income or expense accrued over the previous payment period and paid at the beginning of the current payment period. If you're using the template for liability bookkeeping, this is the amount you enter as the debit to the interest expense account. If you're using the template for receivables or investment bookkeeping, this is the amount you enter as a credit to the interest income account. If you're using the template for a financial forecast, you can include this amount in either the financing income or financing expense portion of your profit and loss statement.

Each period's interest is the previous Principal Balance amount times the Interest Rate value. But because no time has passed between the start of the debt term and the first payment, letting interest accrue, the first period formula is 0. Starting in the second period, the Interest Component amount is the previous period's Principal Balance times the Interest Rate value. Also, the basic formula is enclosed in an IF

> **HINT:** Remember that the balances reported on the amortization schedule are as of the beginning of the payment period. If you need to know the balance at the end of the payment period—as might be the case if you use the amortization template for accounting or financial forecasting—you need to add the interest accrued during the previous period to show the correct balance at the end of the period. For example, the ending balance for the first period is calculated:
>
> =F12+D13
>
> The formula for the second period is:
>
> =F13+D14
>
> and so on. Notice also that any balloon payment is assumed to be made at the beginning of the payment period.

statement that first verifies that the debt term hasn't already expired. Therefore, in the second period of the forecasting horizon, the Total Payment formula is:

=IF(B13<=Debt_Term,F12*Interest_Rate,0)

B13 contains the period identifier. F12 contains the previous period's Principal Balance amount. In subsequent periods, these parts of the formula change so that the formula always uses the current period identifier and the previous period Principal Balance amount.

Principal Component. The principal component is the amount subtracted from the outstanding principal balance when the total payment exceeds the accrued interest. If you're using the template for receivables or investment bookkeeping, this is the amount you enter as the credit to the asset account, reflecting a reduction in the amount owed you. If you're using the template for liability bookkeeping, this is the amount you enter as the debit to the liability account, reflecting a reduction in the amount you owe.

For each period, the Principal Component amount is the Total Payment amount less the Interest Component amount. The first-period formula is:

=C12–D12

The second-period formula is:

=C13–D13

and so on.

Principal Balance. The principal balance is the outstanding balance of the debt at the beginning of the period immediately after the payment is made. If you're using the template for financial forecasts, this is the amount you enter, along with any interest accrued as of the balance sheet date, on the balance sheet as either an asset or a liability. (For example, if you're reporting the balance for the end of

3: Debt Amortization Templates

the first period, you add the beginning Principal Balance amount for the first period and the interest accrued during the first period but paid in the second period.)

The Principal Balance amount is the previous period's Principal Balance amount minus the Principal Component amount for the current period. The formula for the first period is:

    =Principal–E12

The formula for subsequent periods is modified to display 0 after the debt is paid off. This modification is necessary for those situations in which a balloon payment is paid. Starting in the second period, the basic formula is enclosed in an IF statement that verifies that the debt term hasn't already expired. Therefore, in the second period of the forecasting horizon, the Principal Balance formula is:

    =IF(B13<=Debt_Term,F12–E13,0)

Again, B13 contains the period identifier. F12 contains the Principal Balance amount for the previous period. E13 contains the Principal Component amount for the current period. In subsequent periods, these parts of the formula change so that the formula always uses the current period identifier, the Principal Balance amount for the previous period, and the Principal Component amount for the current period.

Balloon Payment Schedule   Use the Balloon Payment Schedule when you're working with debt that contains a balloon payment. The bookkeeping and forecasting methods for balloon payments and principal reduction are the same as the methods for the total payment and principal component described on the amortization schedule. The Balloon Payment Schedule has three columns: Balloon Payment, Full Principal Payment, and True Balance.

Balloon Payment. The balloon payment is the principal balance outstanding when the debt term ends. The formula for the first period is:

=IF(B12=Debt_Term,F12,0)

The second-period formula is:

=IF(B13=Debt_Term,F13,0)

and so on.

Full Principal Payment. The full principal payment is the principal component of the regular payment and any balloon payment. The schedule uses the Full Principal Payment value as the total principal reduction stemming from regular payments and any balloon payment made. The formula for the first period is:

=H12+E12

The formula for the second period is:

=H13+E13

and so on.

True Balance. The true principal balance is the principal balance in the amortization schedule less any balloon payment made. The schedule uses the True Balance value as the principal balance outstanding, because it includes both the principal components of the regular debt service payments and the balloon payment. The formula for the first period is:

=F12–H12

The formula for the second period is:

=F13–H13

and so on.

3: Debt Amortization Templates

Entering Your Own Data

To enter your own data in the fixed rate, annuity due amortization template, follow these steps:

1. Load FIXDUE.XLS from the templates disk. The template initially contains the default inputs shown in Figure 3-3.

2. In cell C4, enter the starting principal balance of the debt.

3. In cell C5, enter the debt term, denominated in payment periods.

4. In cell C6, enter the amortization term, denominated in payment periods.

5. In cell C7, enter the per-period interest rate.

6. Save your changes by saving the spreadsheet and giving it a new filename. Save it on the disk on which you plan to store the financial model you're constructing or on which you plan to store your accounting records.

7. Print the template.

Customizing the Template

You can use the fixed rate, annuity due amortization template without modification for many debt instruments. However, you might want to change the template so that it more closely matches your requirements. For example, you can add text that describes the borrower or lender, the debt contract's other terms, and the supporting documentation for the template. You can also increase or decrease the number of periods.

Before you change anything on the template other than the input parameters, unprotect the document.

Increasing the number of periods

To increase the number of periods, follow these steps:

1. Remove the border from the last row of the schedules.

2. Copy the current last row of the schedules down as needed. (You'll probably want either as many rows in the schedules as there are forecasting periods in your overall model or as many rows as there are payment periods in the debt term.)

Decreasing the number of periods	To decrease the number of periods, follow these steps: 1. Delete any unneeded rows from the bottom of the schedules. 2. Put a border at the new bottom of the schedules. 3. Reinstate cell protection as needed.
Removing the Balloon Payment Schedule	If the debt you want to track doesn't have a balloon payment, you might want to remove the Balloon Payment Schedule. To do so, follow these steps: 1. Clear all the cells in the Balloon Payment Schedule. 2. Reinstate cell protection as needed.

3. Replace the border on the bottom of the schedules.

4. Reinstate cell protection as needed.

VARIABLE RATE, ANNUITY DUE TEMPLATE (VARIDUE.XLS)

You can use the variable rate, annuity due template (VARIDUE.XLS), shown in Figure 3-4, to construct debt amortization schedules for debt instruments with a variable interest rate and payments made at the beginning of each period. The template assumes a balloon payment when regular debt service payments don't completely pay off the outstanding principal by the end of the debt term.

Given the four parameters—principal, debt term, amortization term, and period interest rates—this template calculates payment amounts, the interest and principal components of each payment, outstanding principal balances for each period, and any balloon payments necessary to pay off the unamortized principal at the end of the debt term. You need this information to calculate profits and losses, to calculate cash flows, to report asset or liability balances on the balance sheet, and to calculate gains or losses on the disposal of assets and the refunding of liabilities.

Variable Interest Rate, Annuity Due Amortization Inputs	
Principal	$100,000
Debt Term	15
Amortize Term	20

Variable Interest Rate, Annuity Due Amortization Schedule				
Period	Period Interest Rate	Total Payment	Interest Component	Principal Component	Principal Balance
1	10.00%	$10,678	$0	$10,678	$89,322
2	11.00%	11,291	8,932	2,359	86,963
3	12.00%	11,888	9,566	2,322	84,640
4	13.00%	12,467	10,157	2,310	82,330
5	12.00%	11,911	10,703	1,208	81,122
6	11.00%	11,383	9,735	1,648	79,474
7	10.00%	10,886	8,742	2,144	77,330
8	9.00%	10,423	7,733	2,690	74,639
9	8.00%	9,996	6,718	3,278	71,361
10	8.00%	9,996	5,709	4,287	67,074
11	8.00%	9,996	5,366	4,630	62,444
12	8.00%	9,996	4,995	5,000	57,443
13	8.00%	9,996	4,595	5,401	52,043
14	8.00%	9,996	4,163	5,833	46,210
15	8.00%	9,996	3,697	6,299	39,911
16	8.00%	0	0	0	0
17	8.00%	0	0	0	0
18	8.00%	0	0	0	0
19	8.00%	0	0	0	0
20	8.00%	0	0	0	0

Balloon Payment Schedule		
Balloon Payment	Full Principal Payment	True Balance
$0	$10,678	$89,322
0	2,359	86,963
0	2,322	84,640
0	2,310	82,330
0	1,208	81,122
0	1,648	79,474
0	2,144	77,330
0	2,690	74,639
0	3,278	71,361
0	4,287	67,074
0	4,630	62,444
0	5,000	57,443
0	5,401	52,043
0	5,833	46,210
39,911	46,210	0
0	0	0
0	0	0
0	0	0
0	0	0
0	0	0

Figure 3-4. *The variable interest rate, annuity due amortization template, showing amortization for a debt of $100,000, amortized over 20 periods but with a balloon payment equal to the outstanding balance at period 15 and with varying interest rates.*

What the Template Contains and Does	The three parts of the fixed rate, annuity due amortization template are the Variable Interest Rate, Annuity Due Amortization Inputs box, the Variable Interest Rate, Annuity Due Amortization Schedule, and the Balloon Payment Schedule.
Variable Interest Rate, Annuity Due Amortization Inputs	The amortization inputs, along with the Period Interest Rate values in the amortization schedule, are the variables you enter, and, unless you turn off cell protection, these are the only cells into which you can enter data.
	These variables are defined by the debt contract. In general, the Principal amount is the amount borrowed or loaned at the beginning of the debt term. The Debt Term value is the number of payment periods over which the debt is outstanding. The Amortize Term value is the number of periods over which the calculated payment can fully amortize, or pay off, the principal.
	For convenience and good documentation within the model, cell C4 contains the starting debt amount and is named Principal, cell C5 contains the debt term in payment periods and is named Debt_Term, and cell C6 contains the amortization in payment periods and is named Amortize_Term. The formulas within the actual schedule use these cell names rather than the cell addresses.
Variable Interest Rate, Annuity Due Amortization Schedule	The amortization schedule has six columns: Period, Period Interest Rate, Total Payment, Interest Component, Principal Component, and Principal Balance.
	Period. The period identifier simply numbers the time periods over which the debt is outstanding and paid down. If you're using the template for accounting, use a number of periods that is equal to or greater than the number of periods over which the debt is outstanding. However, if you're using the template as a building block for a financial projection, you'll probably want the number of periods in your amortization schedule to correspond to the number of periods in the other schedules that make up your financial forecasting model.

The first period is stored in cell B11 as the integer 1. Periods that follow are stored as the previous period plus 1. For example, the formula for the second period is:

=B11+1

The formula for the third period is:

=B12+1

and so on.

Period Interest Rate. The period interest rates are the interest rates that, when multiplied by the outstanding balance at the beginning of the payment period, result in the amount of interest expense or interest income for the period. The period interest rates typically are tied to a market-sensitive interest rate index that is based on a widely traded or used interest rate, such as the one-year U.S. treasury bill or one-year London interbank offered rate. You enter actual or forecasted interest rates for each payment period over the debt term in this column. (Although no time has elapsed and no interest has accrued before the first payment is made, you still need the Period Interest Rate value for the first period to calculate the Total Payment amount for the first period.)

Total Payment. The total payment is the current period payment. If you're using the template for liability bookkeeping, this is the amount you enter as a credit to the cash account. If you're using this template for receivables or investment bookkeeping, this is the amount you enter as a debit to your cash account. If you're using the template as part of a financial forecast and, from your perspective, the debt being amortized represents a liability, you can add the payment amount to other debt service payments into the section of a cash flow forecast that details uses of funds. If you're using the template as part of a financial forecast and, from your perspective, the debt being amortized represents an asset, you can add the payment amount to other debt service payments in the section of a cash flow forecast that details sources of funds.

The Total Payment formula for the first period uses the PMT function, as follows:

```
=-PMT(C11,Amortize_Term,Principal,0,1)
```

C11 contains the first-period interest rate. The minus sign to the left of the PMT function is needed because, when the Principal Component amount is a positive number, the Total Payment amount that is calculated is negative. In subsequent periods, this part of the formula changes so that the formula always uses the appropriate period's interest rate. However, the formula is modified in subsequent periods to display 0 after the debt is paid off. The formula also is modified so that the calculated payment amount not only includes the new Period Interest Rate value, but also reflects the remaining amortization term and the current Principal Balance amount. Starting in the second period, then, this formula is enclosed in an IF statement that verifies that the debt term hasn't already expired. In the second period of the forecasting horizon, the Total Payment formula is:

```
=IF(B12<=Debt_Term,-PMT(C12,Amortize_Term-B11,G11+E12,0,1),0)
```

B12 contains the period identifier. The Amortize_Term−B11 portion of the formula calculates the remaining amortization term over which the amount in cells G11 and E12, the previous period's Principal Balance and the current period's Interest Component, must be amortized. In subsequent periods, these parts of the formula are changed so that the formula always uses the current period identifier, the remaining amortization term, and the appropriate principal and accrued interest balances.

Interest Component. The interest component is the amount of income or expense that is accrued over the previous payment period and that is paid at the beginning of the current payment period. If you're using the template for liability bookkeeping, this is the amount you enter as a debit to the interest expense account. If you're using the template for receivables or investment bookkeeping, this is the amount

3: Debt Amortization Templates

you enter as a credit to the interest income account. If you're using the template for a financial forecast, you can add this amount in either the financing income or financing expense portion of your profit and loss statement.

Except for the Interest Component amount for the first period, which is entered as 0, each period's Interest Component amount is the previous period's Principal Balance amount times the previous Period Interest Rate value. However, the formula is modified to display 0 after the debt is paid off. Accordingly, the basic formula is enclosed in an IF statement that verifies that the debt term hasn't already expired. In the second period of the forecasting horizon, the Interest Component formula is:

=IF(B12<=Debt_Term,G11*C11,0)

Again, B12 contains the period identifier. G11 contains the Principal Balance amount for the previous period. C11 contains the Period Interest Rate value for the previous period. In subsequent periods, these parts of the formula change so that the formula always uses the current period identifier, the previous period's Principal Balance amount, and the previous Period Interest Rate value.

Principal Component. The principal component is the amount subtracted from the outstanding principal balance when the total payment exceeds the accrued interest. If you're using the template for receivables or investment bookkeeping, this is the amount you enter as a credit to the asset account, reflecting a reduction in the amount owed you. If you're using the template for liability bookkeeping, this is the amount you enter as a debit to the liability account, reflecting a reduction in the amount you owe.

For each period, the Principal Component amount is the Total Payment amount less the Interest Component amount. The first-period formula is:

=D11−E11

The second-period formula is:

    =D12–E12

and so on.

Principal Balance. The principal balance is the outstanding balance of the debt at the beginning of the period, immediately after the payment is made. If you're using the template for financial forecasts, this amount, plus any accrued interest, is what you include on the balance sheet either as an asset or as a liability.

The Principal Balance amount is the previous period's Principal Balance minus the principal component of the current period's payment. The formula for the first period is:

    =Principal–F11

The formula for subsequent periods is modified to display 0 after the debt term is paid off. Starting in the second period, then, the basic formula is enclosed in an IF statement that verifies that the debt term

> **HINT:** Remember that the balances reported on the amortization schedule are as of the beginning of the period. If you need to know the balances for the end of the period—as might be the case if you use the amortization schedule for accounting—you need to add the interest accrued from the previous period to show the principal balance for the end of the period. For example, the ending balance formula for the first period is:
>
>   =G11+E12
>
> The ending balance formula for the second period is:
>
>   =G12+E13
>
> and so on. Notice that any balloon payment is assumed to be made at the beginning of the payment period.

hasn't already expired. In the second period of the forecasting horizon, the Principal Balance formula is:

=IF(B12<=Debt_Term,G11–F12,0)

Once again, B12 contains the period identifier. G11 contains the Principal Balance amount for the previous period. F12 contains the Principal Component amount for the current period. In subsequent periods, these parts of the formula change so that the formula always uses the current period identifier, the Principal Balance amount for the previous period, and the current Principal Component amount.

Balloon Payment Schedule

Use the Balloon Payment Schedule when you're working with debt that contains a balloon payment. The bookkeeping and forecasting methods for balloon payments and principal reductions are the same as the methods for the total payment and principal component described on the amortization schedule. The Balloon Payment Schedule has three columns: Balloon Payment, Full Principal, and True Balance.

Balloon Payment. The balloon payment is the principal balance outstanding when the debt term ends. The formula for the first period is:

=IF(B11=Debt_Term,G11,0)

The second-period formula is:

=IF(B12=Debt_Term,G12,0)

and so on.

Full Principal Payment. The full principal payment is the principal component of the regular payment plus any balloon payment. The schedule uses this value as the total principal reduction stemming from both regular payments made over the debt term and any balloon payment made during the last payment period of the debt term. The formula for the first period is:

=I11+F11

The formula for the second period is:

=I12+F12

and so on.

True Balance. The true principal balance is the principal balance in the amortization schedule, less any balloon payment made. The schedule uses this value as the principal balance outstanding, including both principal components of the regular debt service payments and the balloon payment. The first-period formula is:

=G11–I11

The formula for the second period is:

=G12–I12

and so on.

Entering Your Own Data

To enter your own data in the variable interest rate, annuity due amortization template, follow these steps:

1. Load VARIDUE.XLS from the templates disk. The template initially contains the default inputs and period interest rates shown in Figure 3-4.

2. In cell C4, enter the starting principal balance of the debt.

3. In cell C5, enter the debt term, denominated in payment periods.

4. In cell C6, enter the amortization term, denominated in payment periods.

5. Starting in cell C11, enter the projected period interest rates in the Period Interest Rate column of the amortization schedule.

6. Save your changes by saving the spreadsheet and giving it a new filename. Save it on the disk on which you plan to store the financial model you're constructing or the disk on which you plan to store your accounting records.

7. Print the template.

3: Debt Amortization Templates

Customizing the Template

You can use the variable rate, annuity due amortization template without modification for many debt instruments. However, you might want to change the template so that it more closely matches your requirements. For example, you can add text that describes the borrower or lender, the debt contract's other terms, the supporting documentation for the template, and assumptions leading to the interest rates forecasted over the debt term. You can also increase or decrease the number of periods.

Before you change anything on the template other than the input parameters, unprotect the document.

Increasing the number of periods

To increase the number of periods, follow these steps:

1. Remove the border from the last row of the schedules.

2. Copy the current last row of the schedules down as needed. (You'll probably want either as many rows in the schedules as there are forecasting periods in your overall model or as many rows as there are payment periods in the debt term.)

3. Replace the border at the bottom of the schedules.

4. Reinstate cell protection as needed.

Decreasing the number of periods

To decrease the number of periods, follow these steps:

1. Delete any unneeded rows from the bottom of the schedules.

2. Add a border at the new bottom of the schedules.

3. Reinstate cell protection as needed.

Removing the Balloon Payment Schedule

If the debt you want to track doesn't have a balloon payment, you might want to remove the Balloon Payment Schedule. To do so, follow these steps:

1. Clear all the cells in the Balloon Payment Schedule.

2. Reinstate cell protection as needed.

LINKING THESE TEMPLATES TO OTHER SPREADSHEETS

Although no other templates in this toolkit are designed to provide data to the amortization templates, you might want to link an amortization template to a subsidiary spreadsheet.

For example, suppose that you calculate the total cost of a new factory in a schedule named FACTORY.XLS, as shown in Figure 3-5, and that you can borrow the total amount at 10 percent per payment period. The debt repayment is amortized over 15 repayment periods, but the actual term of the debt is equal to 10 periods, meaning a balloon payment will be necessary at the end of period 10. Using the fixed rate template (FIXRATE.XLS), you develop an amortization schedule.

However, rather than simply entering $737,500 as the principal, you link this cell to the FACTORY.XLS spreadsheet. Using this approach means that each time you change FACTORY.XLS, your amortization schedule, via the link, also is updated. To construct such a link with a file named FACTORY.XLS, stored in the WINDOWS directory on your hard disk, you'd do the following:

1. Load FIXRATE.XLS from the templates disk. The template initially contains the default inputs shown in Figure 3-1.

2. In cell C4, enter the amount of debt required to purchase the factory by entering the formula:

    ='C:\WINDOWS\FACTORY.XLS'!$B$6

   Cell B6 is the cell that contains the total cost of the factory and, therefore, the amount being borrowed.

	A	B
1	Costs of New Factory	
2		
3	Building	500000
4	Land	100000
5	Machinery	137500
6	Total Factory Costs	737500

Figure 3-5. *The summary of factory costs.*

3. In cell C5, enter 10 as the debt term.

4. In cell C6, enter 15 as the amortization term.

5. In cell C7, enter 10 percent as the interest rate.

6. Save your changes by saving the spreadsheet and giving it a new filename. Save it on the disk on which you plan to store the financial model you're constructing or on which you plan to store your other accounting records.

7. Print the spreadsheet.

The completed amortization schedule might look like the one shown in Figure 3-6 on the following page. The significance of this link is that the value shown in cell C4 ($737,500) isn't a number or formula calculated in this spreadsheet; rather, it is the calculated total debt pulled from FACTORY.XLS.

Fixed Interest Rate Amortization Inputs	
Principal	$737,500
Debt Term	10
Amortize Term	15
Interest Rate	10.00%

Fixed Interest Rate Amortization Schedule				
Period	Total Payment	Interest Component	Principal Component	Principal Balance
1	$96,962	$73,750	$23,212	$714,288
2	96,962	71,429	25,533	688,755
3	96,962	68,875	28,086	660,669
4	96,962	66,067	30,895	629,774
5	96,962	62,977	33,985	595,789
6	96,962	59,579	37,383	558,406
7	96,962	55,841	41,121	517,285
8	96,962	51,728	45,233	472,051
9	96,962	47,205	49,757	422,294
10	96,962	42,229	54,732	367,562
11	0	0	0	0
12	0	0	0	0
13	0	0	0	0
14	0	0	0	0
15	0	0	0	0
16	0	0	0	0
17	0	0	0	0
18	0	0	0	0
19	0	0	0	0
20	0	0	0	0

Balloon Payment Schedule		
Balloon Payment	Full Principal Payment	True Balance
$0	$23,212	$714,288
0	25,533	688,755
0	28,086	660,669
0	30,895	629,774
0	33,985	595,789
0	37,383	558,406
0	41,121	517,285
0	45,233	472,051
0	49,757	422,294
367,562	422,294	0
0	0	0
0	0	0
0	0	0
0	0	0
0	0	0
0	0	0
0	0	0
0	0	0
0	0	0
0	0	0

Figure 3-6. *A fixed rate debt amortization schedule, with the principal calculated in and pulled from a separate spreadsheet.*

4

Future Value Templates

An important part of business planning is ensuring that you are prepared for future cash needs, such as purchasing new business machinery 3 years from now, funding an employee retirement plan 25 years from now, or paying off a bank debt 30 months from now. The three templates described in this chapter provide a framework for you to use in planning for such future cash needs. These templates (and the convention each uses) are:

- FVDPOSIT.XLS (onetime deposit)
- FVORDANN.XLS (ordinary annuity)
- FVANNDUE.XLS (annuity due)

This chapter shows how to use these three templates, print them, modify them, and link them with other spreadsheets.

APPLYING FUTURE VALUE AND PRESENT VALUE CONCEPTS: A SHORT PRIMER

You can take one of two approaches to save money for a future cash need: You can invest an initial lump sum, collect interest income over time, and watch your sum grow to a future cash amount; or you can make regular payments (say, every month or every year), collect interest income over time, and again end up with a future cash amount.

With the first approach, four variables are involved: the amount of cash you need or will have accumulated at some point in the future (the future value), the number of periods you will hold the cash, the interest rate (expressed as a percentage per time period), and the initial cash deposit (the present value). Generally, you assume, or set, three of these variables and then calculate the fourth variable, based on the other three. Using the following formula, you define three of the variables and then solve for the fourth, undefined variable:

$$FV=PV*(1+i)^n$$

where FV equals the future value, PV equals the present value, i equals the period interest rate, and n equals the number time periods.

For example, suppose that you invest $10,000 today, that your investment will earn 10 percent interest each year, and that you will invest the cash for 2 years. Substituting the three variables you know—the present value ($10,000), the interest rate (10 percent), and the number of time periods (2 years)—in the formula gives you the following:

$$FV=\$10{,}000*(1+10\%)^2$$

The result shows that the future value of this investment is $12,100. Similarly, you can use this basic formula to find any of the other three variables. (You don't have to use complex variations of this formula because Microsoft Excel provides four built-in financial functions that let you simply plug in the variables. FV solves for the future value; NPER solves for the number of time periods; RATE solves for the interest rate; and PMT solves for the payment amount.)

With the second approach, four variables also are involved. Three of the variables are the same as in the first approach: the future value, the time periods, and the interest rate. The fourth variable is the amount of your regular payments—called the annuity. Over time, the combination of the payments you make and the interest earnings on those payments grow to a future value, or cash amount. The formula differs from that used to calculate future values for a onetime deposit:

$$FV=P*((1+i)^n-1)/i$$

where FV equals the future value, P equals the payment amount made at the end of each period, i equals the interest rate, and n equals the number of periods.

Here again, you define three of the variables and use the formula to calculate the fourth. For example, if you want to calculate the future value of annual payments of $1,000 made at the end of each of the next 25 years earning 10 percent annually, you substitute the defined variables in the formula and solve for the undefined variable.

FV=$1,000*((1+10%)^25−1)/10%

The result shows that by making this annual stream of payments, you accumulate $98,347.06. One other factor in the future value of an annuity is whether you make the payments at the end of the period or the beginning of the period. Notice in the preceding example that the $1,000 payments are made at the end of the period. This arrangement is called an ordinary annuity. If you make payments at the beginning of the period, it is called an annuity due. Under an annuity due arrangement, you earn an extra period of interest. Accordingly, the formula for the future value of payments made at the beginning of the period is simply the end-of-period formula multiplied by the factor 1 plus the interest rate, as follows:

FV=P*((1+i)^n−1)/i*(1+i)

For example, if you use the same numbers as the defined variables in the preceding example but assume payments are made at the beginning of the period, the formula gives the result $108,181.77. You get the same result when you multiply the calculated result of the formula by the factor 1 plus the interest rate, assuming the payments are made at the end of the period. For example, $98,347.06*(1+10%) equals $108,181.77.

Although these basic future value formulas are simple, they provide you with a wealth of information that is useful in planning for the financial future. Using either approach—the initial deposit or the annuity—you can solve for one of the variables based on the other three. For example, you can compute how much you need to invest at 9 percent either today as a lump sum or as a regular periodic payment to fund a $100,000 expansion two years from now. You can compute the interest rate you must earn on a $300,000 investment to have $1,000,000 at the end of 10 years—or the interest rate you must earn on monthly payments of $5,000 to have $1,000,000 at the end of 10 years. You can compute the number of years that it takes for a $50,000 onetime deposit earning 12 percent annually to grow to $1,000,000 or how many years it takes for annual payments of $11,000 earning 12 percent to grow to $1,000,000.

You now know the mechanics of using the future value formulas and the logic used in the future value templates. But keep in mind three other points when using the future value formulas and templates. First, use the same unit of time for the interest rate that you use for the time periods. For example, if you use an annual interest rate, also measure your time periods in years. If you measure your time in months, use a monthly interest rate. Second, if the interest income generated is subject to income tax, you need to state the interest rate as an after-tax percentage instead of a pretax percentage because income tax reduces the interest income you earn. Third, in defining future values, you might want to make some allowance for inflation, particularly for distant future cash needs. One approach to allowing for inflation in your definition of the future value variable is to use the future value for a onetime deposit formula and specify the interest rate as the inflation rate. For example, if a piece of improved, industrial real estate today costs $500,000 and inflation increases the price 5 percent each year for 10 years, you can calculate the estimated price 10 years in the future by using the following formula for the future value of a onetime deposit:

FV=$500,000*(1+5%)^10

The result shows a calculated future value of $814,447.31. This is the amount you might use as the defined future value in one of the templates, if you plan to accumulate enough cash to purchase the land 10 years from now.

FUTURE VALUE ONETIME DEPOSIT TEMPLATE (FVDPOSIT.XLS)

You can use the template for a future value of a onetime deposit (FVDPOSIT.XLS), shown in Figure 4-1, to plan for financial needs that require a onetime, lump-sum payment. To complete the schedule, you define any three of the following four variables: the onetime initial deposit, the period interest rate, the number of periods, and the future value. The template calculates the undefined fourth variable and produces a schedule that summarizes the interest income and the principal balances for each of the time periods. You can also use this

Future Value Onetime Deposit Inputs & Outputs		
	Input	Output
Future Value	$1,000,000.00	$1,000,000.00
Periods	0	10
Interest	15.00%	15.00%
Deposit	$250,000.00	$250,000.00

Interest Income and Principal Balances Schedule		
Period	Interest Income	Principal Balance
Initial Deposit		$250,000.00
1	$37,500.00	287,500.00
2	$43,125.00	330,625.00
3	$49,593.75	380,218.75
4	$57,032.81	437,251.56
5	$65,587.73	502,839.30
6	$75,425.89	578,265.19
7	$86,739.78	665,004.97
8	$99,750.75	764,755.72
9	$114,713.36	879,469.07
10	$131,920.36	1,011,389.43
11	$0.00	0.00
12	$0.00	0.00
13	$0.00	0.00
14	$0.00	0.00
15	$0.00	0.00
16	$0.00	0.00
17	$0.00	0.00
18	$0.00	0.00
19	$0.00	0.00
20	$0.00	0.00

Figure 4-1. *The template for the future value of an initial, onetime deposit, with example data.*

schedule to calculate the estimated future price of an item, given a present price, an inflation rate, and a number of periods of inflation.

What the Template Contains and Does

The two parts of the template for a future value of a onetime deposit are the inputs and outputs box and the schedule of interest income and principal balances. You enter three of the following four variables:

- Future Value
- Periods
- Interest
- Deposit

Unless you turn off cell protection, these are the only four cells into which you can enter data.

Enter a 0 for the variable you want to find. You can find only one variable at a time, but you can select any variable. Future Value is the amount of cash you need or want in the future. Periods is the number of time periods over which you will invest the initial deposit and any interest income. Interest is the percentage that, when multiplied by the balance at the beginning of the period, calculates the interest income for the period. Deposit is the beginning amount of cash invested.

For convenience and good documentation within the model, cell C4 contains the Future Value input and is named Future_value, cell C5 contains the Periods input and is named Periods, cell C6 contains the Interest input and is named Interest, cell C7 contains the Deposit input and is named Deposit, cell D4 contains the Future Value output and is named Calc_future_value, cell D5 contains the Periods output and is named Calc_periods, cell D6 contains the Interest output and is named Calc_interest, and cell D7 contains the Deposit output and is named Calc_deposit. The formulas within the template use these cell names rather the cell addresses.

Future Value Onetime Deposit Inputs & Outputs

The inputs and outputs box has three columns. The first column holds the text describing the values you can enter and the values the template can calculate. The second column of the schedule holds the input variables. You enter actual values for the three variables that you know and a 0 for the one that you want the template to calculate. The third column of the schedule holds the three variables you enter as inputs and the solution for the fourth variable, based on your inputs.

Future Value input. In this cell, enter the amount you want to accumulate, if you know this value.

Periods input. In this cell, enter the number of periods you will hold the investment, if you know this value.

Interest input. In this cell, enter the interest rate you will earn, if you know this value.

Deposit input. In this cell, enter the initial deposit, if you know this amount.

Future Value output. If you enter an amount other than 0 as the Future Value input, the template uses this amount as the Future Value output. If you enter 0 as the Future Value input, the template calculates the Future Value output by assuming the input initial deposit is invested at the input interest rate and for the input number of periods. The formula uses the FV function to calculate the future value output, as follows:

=IF(C4<>0,C4,–FV(Interest,Periods,,Deposit))

Periods output. If you enter an integer other than 0 as the Periods input, the template uses this integer as the Periods output. If you enter 0 as the Periods input, the template calculates the Periods output as the number of periods for the input initial deposit invested at the input interest rate growing to the input future value. The formula uses the NPER function to calculate the number of periods, as follows:

=ROUND(IF(C5<>0,C5,NPER(Interest,,–Deposit,Future_value)),0)

The formula rounds the number of periods because the NPER function can calculate a non-integer result but the template logic depends on an integer result.

Interest output. If you enter a percentage as the Interest input, the template uses this percentage as the Interest output. If you enter 0 as the Interest input, the template calculates the Interest output as the interest rate that, given the input initial deposit, generates enough interest income to reach the input future value in the input number of periods. The formula uses the RATE function to calculate the interest rate, as follows:

=IF(C6<>0,C6,RATE(Periods,,-Deposit,Future_value))

Deposit output. If you enter an amount other than 0 as the Deposit input, the template uses this amount as the Deposit output. If you enter 0 as the Deposit input, the template calculates the Deposit output as the amount that, if invested for the input number of periods at the input interest rate, grows into the input future value. The formula is:

=IF(C7<>0,C7,Future_value/(1+Interest)^Periods)

Interest Income and Principal Balances Schedule

The Interest Income and Principal Balances Schedule calculates the interest income and the principal balance for each of the time periods. The schedule has three columns that contain calculated data.

Period. The Period identifier simply numbers the periods for which the interest income and the principal balances are reported. The first period is stored in cell B13 as the integer 1. Periods that follow are stored as the previous period plus 1. For example, the formula for the second period is:

=B13+1

The formula for the third period is:

=B14+1

and so on.

Interest Income. The Interest Income column shows the interest earned for the period. The Interest Income value is the previous period's Principal Balance value times the period interest rate. The formula is enclosed in an IF statement that first verifies that the period for which results are calculated is less than or equal to the number of periods specified by the Periods output. For example, the formula for the first period (in cell C13) is:

    =IF(B13<=Calc_periods,D12*Calc_interest,0)

The formula for the second period is:

    =IF(B14<=Calc_periods,D13*Calc_interest,0)

and so on.

Principal Balance. The Principal Balance column shows the initial deposit made and the principal balance at the end of each period. The initial deposit is the Deposit output. The ending principal balance for each period, including the final period, is the previous Principal Balance value plus the interest income for the current period. The formula is enclosed in an IF statement that first verifies that the period for which results are calculated is less than or equal to the number of periods specified by the Periods output. For example, the formula for the first period (in cell D13) is:

    =IF(B13<=Calc_periods,D12+C13,0)

The formula for the second period is:

    =IF(B14<=Calc_periods,D13+C14,0)

and so on.

Entering Your Own Data

To enter your own data in the template for a future value of a onetime deposit, use the following steps:

1. Load the FVDPOSIT.XLS template from the templates disk. The template initially contains the default inputs shown in Figure 4-1.

2. In cell C4, enter the Future Value input if you know the future value you need or want; enter 0 if you want the template to calculate the future value, given the number of periods, the interest rate, and the initial deposit.

3. In cell C5, enter the Periods input as an integer, if you know the number of periods you need or want; enter 0 if you want the template to calculate the number of periods, given the future value, the interest rate, and the initial deposit.

4. In cell C6, enter the Interest input as a percentage, if you know the interest rate you'll earn; enter 0 if you want the template to calculate the interest rate, given the future value, the number of periods, and the initial deposit.

> **HINT:** Specify the interest rate as the rate per period. For example, if your periods are months, use a monthly rate; if your periods are years, use a yearly rate.

5. In cell C7, enter the Deposit input, if you know the amount you'll invest; enter 0 if you want the template to calculate the initial deposit, given the future value, the number of periods, and the interest rate.

> **HINT:** Be sure to enter 0 in the inputs column of the inputs and outputs box for the variable you want to find. If you don't enter 0 for any variables, both the outputs and the compounding schedule might show incorrect results because the four output variables might not agree with the basic formula for the future value of a onetime deposit.

6. Save your changes by saving the spreadsheet and giving it a new filename.

7. Print the spreadsheet.

Customizing the Template

You can use the template for the future value of a onetime deposit for finding any one of the four variables in the basic formula for a future value of a onetime deposit. However, you might want to change the template so that it more closely matches your requirements. For example, you can add text that describes and documents the three variables you define and the fourth variable for which you solve. If you're examining a future value problem that uses more than or less than 20 periods, you can also increase or decrease the number of periods in the schedule. Before you change anything on the schedule other than the future value inputs, unprotect the document.

Increasing the number of periods

To increase the number of periods in the interest income and principal balances schedule, use the following steps:

1. Remove the bottom border from the last row of the schedule.

2. Copy the current last row of the schedule down as needed. (You'll probably want as many rows in your schedule as the number of periods shown in the inputs and outputs box.)

3. Replace the border on the bottom row of the schedule.

4. Reinstate cell protection as needed.

Decreasing the number of periods

To decrease the number of periods in the interest income and principal balances schedule, use the following steps:

1. Delete any unneeded rows from the bottom of the schedule.

2. Add a border to the new bottom of the schedule.

3. Reinstate cell protection as needed.

FUTURE VALUE ORDINARY ANNUITY TEMPLATE (FVORDANN.XLS) You can use the template for the future value of an ordinary annuity (FVORDANN.XLS), shown in Figure 4-2, to plan for financial needs that require a series of equal payments, one at the end of each period. To complete the schedule, you define any three of the following four variables: the amount of the regular payment you will make at the end of each period, the period interest rate, the number of periods, and the future value. The template calculates the undefined, fourth variable and produces a schedule that summarizes the interest income and the principal balances for each of the time periods.

Future Value Ordinary Annuity Inputs & Outputs		
	Inputs	Outputs
Future Value	$0.00	$381,691.91
Periods	15	15
Interest	9.00%	9.00%
Payment	$13,000.00	$13,000.00

Payments, Interest Income, and Principal Balances Schedule			
Period Number	Payment Amount	Interest Income	Principal Balance
1	$13,000.00	$0.00	13,000.00
2	$13,000.00	$1,170.00	27,170.00
3	$13,000.00	$2,445.30	42,615.30
4	$13,000.00	$3,835.38	59,450.68
5	$13,000.00	$5,350.56	77,801.24
6	$13,000.00	$7,002.11	97,803.35
7	$13,000.00	$8,802.30	119,605.65
8	$13,000.00	$10,764.51	143,370.16
9	$13,000.00	$12,903.31	169,273.47
10	$13,000.00	$15,234.61	197,508.09
11	$13,000.00	$17,775.73	228,283.81
12	$13,000.00	$20,545.54	261,829.36
13	$13,000.00	$23,564.64	298,394.00
14	$13,000.00	$26,855.46	338,249.46
15	$13,000.00	$30,442.45	381,691.91
16	$0.00	$0.00	0.00
17	$0.00	$0.00	0.00
18	$0.00	$0.00	0.00
19	$0.00	$0.00	0.00
20	$0.00	$0.00	0.00

Figure 4-2. *The template for the future value of an ordinary annuity, with example data.*

What the Template Contains and Does

The two parts of the template for the future value of an ordinary annuity are the inputs and outputs box and the schedule of payments, interest income, and principal balances. You enter three of the following four variables:

- Future Value
- Periods
- Interest
- Payment

Unless you turn off cell protection, these are the only four cells into which you can enter data.

Enter a 0 for the variable you want to find. You can find only one variable at a time, but you can select any variable. Future Value is the amount of cash you need or want in the future. Periods is the number of time periods. You make the payment amount at the end of each period. Interest is the percentage that, when multiplied by the balance at the beginning of the period, calculates the interest income for the period. Payment is the amount of cash invested at the end of each period.

For convenience and good documentation within the model, cell C4 contains the Future Value input and is named Future_value, cell C5 contains the Periods input and is named Periods, cell C6 contains the Interest input and is named Interest, cell C7 contains the Payment input and is named Payment, cell D4 contains the Future Value output and is named Calc_future_value, cell D5 contains the Periods output and is named Calc_periods, cell D6 contains the Interest output and is named Calc_interest, and cell D7 contains the Payment output and is named Calc_payment. The formulas within the template use these cell names rather than the cell addresses.

Future Value Ordinary Annuity Inputs & Outputs

The inputs and outputs box has three columns. The first column holds the text describing the values you can enter and the values the template can calculate. The second column of the schedule holds the input variables. You enter actual values for the three variables that you know and a 0 for the one that you want the template to calculate. The third column of the schedule holds the three variables you enter as inputs and the solution for the fourth variable, based on your inputs.

Future Value input. In this cell, enter the amount you want to accumulate, if you know this value.

Periods input. In this cell, enter the number of periods in which you will make payments, if you know this value.

Interest input. In this cell, enter the interest rate you will earn, if you know this value.

Payment input. In this cell, enter the amount of the regular payment you will make at the end of each period, if you know this amount.

Future Value output. If you enter an amount other than 0 as the Future Value input, the template uses this amount as the Future Value output. If you enter 0 as the Future Value input, the template calculates the Future Value output by assuming the input payment is made at the end of each of the input number of periods and is invested at the input interest rate. The formula uses the FV function to calculate the future value output, as follows:

```
=IF(C4<>0,C4,-FV(Interest,Periods,Payment))
```

Periods output. If you enter an integer other than 0 as the Periods input, the template uses this integer as the Periods output. If you enter 0 as the Periods input, the template calculates the Periods output as the number of periods needed to return the input future value, given the input interest rate and the input payment amount. The formula uses the NPER function to calculate the number of periods, as follows:

```
=ROUND(IF(C5<>0,C5,NPER(Interest,-Payment,,Future_value)),0)
```

The formula rounds the number of periods because the NPER function can calculate a non-integer result but the template logic depends on an integer result.

Interest output. If you enter a percentage other than 0 as the Interest input, the template uses this percentage as the Interest output. If you enter 0 as the Interest input, the template calculates the Interest output as the rate at which the input payments, made at the end of each of the input number of periods, generate enough interest income to reach the input future value. The formula uses the RATE function to calculate the interest rate, as follows:

=IF(C6<>0,C6,RATE(Periods,–Payment,,Future_value))

Payment output. If you enter an amount other than 0 as the Payment input, the template uses this amount as the Payment output. If you enter 0 as the Payment input, the template calculates the Payment output as the payment amount that you need to invest at the end of each of the input number of periods at the input interest rate to grow into the input future value. The formula uses the PMT function to calculate the payment output, as follows:

=IF(C7<>0,C7,–PMT(Interest,Periods,,Future_value))

Payments, Interest Income, and Principal Balances Schedule

The Payments, Interest Income, and Principal Balances Schedule shows the payment made at the end of each period and calculates the interest income and the principal balance for each period. The schedule has four columns that contain calculated data.

Period. The Period identifier simply numbers the periods for which the payment is shown, the interest income is calculated, and the principal balances are accumulated. The first period is stored in cell B12 as the integer 1. Periods that follow are stored as the previous period plus 1. For example, the formula for the second period is:

=B12+1

The formula for the third period is:

    =B13+1

and so on.

Payment Amount. The Payment Amount column shows the payment made at the end of each of the periods. The payment amount for each period is the Payment output. The formula is enclosed in an IF statement that verifies that the period for which results are calculated is less than or equal to the output number of periods. For example, the formula for the first period (in cell C12) is:

    =IF(B12<=Calc_periods,Calc_payment,0)

The formula for the second period is:

    =IF(B13<=Calc_periods,Calc_payment,0)

and so on.

Interest Income. The Interest Income column shows the interest earned for the period. Because the first period has no beginning balance to earn interest, the template enters the first-period interest income as 0. However, in the second and following periods, the interest income is the previous period's Principal Balance value times the period interest rate. The formula is enclosed in an IF statement that verifies that the period for which results are calculated is less than or equal to the output number of periods. For example, the formula for the second period (in cell D13) is:

    =IF(B13<=Calc_periods,E12*Calc_interest,0)

The formula for the third period is:

    =IF(B14<=Calc_periods,E13*Calc_interest,0)

and so on.

Principal Balance. The Principal Balance column shows payments and interest income accumulated through the end of each period. The principal balance for each period, including the final period, is the previous Principal Balance value—if one exists—plus the payment and the interest income for the current period. The formula is enclosed in an IF statement that verifies that the period for which results are calculated is less than or equal to the output number of periods. For example, the formula for the first period (in cell E12) is:

=IF(B12<=Calc_periods,C12+D12,0)

The formula for the second period is:

=IF(B13<=Calc_periods,E12+C13+D13,0)

The formula for the third period is:

=IF(B14<=Calc_periods,E13+C14+D14,0)

and so on.

Entering Your Own Data

To enter your own data in the template for the future value of an ordinary annuity, use the following steps.

1. Load the FVORDANN.XLS template from the templates disk. The template initially contains the default inputs shown in Figure 4-2.

2. In cell C4, enter the Future Value input, if you know the future value you need or want; enter 0 if you want the template to calculate the future value, given the number of periods, the interest rate, and the payment.

3. In cell C5, enter the Periods input as an integer, if you know the number of periods you need or want; enter 0 if you want the template to calculate the number of periods, given the future value, the interest rate, and the payment.

4. In cell C6, enter the Interest input as a percentage, if you know the interest rate you'll earn; enter 0 if you want the template to calculate the interest rate, given the future value, the number of periods, and the payment.

> **HINT:** Specify the interest rate as the rate per payment period. For example, if you will make a payment at the end of each month, use a monthly interest rate and months as the periods. If you will make a payment at the end of each year, use an annual interest rate and years as the periods.

5. In cell C7, enter the Payment input, if you know the amount you'll invest at the end of each period; enter 0 if you want the template to calculate the payment, given the future value, the number of periods, and the interest rate.

> **HINT:** Be sure to enter 0 in the inputs column of the inputs and outputs box for the variable you want to find. If you don't enter 0 for any variable, both the outputs and the Payments, Interest Income, and Principal Balances Schedule might show incorrect results because the four output variables might not agree with the basic formula for the future value of an ordinary annuity.

6. Save your changes by saving the spreadsheet and giving it a new filename.

7. Print the spreadsheet.

Customizing the Template

You can use the template for the future value of an ordinary annuity for finding any one of the four variables in the basic formula for the future value of an ordinary annuity. However, you might want to change the template so that it more closely matches your requirements. For example, you can add text that describes and documents the three variables you define and the fourth variable for which you solve. If you're examining a future value problem that uses more than or less than 20 periods, you can also increase or decrease the number of periods in the schedule. Before you change anything on the schedule other than the inputs, unprotect the document.

Increasing the number of periods

To increase the number of periods in the schedule of payments, interest income, and principal balances, use the following steps:

1. Remove the bottom border from the last row of the schedule.
2. Copy the current last row of the schedule down as needed. (You'll probably want as many rows in your schedule as the number of periods shown in the inputs and outputs box.)
3. Replace the border on the bottom row of the schedule.
4. Reinstate cell protection as needed.

Decreasing the number of periods

To decrease the number of periods in the schedule of payments, interest income, and principal balances, use the following steps:

1. Delete any unneeded rows from the bottom of the schedule.
2. Add a border to the new bottom of the schedule.
3. Reinstate cell protection as needed.

FUTURE VALUE ANNUITY DUE TEMPLATE (FVANNDUE.XLS)

You can use the template for the future value of an annuity due (FVANNDUE.XLS), shown in Figure 4-3 on the following page, to plan for financial needs that you meet by making a series of equal payments, one at the beginning of each period. To complete the schedule, you define any three of the following four variables: the amount of the regular payment you will make at the beginning of each period, the period interest rate, the number of periods, and the future value. The template calculates the undefined, fourth variable and produces a schedule summarizing the payments, interest income, and principal balances for each of the time periods.

Microsoft Excel Small Business Consultant

Future Value Annuity Due Inputs & Outputs		
	Inputs	Outputs
Future Value	$1,750,000.00	$1,750,000.00
Periods	26	26
Interest	0.00%	11.67%
Payment	$11,000.00	$11,000.00

Payments, Interest Income, and Principal Balances Schedule			
Period Number	Payment Amount	Interest Income	Principal Balance
1	$11,000.00	$1,283.38	12,283.38
2	$11,000.00	$2,716.49	25,999.87
3	$11,000.00	$4,316.81	41,316.68
4	$11,000.00	$6,103.83	58,420.51
5	$11,000.00	$8,099.35	77,519.85
6	$11,000.00	$10,327.68	98,847.54
7	$11,000.00	$12,816.00	122,663.54
8	$11,000.00	$15,594.64	149,258.18
9	$11,000.00	$18,697.45	178,955.63
10	$11,000.00	$22,162.28	212,117.91
11	$11,000.00	$26,031.35	249,149.26
12	$11,000.00	$30,351.83	290,501.09
13	$11,000.00	$35,176.38	336,677.48
14	$11,000.00	$40,563.82	388,241.29
15	$11,000.00	$46,579.81	445,821.11
16	$11,000.00	$53,297.70	510,118.80
17	$11,000.00	$60,799.36	581,918.17
18	$11,000.00	$69,176.25	662,094.42
19	$11,000.00	$78,530.48	751,624.90
20	$11,000.00	$88,976.08	851,600.98

Figure 4-3. *The template for the future value of an annuity, with example data.*

What the Template Contains and Does

The two parts of the template for the future value of an annuity due are the inputs and outputs box and the schedule of payments, interest income, and principal balances. You enter three of the following four variables:

- Future Value

- Periods

- Interest
- Payment

Unless you turn off cell protection, these are the only four cells into which you can enter data.

Enter a 0 for the variable you want to find. You can find only one variable at a time, but you can select any variable. Future Value is the amount of cash you need or want in the future. Periods is the number of time periods. You make the payment amount at the beginning of each. Interest is the percentage that, when multiplied by the balance at the beginning of the period, calculates the interest income for the period. Payment is the amount of cash invested at the beginning of each period.

For convenience and good documentation within the model, cell C4 contains the Future Value input and is named Future_value, cell C5 contains the Periods input and is named Periods, cell C6 contains the Interest input and is named Interest, cell C7 contains the Payment input and is named Payment, cell D4 contains the Future Value output and is named Calc_future_value, cell D5 contains the Periods output and is named Calc_periods, cell D6 contains the Interest output and is named Calc_interest, and cell D7 contains the Payment output and is named Calc_payment. The formulas within the template use these cell names rather the cell addresses.

Future Value Annuity Due Inputs & Outputs

The inputs and outputs box has three columns. The first column holds the text describing the values you can enter and the values the template can calculate. The second column of the schedule holds the input variables. You enter actual values for the three variables that you know and a 0 for the one that you want the template to calculate. The third column of the schedule holds the three variables you enter as inputs and the solution for the fourth variable, based on your inputs.

Future Value input. In this cell, enter the amount you want to accumulate, if you know this value.

Periods input. In this cell, enter the number of periods in which you will make payments, if you know this value.

Interest input. In this cell, enter the interest rate you will earn, if you know this value.

Payment input. In this cell, enter the amount of the regular payment you will make at the beginning of each period, if you know this amount.

Future Value output. If you enter an amount other than 0 as the Future Value input, the template uses this amount as the Future Value output. If you enter 0 as the Future Value input, the template calculates the Future Value output by assuming the input payment is made at the beginning of each of the periods and is invested at the input interest rate. The formula uses the FV function to calculate the output future value, as follows:

```
=IF(C4<>0,C4,-FV(Interest,Periods,Payment,,1))
```

Periods output. If you enter an integer other than 0 as the Periods input, the template uses this integer as the Periods output. If you enter 0 as the Periods input, the template calculates the Periods output as the number of periods needed to return the input future value, given the input interest rate and the input payment amount. The formula uses the NPER function to calculate the output number of periods, as follows:

```
=ROUND(IF(C5<>0,C5,NPER(Interest,-Payment,,Future_value,1)),0)
```

The formula rounds the number of periods because the NPER function can calculate a non-integer result but the template logic depends on an integer result.

Interest output. If you enter a percentage other than 0 as the Interest input, the template uses this percentage as the Interest output. If you enter 0 as the Interest input, the template calculates the Interest output as the interest rate at which the input payments made at the beginning of each of the input number of periods generate enough interest income to reach the input future value. The formula uses the RATE function to calculate the output interest rate, as follows:

=IF(C6<>0,C6,RATE(Periods,−Payment,,Future_value,1))

Payment output. If you enter an amount other than 0 as the Payment input, the template uses this amount as the Payment output. If you enter 0 as the Payment input, the template calculates the Payment output as the payment amount that you need to invest at the beginning of each of the input number of periods at the input interest rate to grow into the input future value. The formula uses the PMT function to calculate the payment output, as follows:

=IF(C7<>0,C7,−PMT(Interest,Periods,,Future_value,1))

Payments, Interest Income, and Principal Balances Schedule

The Payments, Interest Income, and Principal Balances Schedule shows the payment made at the beginning of each period and calculates the interest income and the principal balance for each period. The schedule has four columns that contain calculated data.

Period. The Period identifier simply numbers the periods for which the payment is shown, the interest income is earned, and the principal balances are accumulated. The first period is stored in cell B12 as the integer 1. Periods that follow are stored as the previous period plus 1. For example, the formula for the second period is:

=B12+1

The formula for the third period is:

=B13+1

and so on.

Payment Amount. The Payment Amount column shows the payment made at the beginning of each of the periods. The payment amount for each period is the Payment output. The formula is enclosed in an IF statement that verifies that the period for which results are calculated is less than or equal to the output number of periods. For example, the formula for the first period (in cell C12) is:

    =IF(B12<=Calc_periods,Calc_payment,0)

The formula for the second period is:

    =IF(B13<=Calc_periods,Calc_payment,0)

and so on.

Interest Income. The Interest Income column shows the interest earned for the period. Because the first period has no beginning balance to earn interest, only the first payment, the template enters the first period interest income as the Payment output times the Interest output. However, in the second and following periods, the interest income is the previous period's Principal Balance amount plus that period's Payment output times the Interest output. The formula is enclosed in an IF statement that verifies that the period for which results are calculated is less than or equal to the output number of periods. For example, the formula for the second period (in cell D13) is:

    =IF(B13<=Calc_periods,(E12+Calc_payment)*Calc_interest,0)

The formula for the third period is:

    =IF(B14<=Calc_periods,(E13+Calc_payment)*Calc_interest,0)

and so on.

Principal Balance. The Principal Balance column shows payments and interest income accumulated through the end of each period. The principal balance for each period, including the final period, is the previous Principal Balance amount—if one exists—plus the payment and the interest income for the current period. The formula is enclosed in an IF statement that verifies that the period for which results are calculated is less than or equal to the output number of periods. For example, the formula for the first period (in cell E12) is:

=IF(B12<=Calc_periods,C12+D12,0)

The formula for the second period is:

=IF(B13<=Calc_periods,E12+C13+D13,0)

The formula for the third period is:

=IF(B14<=Calc_periods,E13+C14+D14,0)

and so on.

Entering Your Own Data

To enter your own data in the template for the future value of an annuity due, use the following steps:

1. Load the FVANNDUE.XLS template from the templates disk. The template initially contains the default inputs shown in Figure 4-3.

2. In cell C4, enter the Future Value input, if you know the future value you need or want; enter 0 if you want the template to calculate the future value, given the number of periods, the interest rate, and the payment.

3. In cell C5, enter the Periods input as an integer, if you know the number of periods you need or want; enter 0 if you want the template to calculate the number of periods, given the future value, the interest rate, and the payment.

4. In cell C6, enter the Interest input as a percentage, if you know the interest rate you'll earn; enter 0 if you want the template to calculate the interest rate, given the future value, the number of periods, and the payment.

> **HINT:** Specify the interest rate as the rate per payment period. For example, if you will make a payment at the beginning of each month, use a monthly interest rate and months as the periods. If you will make a payment at the beginning of each year, use an annual interest rate and years as the periods.

5. In cell C7, enter the Payment input, if you know the amount you'll invest at the beginning of each period; enter 0 if you want the template to calculate the payment, given the future value, the number of periods, and the interest rate.

> **HINT:** Be sure to enter 0 in the Input column of the inputs and outputs box for the variable you want to find. If you don't enter 0 for any variable, both the outputs and the Payments, Interest Income, and Principal Balances Schedule might show incorrect results because the four output variables might not agree with the basic formula for the future value of an annuity due.

6. Save your changes by saving the spreadsheet and giving it a new filename.

7. Print the spreadsheet.

Customizing the Template

You can use the template for the future value of an annuity due for finding any one of the four variables in the basic formula for the future value of an annuity due. However, you might want to change the template so that it more closely matches your requirements. For example, you can add text that describes and documents the three variables you define and the fourth variable, which the template calculates. If you're examining a future value problem that uses more than or less than 20 periods, you can also increase or decrease the number of periods on the schedule. Before you change anything on the schedule other than the inputs, unprotect the document.

4: Future Value Templates

Increasing the number of periods To increase the number of periods in the schedule of payments, interest income, and principal balances, use the following steps:

1. Remove the bottom border from the last row of the schedule.

2. Copy the current last row of the schedule down as needed. (You'll probably want as many rows in your schedule as the number of periods shown in the inputs and outputs box.)

3. Replace the border on the bottom row of the schedule.

4. Reinstate cell protection as needed.

Decreasing the number of periods To decrease the number of periods in the schedule of payments, interest income, and principal balances, use the following steps:

1. Delete any unneeded rows from the bottom of the schedule.

2. Add a border to the new bottom of the schedule.

3. Reinstate cell protection as needed.

LINKING THESE TEMPLATES WITH OTHER SPREADSHEETS You might want to calculate some of the Future Value input amounts in subsidiary spreadsheets. For example, assume that you plan to construct a new office building 10 years from now. You estimate it would cost $1,000,000 to build the office building today. However, you estimate that construction costs will inflate 5 percent annually over the next 10 years. Also assume that you plan to make 10 equal annual payments to an investment account, earning 10 percent annual interest to pay for the construction of the office building. Two future value problems exist within this example. You might first use the template for the future value of a onetime deposit (FVDPOSIT.XLS) to estimate the construction costs of the office building 10 years from now. The new inputs to the template to calculate the construction costs are shown in Figure 4-4 on the following page. Rather than enter the calculated future value from this template into the template for the future value of an ordinary annuity (FVORDANN.XLS), you might link

129

the input cell in the template that calculates the future value of the office building to the template that calculates the annual payments necessary to accumulate the future value. You might, for example, use the following steps to model this example and link the two templates:

Future Value Onetime Deposit Inputs & Outputs		
	Input	Output
Future Value	$0.00	$1,628,894.63
Periods	10	10
Interest	5.00%	5.00%
Deposit	$1,000,000.00	$1,000,000.00

Interest Income and Principal Balances Schedule		
Period	Interest Income	Principal Balance
Initial Deposit		$1,000,000.00
1	$50,000.00	1,050,000.00
2	$52,500.00	1,102,500.00
3	$55,125.00	1,157,625.00
4	$57,881.25	1,215,506.25
5	$60,775.31	1,276,281.56
6	$63,814.08	1,340,095.64
7	$67,004.78	1,407,100.42
8	$70,355.02	1,477,455.44
9	$73,872.77	1,551,328.22
10	$77,566.41	1,628,894.63
11	$0.00	0.00
12	$0.00	0.00
13	$0.00	0.00
14	$0.00	0.00
15	$0.00	0.00
16	$0.00	0.00
17	$0.00	0.00
18	$0.00	0.00
19	$0.00	0.00
20	$0.00	0.00

Figure 4-4. *The template for the future value of a onetime deposit, calculating the inflated cost of the factory.*

1. Load FVDPOSIT.XLS from the templates disk and enter the appropriate inputs so that you can solve for the inflated cost of the office building that costs $1,000,000 today but is expected to inflate annually by 5 percent each of the next 10 years.
2. Save the modified template as COST_EST.XLS.
3. Load FVORDANN.XLS from the templates disk and enter 0 as the Payment input (because you want to find this amount), 10 as the Periods input (because you want to construct the factory 10 years from now), 10 percent as the Interest input (because you believe you can earn an after-tax return of 10 percent annually), and the following formula as the estimated future value:

    ='C:\WINDOWS\COST_EST.XLS'!$D$4

This formula assumes that COST_EST.XLS is stored in the WINDOWS directory and supplies the Future Value input amount. Cell D4 in that file is the cell that contains the Future Value amount. The template for the future value of an ordinary annuity with the Future Value input pulled from the template for the future value of a onetime deposit using Microsoft Excel's linking feature is shown in Figure 4-5 on the following page.

Microsoft Excel Small Business Consultant

Future Value Ordinary Annuity Inputs & Outputs		
	Inputs	Outputs
Future Value	$1,628,894.63	$1,628,894.63
Periods	10	10
Interest	10.00%	10.00%
Payment	$0.00	$102,205.64

Payments, Interest Income, and Principal Balances Schedule			
Period Number	Payment Amount	Interest Income	Principal Balance
1	$102,205.64	$0.00	102,205.64
2	$102,205.64	$10,220.56	214,631.84
3	$102,205.64	$21,463.18	338,300.66
4	$102,205.64	$33,830.07	474,336.36
5	$102,205.64	$47,433.64	623,975.63
6	$102,205.64	$62,397.56	788,578.83
7	$102,205.64	$78,857.88	969,642.35
8	$102,205.64	$96,964.24	1,168,812.22
9	$102,205.64	$116,881.22	1,387,899.08
10	$102,205.64	$138,789.91	1,628,894.63
11	$0.00	$0.00	0.00
12	$0.00	$0.00	0.00
13	$0.00	$0.00	0.00
14	$0.00	$0.00	0.00
15	$0.00	$0.00	0.00
16	$0.00	$0.00	0.00
17	$0.00	$0.00	0.00
18	$0.00	$0.00	0.00
19	$0.00	$0.00	0.00
20	$0.00	$0.00	0.00

Figure 4-5. *The template for the future value of an ordinary annuity, calculating the annual payments required to accumulate enough money to construct a new factory 10 years from now.*

5

Cost Center Template

Thorough financial modeling usually requires that you build detailed forecasts of your costs. These forecasts are sometimes called cost center schedules. The simple cost center template (COSTSRPT.XLS) described in this chapter provides a framework for you to use in constructing your own cost center schedules.

This chapter shows you how to use the template to construct specific cost center schedules, print them, modify them, and link them with subsidiary spreadsheets.

COST CENTERS: A SHORT PRIMER

Cost centers are simply business activities or work groups for which costs are separately forecasted and monitored. Standard cost centers include the sales and marketing functions, the finance and administration functions, the manufacturing function, and the product research and development function. Within cost centers, costs are classified by the nature of the expenditure. Standard cost classifications include salaries, rent, advertising, and interest. Accordingly, in using this template, you need to make two decisions either directly or indirectly.

First, you need to define your cost centers. It's difficult to give generic advice about which activities or groups to include in each cost center, but two important considerations are industry standards and your internal management structure. Your industry might use standard cost center definitions. If so, you can compare financial information about your peers, which is often readily available in most libraries, with your own forecasts to check your performance against that of your peers.

Your own internal management structure can also influence your definition of cost centers. By defining a cost center as the work group or activity for which an individual manager is responsible, you can often more easily involve individual managers in the forecasting and monitoring of costs. Involvement often improves the quality of the forecasting and monitoring.

Second, you need to define the cost classifications used within the cost centers. It's also difficult to give generic advice on which classifications to use. Here again, it's important to be cognizant of industry standards for the reason already mentioned. In addition, there are other issues you'll want to thoroughly consider when assigning classifications. You might want to use the same cost classifications for each of the cost centers; by doing so, you can look at the cost classifications company-wide.

> **HINT:** You might want to forecast at a level of detail that is easily reconcilable to your financial and tax accounting records because you'll probably want to compare the budgeted financial performance described in your forecast with the actual financial performance documented in your accounting records.

COST CENTER TEMPLATE (COSTSRPT.XLS)

You can use the cost center template (COSTSRPT.XLS) shown in Figure 5-1 to construct cost center schedules for activities or work groups for which you want to forecast expenses separately. This template provides a framework for the development of your own cost center forecasts.

Given complete cost data, this template details and calculates the total period expenses for each period of the forecasting horizon. You need this information to calculate business profits and losses and to calculate business cash flows.

Cost Center Schedule										
Expense Categories	Period 1	Period 2	Period 3	Period 4	Period 5	Period 6	Period 7	Period 8	Period 9	Period 10
Advertising	$0	$0	$0	$0	$0	$0	$0	$0	$0	$0
Bad Debts from Sales or Services	0	0	0	0	0	0	0	0	0	0
Bank Service Charges	0	0	0	0	0	0	0	0	0	0
Car and Truck Expenses	0	0	0	0	0	0	0	0	0	0
Commissions	0	0	0	0	0	0	0	0	0	0
Depletion	0	0	0	0	0	0	0	0	0	0
Depreciation	0	0	0	0	0	0	0	0	0	0
Dues and Publications	0	0	0	0	0	0	0	0	0	0
Employee Benefit Programs	0	0	0	0	0	0	0	0	0	0
Freight	0	0	0	0	0	0	0	0	0	0
Insurance	0	0	0	0	0	0	0	0	0	0
Interest	0	0	0	0	0	0	0	0	0	0
Laundry and Cleaning	0	0	0	0	0	0	0	0	0	0
Legal and Professional Services	0	0	0	0	0	0	0	0	0	0
Office Expense	0	0	0	0	0	0	0	0	0	0
Pension and Profit Sharing Plans	0	0	0	0	0	0	0	0	0	0
Rent on Business Property	0	0	0	0	0	0	0	0	0	0
Repairs	0	0	0	0	0	0	0	0	0	0
Supplies	0	0	0	0	0	0	0	0	0	0
Taxes	0	0	0	0	0	0	0	0	0	0
Travel	0	0	0	0	0	0	0	0	0	0
Meals and Entertainment	0	0	0	0	0	0	0	0	0	0
Utilities and Telephone	0	0	0	0	0	0	0	0	0	0
Wages	0	0	0	0	0	0	0	0	0	0
Period Expense Total	$0	$0	$0	$0	$0	$0	$0	$0	$0	$0

Figure 5-1. *The cost center template, with example data.*

What the Template Contains and Does

The cost center template consists of a 10-period forecast of costs by classification.

You enter a cost forecast for each cost classification in each period of the forecasting horizon. Unless you turn off cell protection, these are the only cells into which you can enter data.

The values you enter as the forecasted amounts for a given classification in a given period are developed in your budgeting and forecasting research. In general, you base your future cost estimates on your past operating history and adjust them for assumptions about the periods on the forecasting horizon. In addition, if you use industry-standard cost center and cost classification definitions, you might be able to benchmark your forecasted expenses against the historical performance of your peers. The cost classifications initially shown include the expense deductions listed in the U.S. Treasury Internal Revenue Service Schedule C, which is used for reporting taxable profit or loss for a sole proprietorship. This list simply provides a starting point for you to use in constructing your own list of cost classifications. Undoubtedly, you'll want to make changes to this list. Detailed instructions for doing so are included in the section of this chapter titled "Customizing the Template."

The cost center schedule has 11 columns and uses two sets of formulas: one to calculate each period identifier of the forecasting horizon and the other to add the costs entered for a forecasting period.

Period. The period identifier simply numbers the time periods for which costs are forecasted. If you're using the template as a building block for a financial projection, use a number of periods in your cost center schedule that corresponds to the number of periods in the other schedules that make up your financial forecasting model.

The first period identifier is stored in cell B3 as the integer 1. Periods that follow are stored as the previous period plus 1. For example, the formula for the second period is:

```
=B3+1
```

The formula for the third period is:

=C3+1

and so on.

Expense Categories. The expense categories detail your line-by-line forecasts of cost center classifications on the forecasting horizon.

Period Expense Total. The period expense total sums the expense categories by period.

The first-period expense total is calculated by the following formula:

=SUM(B4:B34)

The formula for the second-period formula is:

=SUM(C4:C34)

and so on. Notice that the range being summed includes an extra row above and below the existing expense categories. This extra row lets you insert and delete rows within the current schedule without damaging the formula that calculates the period total expense. Inserting and deleting rows is described in detail in the section of this chapter titled "Customizing the Template."

Entering Your Own Data

To enter your own data in the cost center template, use the following steps:

1. Load COSTSRPT.XLS from the templates disk. The template initially shows all cost forecasts as 0, as shown in Figure 5-1.

2. Enter the forecasted amount of each expense classification for each period in your forecasting horizon.

3. Save your changes by saving the spreadsheet and giving it a new filename. Save it on the disk on which you plan to store the rest of the financial model you're constructing.

4. Print the spreadsheet.

Customizing the Template

You can use the cost center template without modification for many cost centers. However, you might want to change the template so that it more closely matches your requirements. For example, you can add text that describes the work group or activity for which costs are separately forecasted. You can increase or decrease the number of periods.

> **HINT:** You can increase the number of periods to 12 if your periods are months and you want to forecast an entire year. You also can increase or decrease the list of expense categories for which the schedule tracks costs. Before you change anything on the template other than the forecasted costs, unprotect the document.

Increasing the number of periods

To increase the number of periods, follow these steps:

1. Remove the border from the last column of the Cost Center Schedule.

2. Copy the current last column of the Cost Center Schedule to the right as needed. (You'll probably want as many columns in the schedule as there are forecasting periods in your overall model.)

3. Replace the border on the right side of the Cost Center Schedule.

4. Reinstate cell protection as needed.

Decreasing the number of periods

To decrease the number of periods, follow these steps:

1. Delete any unneeded columns from the right side of the schedule.

2. Add a border on the new right side of the Cost Center Schedule.

3. Reinstate cell protection as needed.

Increasing the number of cost categories

To increase the number of cost categories listed, follow these steps:

1. Between (not including) rows 4 and 34 of the schedule, insert as many rows as are needed to accommodate the additional cost categories.

5: Cost Center Template

2. Describe the new cost categories by entering the appropriate text in column A.

3. Verify that the period expense total includes all the cost classification rows. If it does not, correct it.

4. Reinstate cell protection as needed.

Decreasing the number of cost categories

To decrease the number of cost categories listed, follow these steps:

1. Delete rows that contain unneeded cost categories.

2. Verify that the period expense total includes all the cost classification rows. If it does not, correct it.

3. Reinstate cell protection as needed.

Linking This Template to Others in the Toolkit

Other templates in this toolkit are specifically designed to provide data to the cost center schedule template. Notice that two of the standard expense classifications are depreciation and interest, amounts that you might calculate with the depreciation and debt amortization templates.

For example, assume that the calculation inputs in the straight-line depreciation schedule (STRAIGHT.XLS) and the fixed rate debt amortization schedule (FIXRATE.XLS) provide the period expense forecasts for the depreciation and interest expense forecasts for this cost center. Rather than entering these amounts manually, you can link the cells that show the period depreciation and interest expense forecasts to the subsidiary depreciation and debt amortization templates that precisely calculate these variables. Using this approach means that each time you update the depreciation and debt amortization templates, your cost center schedule, via the link, is also updated. Use the following steps to link the subsidiary depreciation and debt amortization templates to the cost center template:

1. Load COSTRPT.XLS from the templates disk. The template initially shows zeros in each expense category, as shown in Figure 5-1.

2. In cell B12, enter the amount of depreciation expense as the period 1 depreciation expense calculated in the straight-line depreciation template by entering the formula:

   ='C:\WINDOWS\STRAIGHT.XLS'!$C$11

   This formula assumes that the straight-line depreciation schedule template (STRAIGHT.XLS) is stored in the WINDOWS directory on your C drive and that it supplies the period depreciation expenses. Cell C11 in that file is the cell that contains the period 1 depreciation expense. In the same way, enter the period 2 through 10 depreciation expenses.

3. In cell B18, enter the amount of interest expense as the period 1 interest expense calculated in the fixed rate debt amortization template (FIXRATE.XLS) by entering the formula:

   ='C:\WINDOWS\FIXRATE.XLS'!$D$12

   This formula assumes that the fixed interest rate debt amortization template (FIXRATE.XLS) is stored in the WINDOWS directory on your C drive and that it supplies the period interest expenses. Cell D12 in that file is the cell that contains the period 1 interest expense. In the same way, enter the period 2 through 10 interest expenses.

The cost center schedule with depreciation and interest expenses pulled from subsidiary templates, via the links, is shown in Figure 5-2. Again, the significance of the link is that the depreciation and interest forecasts are not values entered or formulas calculated in this spreadsheet; rather, the calculated expense amounts are pulled from the straight-line depreciation and fixed interest rate debt amortization templates.

Cost Center Schedule										
Expense Categories	Period 1	Period 2	Period 3	Period 4	Period 5	Period 6	Period 7	Period 8	Period 9	Period 10
Advertising	$0	$0	$0	$0	$0	$0	$0	$0	$0	$0
Bad Debts from Sales or Services	0	0	0	0	0	0	0	0	0	0
Bank Service Charges	0	0	0	0	0	0	0	0	0	0
Car and Truck Expenses	0	0	0	0	0	0	0	0	0	0
Commissions	0	0	0	0	0	0	0	0	0	0
Depletion	0	0	0	0	0	0	0	0	0	0
Depreciation	6,944	6,944	6,944	6,944	6,944	6,944	6,944	6,944	6,944	6,944
Dues and Publications	0	0	0	0	0	0	0	0	0	0
Employee Benefit Programs	0	0	0	0	0	0	0	0	0	0
Freight	0	0	0	0	0	0	0	0	0	0
Insurance	0	0	0	0	0	0	0	0	0	0
Interest	10,000	9,825	9,633	9,422	9,190	8,934	8,653	8,344	8,003	7,629
Laundry and Cleaning	0	0	0	0	0	0	0	0	0	0
Legal and Professional Services	0	0	0	0	0	0	0	0	0	0
Office Expense	0	0	0	0	0	0	0	0	0	0
Pension and Profit Sharing Plans	0	0	0	0	0	0	0	0	0	0
Rent on Business Property	0	0	0	0	0	0	0	0	0	0
Repairs	0	0	0	0	0	0	0	0	0	0
Supplies	0	0	0	0	0	0	0	0	0	0
Taxes	0	0	0	0	0	0	0	0	0	0
Travel	0	0	0	0	0	0	0	0	0	0
Meals and Entertainment	0	0	0	0	0	0	0	0	0	0
Utilities and Telephone	0	0	0	0	0	0	0	0	0	0
Wages	0	0	0	0	0	0	0	0	0	0
Period Expense Total	$16,944	$16,770	$16,578	$16,367	$16,134	$15,879	$15,597	$15,288	$14,948	$14,574

Figure 5-2. *The cost center template, with depreciation and interest calculated and pulled from the straight-line depreciation template and the fixed interest rate debt amortization template.*

6

Sales and Cost of Sales Template

In addition to requiring cost forecasts, as discussed in Chapter 5, financial modeling usually requires detailed forecasts of sales and related variables, such as cost of sales, gross margins, and the inventory levels required to support the forecasted sales. The sales and cost of sales template (SALESRPT.XLS) described in this chapter provides a framework for you to use in forecasting sales, cost of sales, gross margins, and inventory levels in a variety of businesses, including manufacturing, wholesaling and retailing, and service firms. This chapter shows how to use the sales forecast template, print it, modify it, and link it with subsidiary spreadsheets.

SALES AND COST OF SALES FORECASTING: A SHORT PRIMER

Sales forecasting is basic to any business plan or budget and to some investment analysis. Essentially, you need to collect information for or make forecasts concerning as many as five related variables.

First, you need to collect the units and dollars of inventory that you already hold or that you estimate you will hold at the beginning of the sales forecast. In a manufacturing firm, these amounts are the sum of the work in process, or partially manufactured, inventory and the finished goods, or ready to sell, inventory. In a wholesaling or retailing firm, these amounts are the sum of those items purchased for resale. You need to collect both the units of inventory and the dollars of inventory. In a service business, no inventory is manufactured or purchased, so these amounts are 0.

Second, for each period in the forecasting horizon, you need to forecast the number of units produced if you're a manufacturer or the number of units purchased if you're a wholesaler or retailer. Typically, the amounts cannot be forecasted independent of sales, but sales isn't the only variable that affects production or purchases. Other important variables such as manufacturing capacities and availability of inventory items to be purchased also impact planned production and purchases.

Third, you need to forecast the costs of producing or purchasing the inventory for each period over the forecasting horizon. For a manufacturing firm, costs are often forecasted by classifications such as direct labor (the wages and employee benefits incurred in making the item), direct materials (the raw materials and components that go into the finished product), and factory overhead (the miscellaneous and incidental costs associated with making the item, such as electricity to run the manufacturing equipment). For wholesalers and retailers, forecasted costs are the amounts paid to suppliers for those items purchased for resale. In a service business, no inventory is manufactured or purchased, so no production or purchase costs exist.

Fourth, you need to forecast the number of units sold and the price per unit sold for each period over the forecasting horizon. For manufacturers, wholesalers, and retailers, the unit forecast simply is the number of cars, shirts, or basketballs sold; the unit price forecast simply is the price at which these items are sold to the customer. For service firms, the unit forecast simply is the number of times a service is provided or the hours of work performed; the unit price forecast simply is the price at which the service or work is billed to the customer.

Fifth, you need to forecast any other variable costs associated with sales. For any type of business, these other costs might include sales commissions incurred as a result of the sale, taxes on the sale, and any other costs incurred and directly tied to the sale.

With this information, you should be able to forecast total sales, cost of sales, and margins. Usually when you forecast sales and cost of sales, you use either the financial accounting or managerial accounting format. Using the financial accounting format, you calculate sales revenue, cost of goods sold, and gross sales margin.

Using the managerial accounting format, you calculate the marginal sales revenue, the variable costs, and the marginal contribution. The marginal sales revenue is the number of units sold times the unit price at which the sales are made. The variable costs include both the cost of goods sold, which is the sum of the production or purchasing costs of the items sold and also any other variable costs incurred as a result of the sale. The marginal contribution is the marginal sales revenue minus the variable costs. The marginal contribution is that amount generated by your sales to pay your fixed costs, those costs that do not vary with sales volumes. You might want to use a combination of both formats in your forecasting, so the sales and cost of sales template amounts to a hybrid of the two formats. You can use sales revenue for either the financial accounting sales revenue or the managerial accounting marginal sales revenue. You can use the cost of sales for either the financial accounting cost of goods sold or the managerial accounting variable costs. Depending on how you use the template's sales revenue and cost of sales, you can use the gross margin for either the financial accounting gross sales margin or the managerial accounting marginal contribution. Total sales simply are the number of units sold times the unit price at which the sales are made. The cost of the goods sold is the sum of the production or purchasing costs of the items sold. The gross sales margin is the total sales less the cost of sales. The gross sales margin is that amount actually generated by your sales to pay for your operating and financing costs. Any amounts left over after paying these costs represent your profit.

SALES FORECAST TEMPLATE (SALESRPT.XLS)

You can use the sales forecast template (SALESRPT.XLS) shown in Figure 6-1 on page 147 to construct sales forecast schedules for each product or service for which you want to estimate sales and production activity separately. This template provides a framework for the development of your own sales and cost of sales forecasts. To complete it for a product or service line, you develop and then enter your sales forecasts, your manufacturing or purchasing forecasts, and your beginning inventory levels for work in process and finished goods.

Given the beginning inventory (expressed both in units and in dollars), the number of units produced or purchased and their costs by period, and the sales volumes and unit sales prices by period, this template details and calculates the total sales, production activity, and inventory balances by period on the forecasting horizon. You need this information to calculate product sales and gross margins, business profits and losses, and business cash flows, and you need it to report the inventory balance on the balance sheet.

What the Template Contains and Does

The five parts of the sales forecast template are the heading box, the sales forecast inputs, the cost totals and statistics, the sales and gross margins forecasts, and the inventory forecasts. You enter several variables into the Sales Forecast Inputs schedule. For the first period only, you enter:

- Beginning Inventory—Units on Hand.
- Beginning Inventory—Balance in Dollars.

For the first and each succeeding period, you enter:

- Units Produced/Purchased.
- Direct Labor, Direct Material, and Factory Overhead.
- Unit Sales.
- Unit Sales Price.
- Other Variable Costs.

Unless you turn off cell protection, these are the only cells into which you can enter data.

Sales Forecast Schedule	Period 1	Period 2	Period 3	Period 4	Period 5	Period 6	Period 7	Period 8	Period 9	Period 10
Sales Forecast Inputs										
Beginning Inventory										
Units on Hand	1,000									
Balance in Dollars	$10,000									
Units Produced/Purchased	400	400	400	400	400	400	400	400	400	400
Production/Purchase Costs										
Direct Labor	1,800	1,800	1,800	1,800	1,800	1,800	1,800	1,800	1,800	1,800
Direct Material	2,000	2,000	2,000	2,000	2,000	2,000	2,000	2,000	2,000	2,000
Factory Overhead	1,000	1,000	1,000	1,000	1,000	1,000	1,000	1,000	1,000	1,000
Unit Sales	300	600	600	600	300	300	300	300	300	300
Unit Sales Price	$25.00	$25.00	$25.00	$25.00	$25.00	$25.00	$25.00	$25.00	$25.00	$25.00
Other Variable Costs	$0	$0	$0	$0	$0	$0	$0	$0	$0	$0
Cost Totals and Statistics										
Total Production/Purchase Costs	$4,800	$4,800	$4,800	$4,800	$4,800	$4,800	$4,800	$4,800	$4,800	$4,800
Cost Statistics										
Beginning Inventory Unit Cost	$10.00	$10.57	$10.95	$11.27	$11.54	$11.74	$11.85	$11.90	$11.93	$11.95
Produced/Purchased Unit Cost	$12.00	$12.00	$12.00	$12.00	$12.00	$12.00	$12.00	$12.00	$12.00	$12.00
Weighted Average Unit Cost	$10.57	$10.95	$11.27	$11.54	$11.74	$11.85	$11.90	$11.93	$11.95	$11.97
Sales and Gross Margin Forecast										
Total Sales	$7,500	$15,000	$15,000	$15,000	$7,500	$7,500	$7,500	$7,500	$7,500	$7,500
Less:										
Cost of Goods Sold	$3,171	$6,571	$6,765	$6,923	$3,523	$3,554	$3,571	$3,580	$3,586	$3,590
Other Variable Costs	$0	$0	$0	$0	$0	$0	$0	$0	$0	$0
Total Cost of Sales	$3,171	$6,571	$6,765	$6,923	$3,523	$3,554	$3,571	$3,580	$3,586	$3,590
Gross Sales Margin	$4,329	$8,429	$8,235	$8,077	$3,977	$3,946	$3,929	$3,920	$3,914	$3,910

Figure 6-1. *The sales and cost of sales template, with example data.*

(continued)

Figure 6-1. *continued*

Inventory Forecast											
Inventory Changes--Units											
Beginning Units on Hand	1,000	1100	900	700	500	600	700	800	900	1000
Plus: Units Produced/Purchased	400	400	400	400	400	400	400	400	400	400
Less: Units Sold	300	600	600	600	300	300	300	300	300	300
Ending Units on Hand	1,100	900	700	500	600	700	800	900	1,000	1,100
Inventory Changes--Dollars											
Beginning Dollars on Hand	$10,000	$11,629	$9,857	$7,892	$5,769	$7,046	$8,292	$9,522	$10,741	$11,955
Plus: Dollars Produced/Purchased	$4,800	$4,800	$4,800	$4,800	$4,800	$4,800	$4,800	$4,800	$4,800	$4,800
Less: Dollars Sold	$3,171	$6,571	$6,765	$6,923	$3,523	$3,554	$3,571	$3,580	$3,586	$3,590
Ending Dollars on Hand	$11,629	$9,857	$7,892	$5,769	$7,046	$8,292	$9,522	$10,741	$11,955	$13,164

The values you enter for Units on Hand and Balance in Dollars under Beginning Inventory come from your accounting records; they document your starting inventory balances. Inventory balances for succeeding periods are calculated, using the forecasts of sales and manufacturing or purchasing activity. The period production figures stem from your forecasts of the anticipated manufacturing or the anticipated purchasing volumes necessary to support the sales plan. The production costs—Direct Labor, Direct Material, and Factory Overhead—are those costs associated with manufacturing or purchasing the product. If you are in a wholesale or retail business that has no manufacturing activity, enter only the Direct Material value (which should be called purchases). Forecast the units sold and the unit sales price based on your sales and marketing research. In general, you estimate future sales based on your sales history, adjusted for assumptions about the periods of the forecasting horizon.

Sales Forecast Schedule heading box

The Sales Forecast Schedule heading box provides column headings for the schedules in the template. It has two rows. The first row contains the text label Period. The second row identifies the period for which the results are calculated.

Period. The period identifier simply numbers the time periods for which sales, manufacturing or purchasing, and inventory levels are forecasted. You'll probably want the number of periods in your sales forecast schedule to correspond to the number of periods in the other schedules that make up your financial forecasting model.

The first period is stored in cell B2 as the integer 1. Periods that follow are stored as the previous period plus 1. For example, the formula for the second period is:

    =B2+1

The formula for the third period is:

    =C2+1

and so on.

Cost Totals and Statistics

The Cost Totals and Statistics schedule calculates the total production and purchase costs, as well as the beginning, produced or purchased, and weighted average unit costs. It has four rows that contain calculated data.

Total Production/Purchase Costs. The Total Production/Purchase Costs value is simply the sum of the Direct Labor, Direct Material, and Factory Overhead values. For a wholesaler or retailer, because the Direct Labor and Factory Overhead figures, by definition, are 0, the total cost is the same as the Direct Material cost. For a service firm, no inventory might be manufactured or purchased for resale. Therefore, this amount might be 0.

The formula for the first period is:

=B12+B13+B14

The formula for the second period is:

=C12+C13+C14

and so on.

Beginning Inventory Unit Cost. The Beginning Inventory Unit Cost value represents the cost of producing one of the units held in the beginning inventory.

It is calculated by dividing the Beginning Dollars on Hand value by the Beginning Units on Hand value calculated in the Inventory Forecasts schedule. For example, the formula for the first period is:

=B46/B40

The formula for the second period is:

=C46/C40

and so on.

Produced/Purchased Unit Cost. The Produced/Purchased Unit Cost value represents the cost of producing or purchasing one of the units manufactured or bought during the period. Although the inventory balances reported on this schedule use an average cost inventory assumption, you can use this value to construct an alternative inventory costing methods, such as First-In-First-Out (FIFO) and Last-In-First-Out (LIFO). (FIFO assumes that the first items purchased or produced are the first items sold; LIFO assumes that the last items purchased or produced are the first items sold. In a period of rising prices, FIFO calculates lower cost of goods sold and higher ending inventory.)

The formula for the first period is:

=B21/B9

The formula for the second period is:

=C21/C9

and so on.

Weighted Average Unit Cost. The Weighted Average Unit Cost value represents the average cost of the product units, considering both the beginning inventory balance and the period production or purchase inventory. This is the per unit cost used to calculate both the cost of sales and next period's beginning inventory levels.

The formula divides the total of the inventory Beginning Dollars on Hand and the Total Production/Purchase Costs values by the total of the inventory Beginning Units on Hand and the Units Produced/Purchased values. For example, the first-period formula is:

=(B46+B21)/(B40+B9)

The formula for the second period is:

=(C46+C21)/(C40+C9)

and so on.

Sales and Gross Margin Forecast

The Sales and Gross Margin Forecast schedule calculates the total sales, cost of goods sold, other variable costs, total cost of sales, and gross sales margin. It has five rows of data.

Total Sales. The Total Sales figure represents the total sales made over the period.

The Total Sales formula multiplies the Unit Sales value by the Unit Sales Price value. For example, the first-period total sales formula is:

    =B16*B17

The second-period total sales formula is:

    =C16*C17

and so on.

Cost of Goods Sold. The Cost of Goods Sold figure shows the total cost of manufacturing or purchasing the items sold during the period.

The formula multiplies the Unit Sales value for the period by the Weighted Average Unit Cost value for the period. For example, the formula for the first period is:

    =B16*B26

The formula for the second period is:

    =C16*C26

and so on.

Other Variable Costs. The Other Variable Costs figure shows the other direct costs associated with consummating a sale.

The value is simply pulled from the cell in which you entered this figure in the Sales Forecast Inputs schedule.

Total Cost of Sales. The Total Cost of Sales figure shows the total cost of goods sold and other costs related to the sales.

The value is the sum of the Cost of Goods Sold and Other Variable Costs values. For example, the formula for the first period is:

=B32+B33

The formula for the second period is:

=C32+C33

and so on.

Gross Sales Margin. The Gross Sales Margin figure shows the amount remaining from sale proceeds after deducting the cost of sales. The Gross Sales Margin figure represents the funds that go toward paying your fixed costs and profits.

The formula is the Total Sales value less the Total Cost of Sales value. For example, the formula for the first period is:

=B29−B34

The formula for the second period is:

=C29−C34

and so on.

Inventory Forecast The Inventory Forecast schedule calculates the beginning inventory balance, the change in inventory balance, and the ending inventory balance, each in dollars and in units. The schedule has eight rows that contain calculated data.

Beginning Units on Hand. The Beginning Units on Hand figure shows the number of completed products you have available for resale at the beginning of the period.

For the first forecasting period, the Beginning Units on Hand figure is simply pulled from the Sales Forecast Inputs schedule. In subsequent periods, it is taken from the cell containing the previous period's Ending Units on Hand.

Units Produced/Purchased. The Units Produced/Purchased figure shows the number of equivalent units manufactured or the number of units bought during the period.

The number is pulled from the Sales Forecast Inputs schedule.

Units Sold. The Units Sold figure shows the number of units of inventory sold during the period.

The number is pulled from the Unit Sales forecast in the Sales Forecast Inputs schedule.

Ending Units on Hand. The Ending Units on Hand figure shows the number of units of inventory held at the end of the period. This number is always the same as the number of units held at the beginning of the next period.

The number is the Beginning Units on Hand value plus the Units Produced/Purchased value for the period minus the Units Sold value for the period. For example, the formula for the first period is:

```
=B40+B41-B42
```

The formula for the second period is:

```
=C40+C41-C42
```

and so on.

Beginning Dollars on Hand. The Beginning Dollars on Hand figure shows the dollar cost of the completed and partially completed products that you have available in inventory for resale.

The number for the first period is pulled from the Sales Forecast Inputs schedule. In subsequent periods, the number is taken from the previous period's Ending Dollars on Hand.

Dollars Produced/Purchased. The Dollars Produced/Purchased figure shows the dollar cost of the units manufactured or bought during the period, using the weighted average unit cost as the cost per unit.

The number is pulled from Total Production/Purchase Costs in the Cost Totals and Statistics schedule.

Dollars Sold. The Dollars Sold figure shows the dollar cost of the units sold during the period, using the weighted average unit cost as the cost per unit. This amount is pulled from Cost of Goods Sold in the Sales and Gross Margin schedule.

Ending Dollars on Hand. The Ending Dollars on Hand figure shows the dollar cost of the inventory held at the end of the period. This number is always the same as the dollar cost of the inventory held at the beginning of the next period.

If you are in a manufacturing business, you can use this amount as the dollar cost of the work in process and finished inventory that is included in the balance sheet. If you are in a wholesale or retail business, you use this amount as the dollar cost of all the inventory that is included in the balance sheet.

The Ending Dollars on Hand formula adds the Beginning Dollars on Hand and Dollars Produced/Purchased values and then subtracts the Dollars Sold value. For example, the formula for the first period is:

    =B46+B47–B48

The formula for the second period is:

    =C46+C47–C48

and so on.

Entering Your Own Data

Using the sales and cost of sales template involves eight steps.

1. Load SALESRPT.XLS from the templates disk. The template initially contains the default inputs shown in Figure 6-1.

2. Enter the beginning inventory balance in dollars and in units on hand for the first period. (Notice that subsequent periods' beginning inventory figures are calculated, not entered.)

3. Enter the units produced or purchased for each period over the forecasting horizon.

> **HINT:** For manufacturing firms, the number of units in the starting inventory balance and the number of units produced should be expressed in equivalent units. For example, 100 units that are 50 percent complete are included in the schedule instead as 50 units that are 100 percent complete. This approach is necessary because if you don't use equivalent units, only a percentage of the costs are included and the calculated unit cost will be too low.

4. Enter the production costs (direct labor, direct material, and factory overhead) associated with manufacturing or purchasing volumes forecasted for each period over the forecasting horizon.

5. Enter the units sold and the unit sales price forecasted for each period over the forecasting horizon.

6. Enter any other variable costs associated with consummating a sale for each period over the forecasting horizon.

> **HINT:** Other variable costs associated with a sale might include commissions or bonuses owed to the salespeople who close the sales, bad debt expense that might be expressed as a function of the sales, and marketing costs related to packaging and distributing the product. You'll often enter this item as a formula that is calculated from unit sales, unit sales price, or the production/purchase costs.

7. Save your changes by saving the spreadsheet and giving it a new filename. Save it on the disk on which you plan to store the financial model you're constructing.

8. Print the spreadsheet.

6: Sales and Cost of Sales Template

Customizing the Template

You can use the sales forecast schedule without modification for many sales forecasts. However, you might want to change the template so that it more closely matches your requirements. For example, you can add text that describes the product being manufactured or purchased and for which sales are forecasted. You can also increase or decrease the number of periods. For example, you can increase the number of periods to 12 if your periods are months and you want to forecast an entire year. Before you change anything on the template other than the sales forecast inputs, unprotect the document.

Increasing the number of periods

To increase the number of periods, follow these steps:

1. Remove the border from the last column of the sales forecast schedule.

2. Copy the current last column of the sales forecast schedule to the right as needed. (You'll probably want as many columns in the schedule as there are forecasting periods in your overall model.)

3. Replace the border on the right side of the sales forecast schedule.

4. Reinstate cell protection as needed.

Decreasing the number of periods

To decrease the number of periods, follow these steps:

1. Delete any unneeded columns from the right side of the schedule.

2. Add a border on the new right side of the sales forecast schedule.

3. Reinstate cell protection as needed.

LINKING THIS TEMPLATE TO OTHER SPREADSHEETS

Other templates in this toolkit are designed to provide data to the sales forecast template.

For example, suppose that you forecast the factory overhead component of your production costs as equal to the total overhead cost center expenses as calculated in the modified cost center template shown in Figure 6-2 on the following page.

Factory Overhead Cost Center Report										
Expense Categories	Period 1	Period 2	Period 3	Period 4	Period 5	Period 6	Period 7	Period 8	Period 9	Period 10
Depreciation	150	150	150	150	150	150	150	150	150	150
Freight	25	25	25	25	25	25	25	25	25	25
Insurance	45	45	45	45	45	45	45	45	45	45
Laundry and Cleaning	15	15	15	15	15	15	15	15	15	15
Legal and Professional Services	75	75	75	75	75	75	75	75	75	75
Office Expense	150	150	150	150	150	150	150	150	150	150
Rent on Business Property	125	125	125	125	125	125	125	125	125	125
Repairs	75	75	75	75	75	75	75	75	75	75
Supplies	100	100	100	100	100	100	100	100	100	100
Utilities and Telephone	250	250	250	250	250	250	250	250	250	250
Period Expense Total	$1,010	$1,010	$1,010	$1,010	$1,010	$1,010	$1,010	$1,010	$1,010	$1,010

Figure 6-2. *A modified cost center template, showing factory overhead.*

However, rather than simply entering the forecasted factory overhead amounts as the total overhead cost center expenses calculated, you link the cells that contain the factory overhead forecasts to the modified cost center template. Using this approach means that each time you update the overhead cost center template, your sales forecast schedule, via the link, is also updated. To construct such a link with OVERHEAD.XLS stored in the WINDOWS directory on your hard disk, you do the following:

1. Load SALESRPT.XLS from the templates disk. The template initially contains the inputs shown in Figure 6-1.

2. In cell B14, enter the amount of factory overhead for the first period by entering the following formula.

    ='C:\WINDOWS\OVERHEAD.XLS'!$B$16

    This formula assumes that OVERHEAD.XLS supplies the period overhead expense. Cell B16 in that file is the cell that contains the first-period overhead expense. In the same way, you can enter the forecasted factory overhead amounts for periods 2 through 10.

The sales forecast schedule with factory overhead amounts pulled from a subsidiary template, via a link, is shown in Figure 6-3 on the following page. Again, the significance of the link is that the contents of row 14 are not values entered or formulas calculated in this spreadsheet; rather the calculated expense amounts are pulled from the overhead cost center template.

Sales Forecast Schedule	Period 1	Period 2	Period 3	Period 4	Period 5	Period 6	Period 7	Period 8	Period 9	Period 10
Sales Forecast Inputs										
Beginning Inventory										
Units on Hand	1,000									
Balance in Dollars	$10,000									
Units Produced/Purchased	400	400	400	400	400	400	400	400	400	400
Production/Purchase Costs										
Direct Labor	1,800	1,800	1,800	1,800	1,800	1,800	1,800	1,800	1,800	1,800
Direct Material	2,000	2,000	2,000	2,000	2,000	2,000	2,000	2,000	2,000	2,000
Factory Overhead	1,000	1,000	1,000	1,000	1,000	1,000	1,000	1,000	1,000	1,000
Unit Sales	300	600	600	600	300	300	300	300	300	300
Unit Sales Price	$25.00	$25.00	$25.00	$25.00	$25.00	$25.00	$25.00	$25.00	$25.00	$25.00
Other Variable Costs	$0	$0	$0	$0	$0	$0	$0	$0	$0	$0

Cost Totals and Statistics	Period 1	Period 2	Period 3	Period 4	Period 5	Period 6	Period 7	Period 8	Period 9	Period 10
Total Production/Purchase Costs	$4,800	$4,800	$4,800	$4,800	$4,800	$4,800	$4,800	$4,800	$4,800	$4,800
Cost Statistics										
Beginning Inventory Unit Cost	$10.00	$10.57	$10.95	$11.27	$11.54	$11.74	$11.85	$11.90	$11.93	$11.95
Produced/Purchased Unit Cost	$12.00	$12.00	$12.00	$12.00	$12.00	$12.00	$12.00	$12.00	$12.00	$12.00
Weighted Average Unit Cost	$10.57	$10.95	$11.27	$11.54	$11.74	$11.85	$11.90	$11.93	$11.95	$11.97

Sales and Gross Margin Forecast	Period 1	Period 2	Period 3	Period 4	Period 5	Period 6	Period 7	Period 8	Period 9	Period 10
Total Sales	$7,500	$15,000	$15,000	$15,000	$7,500	$7,500	$7,500	$7,500	$7,500	$7,500
Less:										
Cost of Goods Sold	$3,171	$6,571	$6,765	$6,923	$3,523	$3,554	$3,571	$3,580	$3,586	$3,590
Other Variable Costs	$0	$0	$0	$0	$0	$0	$0	$0	$0	$0
Total Cost of Sales	$3,171	$6,571	$6,765	$6,923	$3,523	$3,554	$3,571	$3,580	$3,586	$3,590
Gross Sales Margin	$4,329	$8,429	$8,235	$8,077	$3,977	$3,946	$3,929	$3,920	$3,914	$3,910

Figure 6-3. *The sales forecast template with the factory overhead inputs provided through a link from the modified cost center template shown in Figure 6-2.*

Inventory Forecast

Inventory Changes--Units											
Beginning Units on Hand	1,000	1100	900	700	500	600	700	800	900	1000
Plus: Units Produced/Purchased	400	400	400	400	400	400	400	400	400	400
Less: Units Sold	300	600	600	600	300	300	300	300	300	300
Ending Units on Hand	1,100	900	700	500	600	700	800	900	1,000	1,100

Inventory Changes--Dollars											
Beginning Dollars on Hand	$10,000	$11,636	$9,868	$7,903	$5,779	$7,059	$8,308	$9,541	$10,763	$11,979
Plus: Dollars Produced/Purchased	$4,810	$4,810	$4,810	$4,810	$4,810	$4,810	$4,810	$4,810	$4,810	$4,810
Less: Dollars Sold	$3,174	$6,579	$6,774	$6,935	$3,530	$3,561	$3,578	$3,588	$3,594	$3,598
Ending Dollars on Hand	$11,636	$9,868	$7,903	$5,779	$7,059	$8,308	$9,541	$10,763	$11,979	$13,192

7

Profit Volume and Break-Even Analysis Template

Profit volume analysis lets you look at the revenues, costs, and profits of your business for a range of business volumes, or revenues. By using profit volume analysis, you can see how sensitive to changes in business volume profits are and where break-even points occur. The break-even point is the business volume at which revenues equal costs. The profit volume and break-even analysis template described in this chapter provides a framework to use in performing profit volume analysis and in calculating break-even points. This chapter shows how to use the template, print it, modify it, and link it with other spreadsheets. In addition, this chapter includes two charts useful in portraying profit volume and break-even analysis data and briefly describes how to use Microsoft Excel's charting features to communicate financial information.

PROFIT VOLUME AND BREAK-EVEN ANALYSIS: A SHORT PRIMER

Profit volume analysis, sometimes called cost-profit-volume analysis, is the process of calculating the profits of a business at different volumes, or revenue levels. Break-even analysis, a component of profit volume analysis, is simply the calculation of the revenue level at which a business shows neither a profit nor a loss.

Generally, profit volume analysis involves five steps. First, set a range of business volumes for which you examine costs and profits. This step is probably one of the most critical because all the information you input—unit sales price, variable costs, fixed costs, and costs varying with profits—is usually valid only over a limited range of volumes. By carefully considering the relationships between costs and changes in volume, you can increase the accuracy of your analysis.

Second, calculate the unit sales price, the amount for which you sell your product or service. For example, if you build and sell single-family homes and your average sales price is $100,000, your unit sales price is $100,000.

Third, identify the costs that vary with revenue, the variable costs. Typically, it's easiest to express and calculate these variable costs either as an amount determined per unit or as an amount determined as a percentage of revenues. For example, if you build houses, many of your costs are best described as an amount per house. For example, your land costs might average $25,000 per house and your material costs and your labor costs each might average $40,000. Other costs, however, are better described as a percentage of revenues. For example, you might calculate sales commissions as 7 percent of the sales price and a state sales tax as $1\frac{1}{2}$ percent of the sales price. The key assumption for the purpose of profit volume analysis, however, is that within the range of business volumes you define, the variable costs change proportionally, based on revenue.

Fourth, determine your fixed costs. Fixed costs are those that stay constant, within the range of business volumes you define. You label these costs "fixed," not because you cannot change them, but because changes in revenue don't change them. Examples of fixed costs are salaries of administrative personnel, office rent, and business insurance.

Fifth, calculate your profits and any costs that vary with profits. Examples of these costs are income taxes and profit-sharing plans. Obviously, the precise determination of income taxes and similar costs requires detailed tax accounting. But you might be able to estimate these income taxes and costs by applying an appropriate percentage to the profits before income taxes and other costs that vary with profits.

You can calculate the contribution margin (the revenues minus the variable costs) and profit at any volume within the range for which your inputs are valid. Although the analysis is only as good as your assumptions and is subject to the inevitable inaccuracies that creep into any projection of the future, profit volume analysis allows you to see roughly what happens to your profits over the likely range of business volumes.

One common profit volume analysis calculation is estimating the revenue level that provides exactly enough contribution margin to cover fixed costs. In this calculation, because no profits exist, none of the costs that vary with profits exist. At the break-even point, revenues leave exactly enough contribution margin to cover fixed costs. The general formula used to calculate the break-even point is as follows:

Break-even point in units=Fixed costs/Contribution margin per unit

If you use more than one of the vary-with-profit cost categories presented in the profit volume and break-even analysis template, you need to recognize the correct relationships between variables as you input them. Basically, three types of relationships exist: independent-independent, independent-dependent, and dependent-dependent. Independent-independent is easiest to calculate because all of the costs that vary with profits are calculated independent of the other. The other two types of relationships can be more difficult. With the independent-dependent relationship, you need to calculate one cost so that you can calculate the next. As an example of this relationship and how you might recognize it in your inputs, suppose that the state income tax rate is 10 percent and is deducted from the Profit Before Vary-with-Profits Costs (PBVPC) and that after deducting the state income tax from the PBVPC, the federal income tax rate of 20 percent is applied to the PBVPC. The correct input percentage for the state income tax rate is 10 percent, because 10 percent of the PBVPC calculates the correct state income tax cost, as follows:

State Income Tax=10%*PBVPC

However, the federal income tax percentage must recognize the state income tax costs:

Federal Income Tax=20%*(PBVPC−State Income Tax)

So you need to calculate the percentage that, when multiplied by the PBVPC, shows the correct federal income tax expense. You can do this by substituting the state income tax formula in the federal income tax formula:

Federal Income Tax=20%*(PBVPC−(10%*PBVPC))

This formula can be further modified as follows to express the federal income tax rate as a percentage of the PBVPC and, therefore, your input to the profit volume and break-even analysis template:

Federal Income Tax=18%*PBVPC

A second type of relationship that might exist between the costs that vary with profits is a dependent-dependent, or circular, relationship. For example, suppose you have an employee bonus cost equal to 10 percent of the after-tax profits. You need to know the amount of the bonus before you can calculate the federal income taxes because it's a tax-deductible expense, and you need to know the federal income tax, because it determines the after-tax profits, upon which the bonus is calculated, before you can calculate the bonus. Assuming that your only tax is a federal income tax rate of 20 percent, you calculate your federal income tax as follows:

Federal Income Tax=20%*(PBVPC−bonus)

Assuming that the employee bonus is 10 percent of the after-tax profits, your employee bonus cost equals:

Bonus=10%*(PBVPC−Federal Income Tax)

Given these definitions, you can define the federal income tax percentage by substituting the formula for the bonus in the federal income tax formula, as follows:

Federal Income Tax=20%*(PBVPC−(10%*(PBVPC−Federal Income Tax)))

You could state this formula algebraically as:

Federal Income Tax=20%*(PBVPC−(10%*PBVPC)+ (10%*Federal Income Tax))

or:

Federal Income Tax=20%*((90%*PBVPC)+(10%*Federal Income Tax))

or:

Federal Income Tax=(18%*PBVPC)+(2%*Federal Income Tax)

or:

98%*Federal Income Tax=18%*PBVPC

or, to show the federal income tax as a percentage of the PBVPC:

Federal Income Tax=18.3673%*PBVPC

Given this number, it's easy to define the bonus as a percentage of the PBVPC by substituting the following formula for federal income tax in the bonus formula:

Bonus=10%*(PBVPC−(18.3673%*PBVPC))

or, to show the bonus as a percentage of the PBVPC:

Bonus=10%*(81.6327%*PBVPC)

or, to show the bonus as a percentage of the PBVPC in another way:

Bonus=8.16372%*PBVPC

PROFIT VOLUME AND BREAK-EVEN ANALYSIS TEMPLATE (PROFT-VOL.XLS)

You can use the profit volume and break-even analysis template (PROFTVOL.XLS), shown in Figure 7-1, to test the effect of changing revenues on business profits. To complete the schedule, you define:

- Revenue variables, including the unit sales price, the low revenue in unit volume tested, and the high revenue in unit volume tested
- Variable costs best expressed as an amount per unit, including the direct labor, the direct materials, and the factory overhead
- Variable costs best expressed as a percentage of revenue, including sales commissions and sales tax
- Any costs commonly calculated as a percentage of profits, including state income tax and federal income tax

The template calculates the break-even point in units; shows the revenues, costs, and profits for the break-even point; and calculates the revenues, costs, and profits for the low units volume, the high units volume, and four intervals between the low and high volumes.

Two charts are included on the templates disk and are linked to the profit volume analysis template. The first chart (COSTPROF.XLC) shows the revenues, costs, and profits at various revenue levels. The second (BREAKEVN.XLC) shows the revenues plotted against the total fixed and variable costs; the point at which the revenue line intersects the total fixed and variable costs identifies the break-even point.

Profit Volume Inputs	
Revenues	
Unit Sales Price	$15.00
Low Unit Volume Tested	15,000
High Unit Volume Tested	75,000
Variable Costs	
Vary-with-Unit Costs	
Direct Labor	$2.00
Direct Material	$2.00
Factory Overhead	$1.00
Other Vary-with-Unit Costs	$0.50
Vary-with-Revenue Costs	
Sales Commissions	5.00%
Sales Tax	8.00%
Other Vary-with-Revenue Costs	1.50%
Fixed Costs	150,000
Vary-with-Profit Costs	
State Income Tax	10.00%
Federal Income Tax	20.00%
Other Vary-with-Profit Costs	5.00%

Break-Even Analysis Forecast	
Volume in Units	20,478
Total Sales	$307,170
Variable Costs	
Direct Labor	(40,956)
Direct Material	(40,956)
Factory Overhead	(20,478)
Other Vary-with-Unit Costs	(10,239)
Sales Commissions	(15,359)
Sales Tax	(24,574)
Other Vary-with-Revenue Costs	(4,608)
Total Variable Costs	(157,169)
Contribution Margin	150,001
Fixed Costs	(150,000)
Profit Before Vary-with-Profit Costs	$1

Profit Volume Forecast						
Volume in Units	15,000	27,000	39,000	51,000	63,000	75,000
Total Sales	$225,000	$405,000	$585,000	$765,000	$945,000	$1,125,000
Variable Costs						
Direct Labor	(30,000)	(54,000)	(78,000)	(102,000)	(126,000)	(150,000)
Direct Material	(30,000)	(54,000)	(78,000)	(102,000)	(126,000)	(150,000)
Factory Overhead	(15,000)	(27,000)	(39,000)	(51,000)	(63,000)	(75,000)
Other Vary-with-Unit Costs	(7,500)	(13,500)	(19,500)	(25,500)	(31,500)	(37,500)
Sales Commissions	(11,250)	(20,250)	(29,250)	(38,250)	(47,250)	(56,250)
Sales Tax	(18,000)	(32,400)	(46,800)	(61,200)	(75,600)	(90,000)
Other Vary-with-Revenue Costs	(3,375)	(6,075)	(8,775)	(11,475)	(14,175)	(16,875)
Total Variable Costs	(115,125)	(207,225)	(299,325)	(391,425)	(483,525)	(575,625)
Contribution Margin	109,875	197,775	285,675	373,575	461,475	549,375
Fixed Costs	(150,000)	(150,000)	(150,000)	(150,000)	(150,000)	(150,000)
Contribution Margin - Fixed Costs	(40,125)	47,775	135,675	223,575	311,475	399,375
Vary-with-Profit Costs						
State Income Tax	4,013	(4,778)	(13,568)	(22,358)	(31,148)	(39,938)
Federal Income Tax	8,025	(9,555)	(27,135)	(44,715)	(62,295)	(79,875)
Other Vary-with-Profit Costs	2,006	(2,389)	(6,784)	(11,179)	(15,574)	(19,969)
Total Vary-with-Profit Costs	14,044	(16,721)	(47,486)	(78,251)	(109,016)	(139,781)
Profits	($26,081)	$31,054	$88,189	$145,324	$202,459	$259,594

Figure 7-1. *The profit volume and break-even analysis template, with sample data.* *(continued)*

Microsoft Excel Small Business Consultant

Figure 7-1. *continued*

Common Size Profit Volume Forecast						
Volume in Units	15,000	27,000	39,000	51,000	63,000	75,000
Total Sales	100.00%	100.00%	100.00%	100.00%	100.00%	100.00%
Variable Costs						
Direct Labor	-13.33%	-13.33%	-13.33%	-13.33%	-13.33%	-13.33%
Direct Material	-13.33%	-13.33%	-13.33%	-13.33%	-13.33%	-13.33%
Factory Overhead	-6.67%	-6.67%	-6.67%	-6.67%	-6.67%	-6.67%
Other Vary-with-Unit Costs	-3.33%	-3.33%	-3.33%	-3.33%	-3.33%	-3.33%
Sales Commissions	-5.00%	-5.00%	-5.00%	-5.00%	-5.00%	-5.00%
Sales Tax	-8.00%	-8.00%	-8.00%	-8.00%	-8.00%	-8.00%
Other Vary-with-Revenue Costs	-1.50%	-1.50%	-1.50%	-1.50%	-1.50%	-1.50%
Total Variable Costs	-51.17%	-51.17%	-51.17%	-51.17%	-51.17%	-51.17%
Contribution Margin	48.83%	48.83%	48.83%	48.83%	48.83%	48.83%
Fixed Costs	-66.67%	-37.04%	-25.64%	-19.61%	-15.87%	-13.33%
Contribution Margin - Fixed Costs	-17.83%	11.80%	23.19%	29.23%	32.96%	35.50%
Vary-with-Profit Costs						
State Income Tax	1.78%	-1.18%	-2.32%	-2.92%	-3.30%	-3.55%
Federal Income Tax	3.57%	-2.36%	-4.64%	-5.85%	-6.59%	-7.10%
Other Vary-with-Profit Costs	0.89%	-0.59%	-1.16%	-1.46%	-1.65%	-1.78%
Total Vary-with-Profit Costs	6.24%	-4.13%	-8.12%	-10.23%	-11.54%	-12.43%
Profits	-11.59%	7.67%	15.08%	19.00%	21.42%	23.08%

Profit Volume Area Chart Data						
Volumes in Units	15,000	27,000	39,000	51,000	63,000	75,000
Fixed Costs	150,000	150,000	150,000	150,000	150,000	150,000
Variable Costs	115,125	207,225	299,325	391,425	483,525	575,625
Costs Varying with Profits	(14,044)	16,721	47,486	78,251	109,016	139,781
Profit	(26,081)	31,054	88,189	145,324	202,459	259,594
Break-Even Analysis Line Chart Data						
Volumes in Units	15,000	27,000	39,000	51,000	63,000	75,000
Total Fixed Costs	150,000	150,000	150,000	150,000	150,000	150,000
Total Variable Costs	251,081	373,946	496,811	619,676	742,541	865,406
Total Sales	225,000	405,000	585,000	765,000	945,000	1,125,000

7: Profit Volume and Break-Even Analysis Template

What the Template Contains and Does

The six parts of the profit volume and break-even analysis template are the Profit Volume Inputs box, the Break-Even Analysis Forecast, the Profit Volume Forecast, the Common Size Profit Volume Forecast, the Profit Volume Area Chart Data, and the Break-Even Analysis Line Chart Data.

Profit Volume Inputs

You enter the following 13 variables in the Profit Volume Inputs schedule:

- Unit Sales Price
- Low Unit Volume Tested
- High Unit Volume Tested
- Direct Labor
- Direct Material
- Factory Overhead
- Other Vary-with-Unit Costs
- Sales Commissions
- Sales Tax
- Other Vary-with-Revenue Costs
- State Income Tax
- Federal Income Tax
- Other Vary-with-Profit Costs

Unless you turn off cell protection, these are the only cells into which you enter data.

Estimate the Unit Sales Price value as the amount per unit you will receive from sales of the product or service for which you are performing profit volume and break-even analysis. Low Unit Volume Tested is the minimum revenue level (in units) for which you will calculate revenues, costs, and profits; High Unit Volume Tested is the maximum revenue level (in units) for which you will calculate

171

revenues, costs, and profits. Direct Labor is the dollar amount of labor per unit, Direct Material is the dollar amount of materials per unit, and Factory Overhead is the dollar amount of factory overhead per unit. If you have other costs that you want to express as a dollar amount per unit, enter the dollar amount of these other costs as the Other Vary-with-Unit Costs amount. Enter Sales Commissions and Sales Tax as percentages of revenue. If you have other costs that you want to express as a percentage of revenues, enter that percentage as the Other Vary-with-Revenue Costs amount. Fixed Costs are those costs that will not change, given the range of revenue levels for which you are testing. State Income Tax and Federal Income Tax are percentages of profits. If you have other costs that you want to express as a percentage of profits, enter that percentage as the Other Vary-with-Profit Costs amount.

For convenience and good documentation within the model, cell C4 contains the Unit Sales Price amount and is named Unit_Sales_Price, cell C5 contains the Low Unit Volume Tested amount and is named Low_Unit_Volume_Tested, cell C6 contains the High Unit Volume Tested amount and is named High_Unit_Volume_Tested, cell C10 contains the Direct Labor amount and is named Direct_Labor, cell C11 contains the Direct Material amount and is named Direct_Material, cell C12 contains the factory overhead amount and is named Factory_Overhead, cell C13 contains the Other Vary-with-Units Costs amount and is named Other_Vary_Unit_Costs, cell C15 contains the Sales Commissions percentage and is named Sales_Commissions, cell C16 contains the Sales Tax percentage and is named Sales_Tax, cell C17 contains the Other Vary-with-Revenue Costs percentage and is named Other_Vary_Revenue_Costs, cell C19 contains the Fixed Costs amount and is named Fixed_Costs, cell C22 contains the State Income Tax percentage and is named State_Income_Tax, cell C23 contains the Federal Income Tax percentage and is named Federal_Income_Tax, and cell C24 contains the Other Vary-with-Profit Costs percentage and is named Other_Vary_Profit_Costs. The formulas within the template use these cell names rather than the cell addresses.

Break-Even Analysis Forecast

The Break-Even Analysis Forecast calculates the volume level in units at which you break even and displays the revenues, variable costs, and fixed costs forecasted at this volume level. The schedule has only one column containing calculated data. Within it, revenues appear as positive amounts, and expenses appear as negative amounts.

Volume in Units. The Volume in Units amount is the number of units at which the break-even point occurs. The amount is rounded to the nearest whole unit, because selling partial units usually is impossible. This Volume in Units amount is calculated by dividing the Fixed Costs amount by the contribution margin per unit. The contribution margin per unit is calculated by subtracting each of the variable costs (expressed as an amount per unit) from the Unit Sales Price value. Those variable costs, which you enter as a percentage of the Unit Sales Price amount, are converted to an amount per unit. Because the calculated revenue level is the level at which no profits are generated, no costs based on profits are included in the formula or are shown in the forecast of revenues and costs at the break-even point. The formula for the break-even point in units (in cell H3) is:

```
=ROUND(Fixed_Costs/(Unit_Sales_Price-(Direct_Labor
+Direct_Material+Factory_Overhead+Other_Vary_Unit_Costs)
-(Unit_Sales_Price*(Sales_Commissions_+Sales_Taxes
+Other_Vary_Revenue_Costs))),0)
```

Total Sales. The Total Sales amount shows the revenue in dollars for the break-even point. The Total Sales amount is the break-even Volume in Units times the Unit Sales Price value. The Total Sales formula (in cell H4) is:

```
=H3*Unit_Sales_Price
```

Direct Labor. The Direct Labor figure shows the direct labor costs for the break-even volume. The amount is the break-even Volume in Units amount times the Direct Labor cost per unit. The Direct Labor formula (in cell H7) is:

```
=-H3*Direct_Labor
```

Direct Material. The Direct Material figure shows the direct material costs for the break-even volume. The amount is the break-even Volume in Units amount times the Direct Material cost per unit. The Direct Material formula (in cell H8) is:

```
=-H3*Direct_Material
```

Factory Overhead. The Factory Overhead figure shows the factory overhead costs for the break-even volume. The amount is the break-even Volume in Units amount times the Factory Overhead cost per unit. The Factory Overhead formula (in cell H9) is:

```
=-H3*Factory_Overhead
```

Other Vary-with-Unit Costs. The Other Vary-with-Unit Costs figure shows any other costs you have expressed as an amount per unit for the break-even volume. The amount is the break-even Volume in Units amount times the Other Vary-with-Unit Costs per unit. The Other Vary-with-Unit Costs formula (in cell H10) is:

```
=-H3*Other_Vary_Unit_Costs
```

Sales Commissions. The Sales Commissions figure shows the sales commissions costs for the break-even volume. The amount is the break-even revenue level times the Sales Commissions percentage. The Sales Commissions formula (in cell H11) is:

```
=-H4*Sales_Commissions
```

Sales Tax. The Sales Tax figure shows the sales tax costs for the break-even volume. The amount is the break-even revenue level times the Sales Tax percentage. The Sales Tax formula (in cell H12) is:

```
=-H4*Sales_Tax
```

Other Vary-with-Revenue Costs. The Other Vary-with-Revenue Costs figure shows any other costs you have expressed as a percentage of revenues for the break-even volume. The amount is the break-even revenue level times the Other Vary-with-Revenue Costs percentage. The Other Vary-with-Revenue Costs formula (in cell H13) is:

    =–H4*Other_Vary_Revenue_Costs

Total Variable Costs. The Total Variable Costs figure shows the total variable costs for the break-even volume. The Total Variable Costs formula (in cell H14) is:

    =SUM(H7:H13)

Contribution Margin. The Contribution Margin figure shows the difference between the total sales and the total variable costs. For break-even analysis, this amount must equal the fixed costs. However, because the break-even point in unit volume is rounded to an integer, this amount might differ. The formula (in cell H15) is:

    =H4+H14

Fixed Costs. The Fixed Costs figure shows the fixed costs at the break-even volume. The formula (in cell H17) is:

    =–Fixed_Costs

Profit Before Vary-with-Profit Costs. The Profit Before Vary-with-Profit Costs figure shows the amount of profit for the break-even volume and is the Contribution Margin amount minus the Fixed Costs figure. None of the costs that vary with profits are included, because profits must equal 0. In some situations, the profit will equal some amount other than 0, even though, by definition, the true break-even point is the revenue volume at which profits equal 0. Typically, however, firms cannot sell fractional units of products or services. Accordingly, the break-even Volume in Units is rounded to an integer, and the template assumes that this is the closest to a break-even volume that you can actually operate. The Profit Before Vary-with-Profit Costs formula (in cell H18) is:

    =H15+H17

Profit Volume Forecast

The Profit Volume Forecast calculates the revenue, costs, and profits at the low unit volume you specify, the high unit volume you specify, and four intermediate volumes between these two boundaries. In the forecast, revenues appear as positive amounts and expenses appear as negative amounts.

Volume in Units. The Volume in Units figure shows the business volume in units for each of the six volume levels for which revenues, costs, and profits are calculated. The first Volume in Units amount is pulled into the Profit Volume Forecast as the Low Unit Volume Tested amount you enter in the Profit Volume Inputs box. The second through the sixth Volume in Units amounts, however, are calculated as the previous Volume in Units amounts plus an increase equal to the range of volumes tested, divided by the number of volumes tested. The range of volumes tested is the High Unit Volume Tested figure minus the Low Unit Volume Tested figure. The number of volumes tested is set at 5 and is defined with the reference name Increments within the template. The formula for the second Volume in Units figure (in cell D27) is:

```
=C27+((High_Unit_Volume_Tested-Low_Unit_Volume_Tested)/Increments
```

The formula for the third volume is:

```
=D27+((High_Unit_Volume_Tested-Low_Unit_Volume_Tested)/Increments)
```

and so on.

Total Sales. The Total Sales amount shows the revenue in dollars for each volume tested. The Total Sales figure is the Volume in Units figure times the Unit Sales Price figure. For example, the Total Sales formula for the first volume tested (in cell C28) is:

```
=C27*Unit_Sales_Price
```

The formula for the second volume tested is:

    D27*Unit_Sales_Price

and so on.

Direct Labor. The Direct Labor figure shows the direct labor costs for each of the volumes tested. The amount is the Volume in Units figure times the Direct Labor cost per unit. The Direct Labor formula for the first volume (in cell C31) is:

    =–C27*Direct_Labor

The formula for the second volume is:

    =–D27*Direct_Labor

and so on.

Direct Material. The Direct Material figure shows the direct material costs for each of the volumes. The amount is the Volume in Units figure times the Direct Material cost per unit. The Direct Material formula for the first volume (in cell C32) is:

    =–C27*Direct_Material

The formula for the second volume is:

    =–D27*Direct_Material

and so on.

Factory Overhead. The Factory Overhead figure shows the factory overhead costs for each of the volumes. The amount is the Volume in Units figure times the Factory Overhead cost per unit. The Factory Overhead formula for the first volume (in cell C33) is:

    =–C27*Factory_Overhead

The formula for the second volume is:

    =-D27*Factory_Overhead

and so on.

Other Vary-with-Unit Costs. The Other Vary-with-Unit Costs figure shows any other costs you have expressed as an amount per unit for each volume tested. The amount is the Volume in Units figure times the Other Vary-with-Unit Costs per unit. The Other Vary-with-Unit Costs formula (in cell C34) is:

    =-C27*Other_Vary_Unit_Costs

The formula for the second volume is:

    =-D27*Other_Vary_Unit_Costs

and so on.

Sales Commissions. The Sales Commissions figure shows the sales commissions costs for each of the volumes tested. The amount is the Total Sales figure times the Sales Commissions percentage. The Sales Commissions formula for the first volume (in cell C35) is:

    =-C28*Sales_Commissions

The formula for the second volume is:

    =-D28*Sales_Commissions

and so on.

Sales Tax. The Sales Tax figure shows the sales tax costs for each of the volumes tested. The amount is the Total Sales figure times the Sales Tax percentage. The Sales Tax formula for the first volume (in cell C36) is:

    =-C28*Sales_Tax

The formula for the second volume is:

=-D28*Sales_Tax

and so on.

Other Vary-with-Revenue Costs. The Other Vary-with-Revenue Costs figure shows any other costs you have expressed as a percentage of revenues for each of the volumes tested. The amount is the Total Sales figure times the Other Vary-with-Revenue Costs percentage. The Other Vary-with-Revenue Costs formula for the first volume (in cell C37) is:

=-C28*Other_Vary_Revenue_Costs

The formula for the second volume is:

=-D28*Other_Vary_Revenue_Costs

and so on.

Total Variable Costs. The Total Variable Costs figure shows the total variable costs for each of the volumes tested. The Total Variable Costs formula for the first volume (in cell C38) is:

=SUM(C31:C37)

The formula for the second volume is:

=SUM(D31:D37)

and so on.

Contribution Margin. The Contribution Margin figure shows the difference between the Total Sales figure and the Total Variable Costs figure. The Contribution Margin formula for the first volume (in cell C39) is:

=C28+C38

The formula for the second volume is:

```
=D28+D38
```

and so on.

Fixed Costs. The Fixed Costs figure shows the fixed costs you enter for the range of volumes tested. The formula is simply a named cell reference and is the same for each of the volumes tested. The formula for the first volume (in cell C41) is:

```
=-Fixed_Costs
```

Contribution Margin – Fixed Costs. This figure is the Contribution Margin figure minus the Fixed Costs figure. It is the amount used to calculate any costs that vary with profits. The Contribution Margin – Fixed Costs formula for the first volume (in cell C42) is:

```
=C39+C41
```

The formula for the second volume is:

```
=D39+D41
```

and so on.

State Income Tax. The State Income Tax figure shows the state income tax costs for each of the volumes tested. The amount is the Contribution Margin – Fixed Costs figure times the State Income Tax percentage. The State Income Tax formula for the first volume (in cell C45) is:

```
=-C42*State_Income_Tax
```

The formula for the second volume is:

```
=-D42*State_Income_Tax
```

and so on.

Federal Income Tax. The Federal Income Tax figure shows the federal income tax costs for each of the volumes tested. The amount is the Contribution Margin – Fixed Costs figure times the Federal Income Tax percentage. The Federal Income Tax formula for the first volume (in cell C46) is:

=-C42*Federal_Income_Tax

The formula for the second volume is:

=-D42*Federal_Income_Tax

and so on.

Other Vary-with-Profit Costs. The Other Vary-with-Profit Costs figure shows any other costs that are calculated as a percentage of profits for each of the volumes tested. The amount is the Contribution Margin – Fixed Costs figure times the Other Vary-with-Profit Costs percentage. The Other Vary-with-Profit Costs formula for the first volume (in cell C47) is:

=-C42*Other_Vary_Profit_Costs

The formula for the second volume is:

=-D42*Other_Vary_Profit_Costs

and so on.

Total Vary-with-Profit Costs. The Total Vary-with-Profit Costs figure shows the total of the costs that vary with profits for each of the volumes tested. The formula for the first volume (in cell C48) is:

=SUM(C45:C47)

The formula for the second volume is:

=SUM(D45:D47)

and so on.

Profits. The Profits figure shows the profits for each of the volumes tested and is the Contribution Margin − Fixed Costs amount minus the Total Vary-with-Profit Costs amount. The Profits formula for the first volume (in cell C49) is:

=C42+C48

The formula for profits for the second volume is:

=D42+D48

and so on.

Common Size Profit Volume Forecast The Common Size Profit Volume Forecast simply converts the costs and profits in the Profit Volume Forecast to percentages of the total sales for each of the volumes for which revenue, costs, and profits are calculated. For example, the formula for the Total Sales percentage for the first volume shown (in cell C55) is:

=C28/C$28

The Volume in Units formulas are simply cell references to the Volume in Units figures calculated in the Break-Even Analysis Forecast. For example, the Volume in Units formula for the first volume shown (in cell C54) is:

=C27

Profit Volume Area Chart Data The Profit Volume Area Chart Data provides the data graphed in the profit volume area chart discussed later in the chapter. All of the figures are simply pulled from the Profit Volume Forecast by cell references. For example, the Volume in Units figure for the first volume is pulled from the Profit Volume Forecast by the following formula:

=C27

The Fixed Costs, Variable Costs, and Costs Varying with Profits figures are pulled as positive numbers from the Profit Volume

Forecast, in which they appear as negative numbers. For example, the formula for the first volume of the Fixed Costs row is:

=–C41

Break-Even Analysis Line Chart Data

The Break-Even Analysis Line Chart Data provides the data to the line chart discussed later in the chapter, which identifies the break-even point by showing the intersection of the total sales line with the total costs line. The Volume in Units, Total Fixed Costs, and Total Sales figures are pulled from the Profit Volume Forecast by cell references. For example, the formula for the first volume of the Volume in Units row is:

=C27

The Fixed Costs figure is pulled as a positive number from the Profit Volume Forecast, in which it appears as a negative number. For example, the formula for the first volume is:

=–C41

Total Variable Costs. The Total Variable Costs figure includes those costs that vary with profits. The figure is the sum of the Fixed Costs, the Total Variable Costs, and the Total Vary-with-Profit Costs figures calculated in the Profit Volume Forecast. Fixed costs are included because the line chart plots total cost data against fixed cost data. You see the difference between the two lines, or the total variable costs. The formula for the first volume is:

=–C38–C41–C48

Entering Your Own Data

To enter your own data in the profit volume and break-even analysis template, follow these steps:

1. Load the PROFTVOL.XLS template from the templates disk. The template initially contains the default inputs shown in Figure 7-1.

2. In cell C4, enter the unit sales price of the product or service you sell.

3. In cell C5, enter the lowest business volume in units for which you want to calculate total sales, costs, and profits.

4. In cell C6, enter the highest business volume in units for which you want to calculate total sales, costs, and profits.

5. In cell C10, enter any direct labor costs that vary with the units sold and that are calculated as an amount per unit.

6. In cell C11, enter any direct material costs that vary with the units sold and that are calculated as an amount per unit.

7. In cell C12, enter any factory overhead costs that vary with the units sold and that are calculated as an amount per unit.

8. In cell C13, enter any other costs that vary with the units sold and that are calculated as an amount per unit.

9. In cell C15, enter any sales commissions as a percentage of the unit sales price or the total sales.

10. In cell C16, enter any sales tax as a percentage of the unit sales price or the total sales.

11. In cell C17, enter any other costs that vary with revenues as a percentage of the unit sales price or the total sales.

12. In cell C19, enter the total fixed costs.

13. In cell C22, enter the state income tax as a percentage of profits before federal income tax and other costs that vary with profits.

14. In cell C23, enter the federal income tax as a percentage of profits before state income tax and other costs that vary with profits.

15. In cell C24, enter as a percentage any other costs that vary with the profits before taxes.

16. Save your changes by saving the spreadsheet and giving it a new filename.

17. Print the spreadsheet.

Customizing the Template

You can use the profit volume and break-even analysis template for testing the sensitivity of your costs and profits to changes in revenues and for calculating your break-even point. However, you might want to change the template so that it more closely matches your requirements. For example, if you want to test more than six volumes at one time, you can increase or decrease the number of volumes for which revenue, costs, and profits are calculated. You can change the text describing the revenue, costs, and profits, or you can remove those cost categories unnecessary to your profit volume and break-even analysis. You can define minimums and maximums for specific costs and then include these minimums and maximums in your profit volume analysis. Before you change anything on the schedule other than the inputs, unprotect the document.

Increasing the number of volumes tested

To increase the number of volumes for which you test revenue, costs, and profits, follow these steps:

1. Remove the right border from the last column of the Profit Volume Forecast.

2. Copy the current last column to the right into as many additional columns as there are additional volumes for which you want to test revenue, costs, and profits.

3. Replace the border on the right column of the schedule.

4. Redefine the reference name Increment so that it equals one number less than the number of different unit volumes you show in your new Profit Volume Forecast. (For example, with six unit volumes in the Profit Volume Forecast, Increment is set to 5.)

5. Reinstate cell protection as needed.

Decreasing the number of volumes To decrease the number of volumes in the Profit Volume Forecast, follow these steps:

1. Clear any unneeded columns from the right side of the forecast.

2. Add a border to the right side of the forecast.

3. Redefine the reference name Increments so that it equals the one number less than the number of different unit volumes you now show in your new profit volume forecast. (For example, with six unit volumes in the schedule, Increments is set to 5.)

4. Reinstate cell protection as needed.

Removing the Break-Even Analysis Forecast, the Profit Volume Forecast, or the Common Size Profit Volume Forecast You can remove the Break-Even Analysis Forecast, the Common Size Profit Volume Forecast, or both the Profit Volume Forecast and the Common Size Profit Volume Forecast. (The Common Size Profit Volume Forecast uses information in the Profit Volume Forecast, so if you remove the Profit Volume Forecast, also remove the Common Size Profit Volume Forecast.) To remove any of these forecasts from the template, follow these steps:

1. Clear the forecast you want to remove.

2. Reinstate cell protection as needed.

Adding minimums and maximums to the Profit Volume Forecast In your business, you might need to keep certain expenses below or above certain amounts. If so, you can, for example, specify that those costs the template calculates as a percentage of profits not become positive if the expenses should be expressed as negatives. To set a minimum expense as 0, use the following step:

1. Edit the formula in the first volume column in the Profit Volume Forecast so that it checks for a minimum, as follows:

    =MIN("old formula","minimum amount")

    where the old formula is the formula currently in the cell and the minimum amount is the dollar amount shown as 0, or a negative value, which you don't want the calculated result to fall below. For example, you could set the State Income Tax formula to never fall below 0 by editing the formula currently in cell C45 to read:

=MIN(−C42*State_Income_Tax,0)

Notice that to keep an expense amount from falling below a certain floor value you use a MIN function because the template calculates expenses as negative amounts. To set a maximum amount, use a MAX function, with the maximum amount specified as 0, or a negative value in the formula:

=MAX("old formula","maximum amount")

> **HINT:** Because expenses are expressed as negative amounts, setting an amount above which an expense should not rise uses a MAX function with one of the arguments set as 0 or a negative "ceiling" value. Setting an amount below which an expense should never fall uses a MIN function, with one of the arguments set as 0 or a negative "floor" value.

Changing the revenue, costs, and profit descriptions

To change the revenue, costs, and profits descriptions on the forecasts, use the following steps:

1. Edit the revenue, costs, or profits description on each of the forecasts so that it agrees with your use.

2. Reinstate cell protection as needed.

LINKING THIS TEMPLATE WITH OTHER SPREADSHEETS

You can add detail to many of your inputs by having the input be the result of other calculations and analyses. For example, you will probably want to provide more detail than simply a lump sum amount for fixed costs. Using Microsoft Excel's ability to link spreadsheets, you can forecast the fixed costs in a separate spreadsheet and pull the fixed costs total from that spreadsheet rather than simply enter the fixed costs into your profit volume and break-even analysis template. The benefit of linking is that as you update and modify your fixed costs spreadsheet, your profit volume and break-even analysis is updated. For example, assume that you forecast your fixed costs by using the modified version of the cost center template (COSTS-RPT.XLS), as shown in Figure 7-2. Rather than enter the fixed costs total from this spreadsheet, you could link the input cell in the profit volume and break-even analysis template (PROFTVOL.XLS) to the spreadsheet that calculates the fixed costs. To complete such a link, you would use the following steps:

1. Load PROFTVOL.XLS from the templates disk.

2. Enter the fixed costs amount into the Profit Volume Forecast as the following formula:

   ='C:\WINDOWS\FIXCOSTS.XLS'!$B$20

Fixed Costs Summary	
Advertising	$5,000
Car and Truck Expenses	5,324
Depreciation	15,000
Dues and Publications	4,300
Employee Benefit Programs	12,987
Insurance	8,760
Interest	7,463
Laundry and Cleaning	543
Legal and Professional Services	12,005
Office Expense	12,000
Rent on Business Property	1,345
Repairs	5,432
Supplies	4,356
Taxes	6,574
Utilities and Telephone	5,432
Wages	43,242
Total Fixed Costs	$149,763

Figure 7-2. *A sample spreadsheet called FIXCOSTS.XLS, which details and totals fixed costs.*

This formula assumes that FIXCOSTS.XLS is stored in the WINDOWS directory and that it supplies the input Fixed Costs amount. Figure 7-3 shows the Profit Volume Inputs box, with the Fixed Costs entered as an amount linked to the spreadsheet FIXCOSTS.XLS.

Profit Volume Inputs	
Revenues	
Unit Sales Price	$15.00
Low Unit Volume Tested	15,000
High Unit Volume Tested	75,000
Variable Costs	
Vary-with-Unit Costs	
Direct Labor	$2.00
Direct Material	$2.00
Factory Overhead	$1.00
Other Vary-with-Unit Costs	$0.50
Vary-with-Revenue Costs	
Sales Commissions	5.00%
Sales Tax	8.00%
Other Vary-with-Revenue Costs	1.50%
Fixed Costs	149,763
Vary-with-Profit Costs	
State Income Tax	10.00%
Federal Income Tax	20.00%
Other Vary-with-Profit Costs	5.00%

Figure 7-3. *The Profit Volume Inputs box of the PROFTVOL.XLS template, with the fixed costs entered by means of a linked spreadsheet.*

CHARTING PROFIT VOLUME AND BREAK-EVEN ANALYSIS DATA

Microsoft Excel provides a rich palette of charting features that you can use both with this template and those described in the other chapters. Because profit volume data and break-even analyses are often displayed using fairly standard approaches, I've included on the templates disk two charts based on the profit volume with break-even analysis template. The first chart, shown in Figure 7-4 on the following page, is an area chart that shows the variable costs, fixed costs, costs varying with profits, and profits over the range of business

Microsoft Excel Small Business Consultant

volumes for a sample profit volume analysis. The second chart, shown in Figure 7-5, is a line chart that shows sample total sales plotted against total costs. (The intersection of the two lines identifies the break-even point.) Area charts and line charts provide a way of quickly showing trends and changes in a variable or variables over time. Although the data graphed in the charts in Figures 7-4 and 7-5 reflects the default inputs in the profit volume and break-even analysis template, any changes you make to the data in the template are reflected in the charts because the charts are dynamically linked to the template.

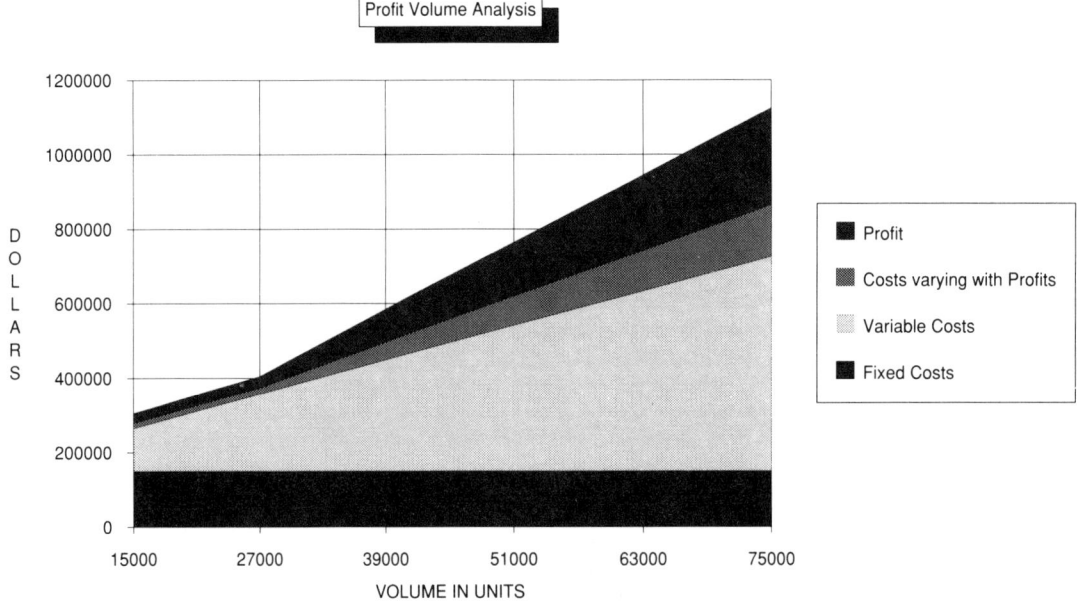

Figure 7-4. *The area chart (COSTPROF.XLC), showing sample variable costs, fixed costs, costs varying with profits, and profit data for different volumes tested.*

Using the Profit Volume Area Chart (COST-PROF.XLC)

Figure 7-4 shows an area chart of the variable costs, fixed costs, costs varying with profits, and profits forecasted for volumes modeled in a profit volume analysis. To use the area chart for your own profit volume analysis, follow these steps:

7: Profit Volume and Break-Even Analysis Template

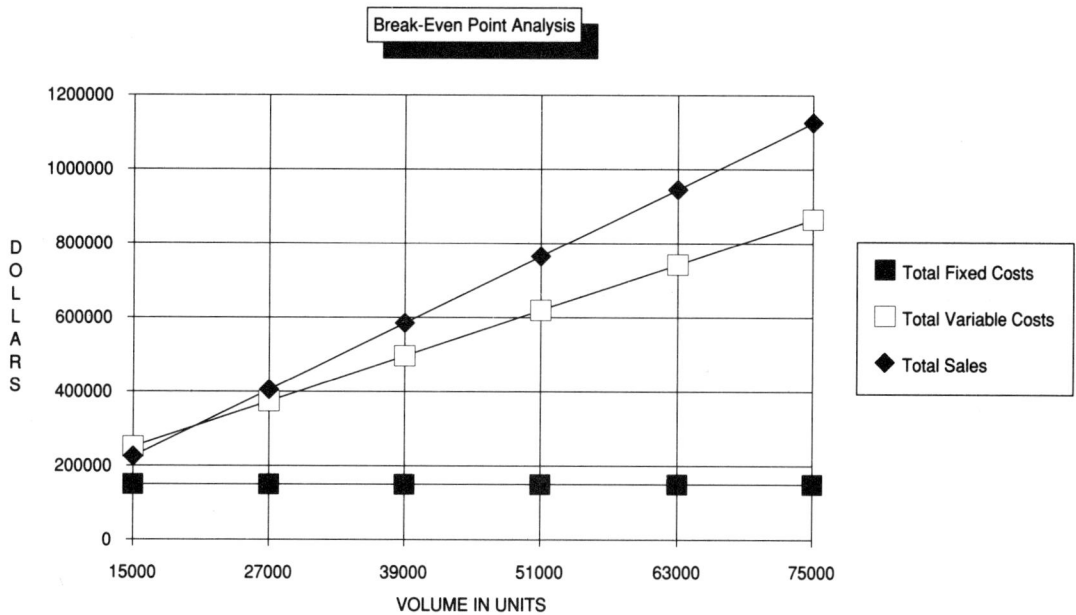

Figure 7-5. *The line chart (BREAKEVN.XLC), showing sample total sales plotted against total variable and total fixed costs.*

1. Follow the instructions in the section of this chapter titled "Entering Your Own Data" to enter inputs for the profit volume and break-even analysis template (PROFTVOL.XLS).

2. Open the chart file (COSTPROF.XLC). (Your data is reflected in the chart.)

3. Save your changes by saving the spreadsheet and giving it a new filename and by saving the chart and giving it a new filename. As long as you save first the template (while the original chart is open) and then the second chart, the links between the chart file and the spreadsheet file will be updated to reflect your new filenames.

4. Print the chart.

Notice that although the total sales are not explicitly included in the chart, they are implicitly included because the sum of the variable costs, fixed costs, costs varying with profits, and profits add up to the total sales.

Using the Break-Even Point Line Chart (BREAK-EVN.XLC)

Figure 7-5 shows a line chart of total sales plotted against total costs, including variable costs, fixed costs, and costs varying with profits. To use the line chart for your own break-even analysis, follow these steps:

1. Follow the instructions in the section of this chapter titled "Entering Your Own Data" to enter inputs for the Profit Volume and Break-Even Analysis template (PROFTVOL.XLS).

2. Open the chart file (BREAKEVN.XLC). (Your data is reflected in the chart.)

3. Save your changes by saving the spreadsheet and giving it a new filename and by saving the chart and giving it a new name. As long as you first save both the template (while the original chart is open) and second the chart, the links between the chart file and the spreadsheet file will be updated to reflect your new filenames.

4. Print the chart.

> **HINT:** Because area and line charts emphasize differences in a variable or variables over time, the scaling for the values axis greatly affects the perceived differences. By using small scaling units, you increase the perceived change in the variable or variables. By using large scaling units, you decrease the perceived change. In general, common sense dictates that the scaling units for charts of financial information be determined by the materiality of the changes. This means that you might need to override the automatic scaling provided by Microsoft Excel, because it scales the data based on the minimum and maximum values, not on your subjective definition of materiality.

An Overview of Other Microsoft Excel Chart Features

Microsoft Excel provides several other chart types that provide powerful alternative methods for communicating the results of your business planning and analysis. You can use these other chart types to show the same information as is graphed in the profit volume area chart and the break-even analysis chart included on the templates disk. Or you can use these other chart types to show information from other spreadsheets. The following sections describe briefly why you might use each chart type and gives examples of the financial data you might show with each chart type.

Bar charts and column charts

Bar charts and column charts show an individual variable, or variables, at a point in time or at points over time. Accordingly, they tend to be best for showing comparisons among items. Figure 7-6 on the following page shows a bar chart of sample starting current asset balances. You can also use a bar chart to display sales revenues across business divisions or product lines or to display competitors' net income after taxes. Notice that because the values axes for bar charts are horizontal, bar charts are less effective than column charts for comparing amounts over time. The reason is that horizontal movement on a graph usually denotes the passage of time. Figure 7-7 on the following page shows a column chart of sample net income after taxes and interest expense for each of the periods for a forecasting horizon. You can also use a column chart to show owner equity over time or after-tax profits among competitors over time. Because bar charts and column charts draw comparisons between variables at a point in time or at points over time, they present an alternative to financial ratios and are another method for drawing comparisons between items. For example, the column chart in Figure 7-7 shows a times interest earned ratio, except that the graph simultaneously communicates both the ratio and the mechanics of calculating the ratio. (For a discussion of times interest earned ratios, see Chapter 9.) The ramifications of this characteristic are significant: You have the ability to present a financial ratio to someone who hasn't been exposed to financial ratios before. In a single chart, you can show the underlying relationship being examined and the nature of the examination.

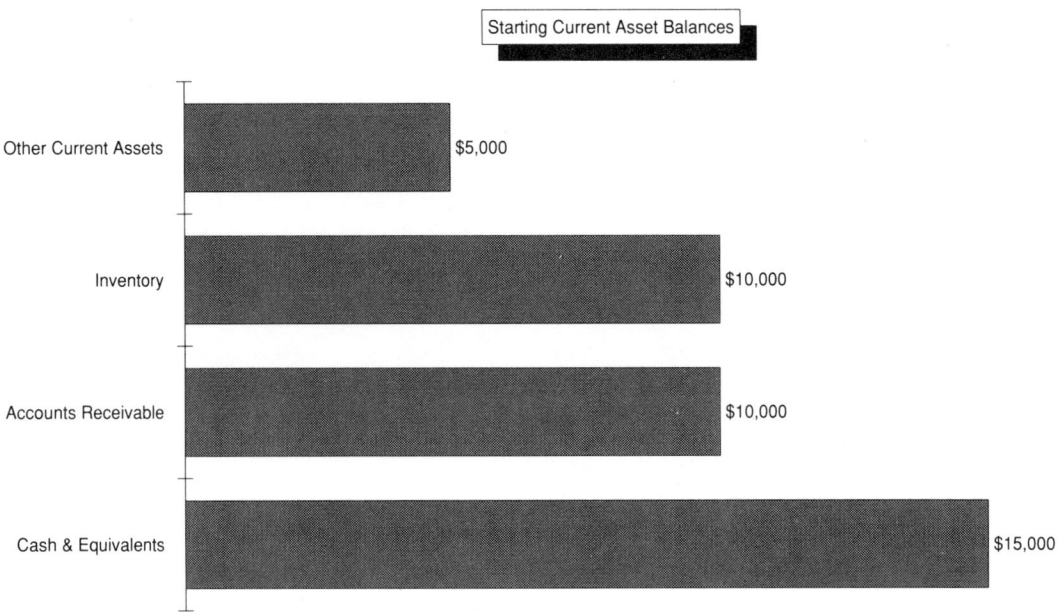

Figure 7-6. *A sample bar chart of starting current asset balances.*

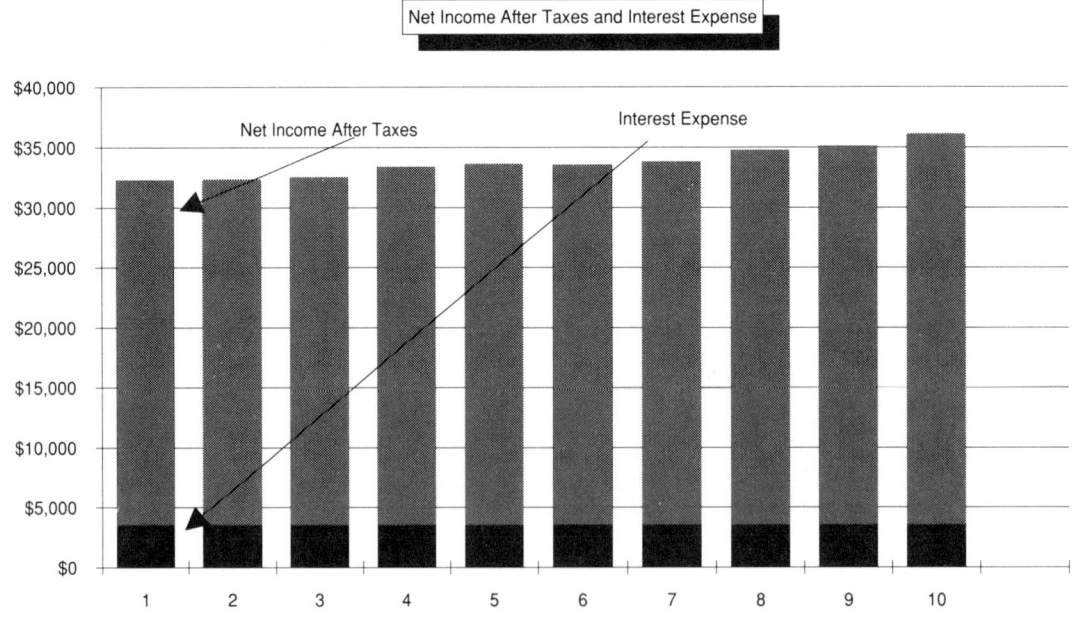

Figure 7-7. *A sample column chart of net income after taxes and interest expense.*

Pie charts   Pie charts draw comparisons between individual variables and the sum of the variables. Pie charts, unlike area, line, bar, or column charts, don't recognize time as a dimension. Figure 7-8 shows a pie chart that depicts the relationship between sample individual current asset percentages and proportional shares to total current assets. You can also use a pie chart to show the proportional shares of revenue generated by various products or the proportional breakdown of cash flow into its components.

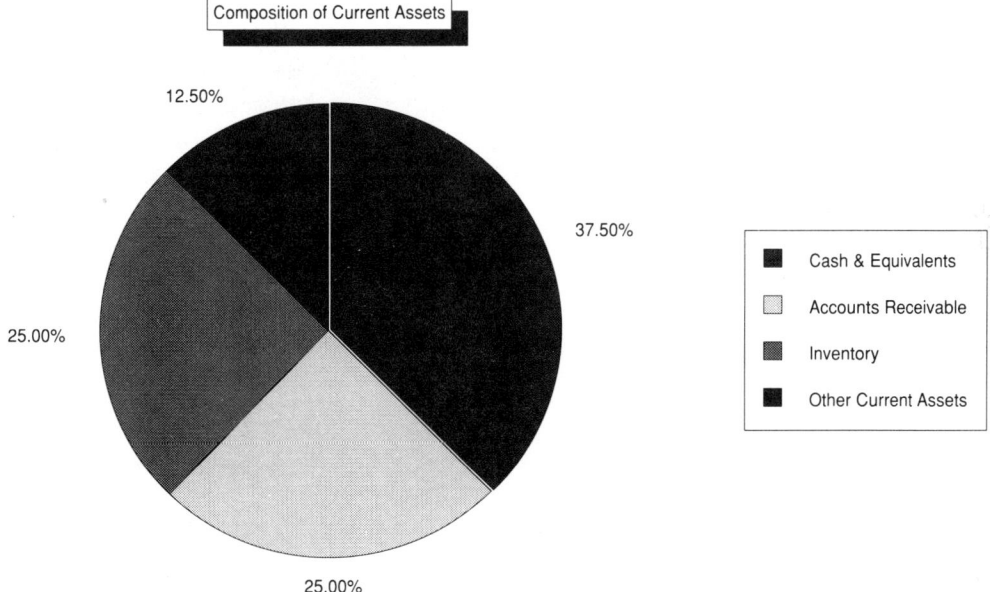

Figure 7-8. *A sample pie chart showing the composition of current assets at a point in time.*

Scatter charts   Scatter charts show the relationships between sets of variables. Scatter charts look similar to area and line charts. However, in a scatter chart, the horizontal axis, which in other chart types represents the time dimension, has numeric significance instead. You can use scatter charts for examining the relationships and assessing any correlations between variables. Figure 7-9 shows a scatter chart of the relationship between sample interest income and beginning cash balances, using the financial statements with ratios template (FINANCLS.XLS), described in Chapter 9, and its default inputs. Predictably, because the template forecasts interest income as the interest rate times the beginning cash balance, the scatter chart shows that a perfect correlation exists between the beginning cash balance and interest income when interest rates remain level. You can also use a scatter chart to show the relationships between your investments in your plant, property, and equipment and your manufacturing efficiencies or between sales revenue and marketing expenses.

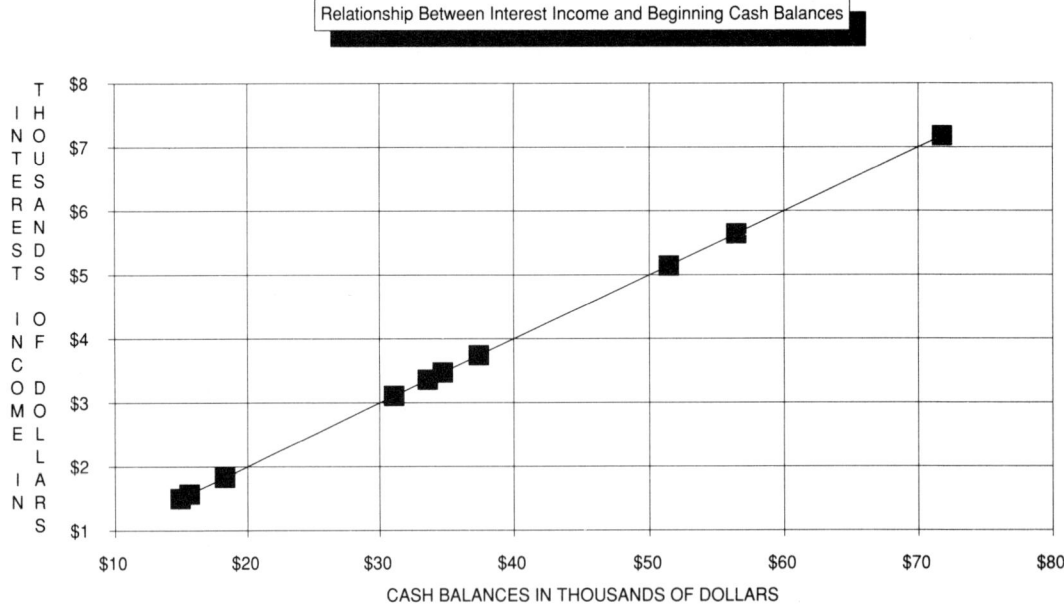

Figure 7-9. *A sample scatter chart of interest income and beginning cash balances.*

Combination charts   Combination charts allow for multiple value axes and for different chart representations of different data series. Figure 7-10 shows a combination chart of the same information that is presented in Figure 7-9: beginning cash balances and interest income. Beginning cash balances are plotted in a column chart and are calibrated by the left vertical axis; the interest income figures are plotted in a line chart and are calibrated by the right vertical axis. You can also use a combination chart to show relationships between two series of values of dissimilar scale or to show correlations between two different types of data best presented in different chart formats.

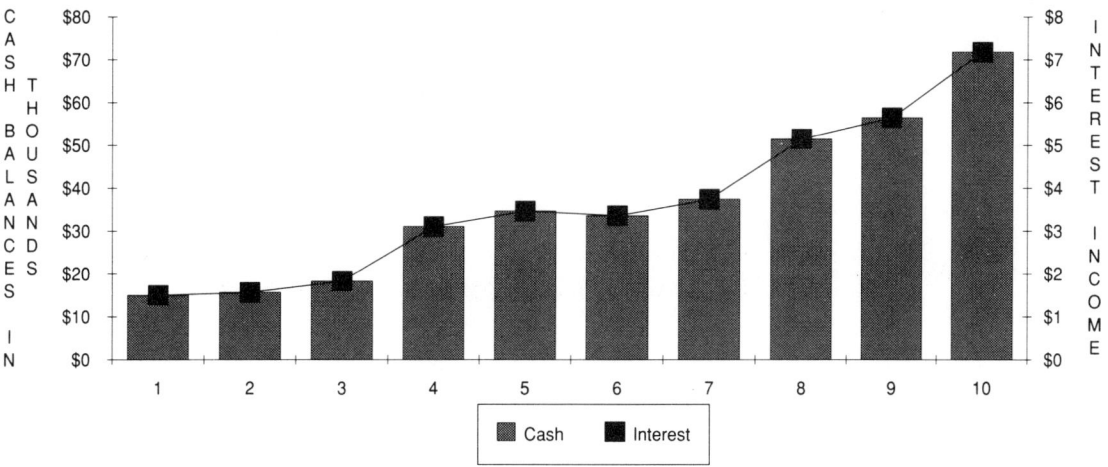

Figure 7-10. *A sample combination chart of interest income and beginning cash balances.*

8

Cash Flow Forecast and Analysis Template

Capital budgeting and investment analysis require that you forecast pretax and after-tax cash flows based on both holding and disposing of each asset or investment. Financial measures of profitability and liquidity are applied to these cash flows. The cash flow forecast and analysis template (CASHFLOW.XLS) described in this chapter provides a framework for forecasting pretax and after-tax cash flows, internal rates of return, internal rates of return adjusted for reinvestment of interim cash flows, net present values, and payback periods. This template is useful for cash flow forecasts for both capital assets and financial investments. This chapter shows how to use the cash flow forecast and analysis template, print it, modify it, and link it with subsidiary spreadsheets.

CASH FLOW FORECASTING AND ANALYSIS: A SHORT PRIMER

Cash flow forecasting and analysis, a basic component of capital budgeting and investment analysis, requires that you forecast each of the variables that might affect cash flows on the forecasting horizon. These variables include the initial outlay to acquire an asset or investment, the cash inflows and the cash outflows from holding an asset or investment, and any cash flows from disposing of an asset or investment. Using these variables, you can forecast the initial cash investment, the operating cash flows, and any liquidation cash flows.

To these cash flows, you apply profitability and liquidity measures. Because all the common profitability measures use discounting, it's important to understand what discounting means. Discounting is the technique of reducing future cash to its equivalent in current cash, thereby providing a basis for an "apples-to-apples" comparison. To convert future cash amounts to current cash amounts, you first need to determine the time value of money, commonly called the interest rate, or the discount rate. The discount rate applied one period at a time is the period discount rate. To discount future cash into equivalent current cash, you divide the cash flow by the sum of one plus the period discount rate as many times as there are periods. For example, if the period discount rate equals 10 percent and you want to convert a $2,300 cash flow two years from now into equivalent current cash, you make the following calculation:

2300/(1+10%)/(1+10%)

or:

$2300/(1+10\%)^2$

Similarly, if you have a cash flow of $5,000 occurring five years from now, you make the following calculation:

5000/(1+10%)/(1+10%)/(1+10%)/(1+10%)/(1+10%)

or:

$5000/(1+10\%)^5$

In any of the discounted cash flow profitability measures, this is the basic calculation: discounting future cash into its equivalent in current cash by using the time value of money expressed as an interest rate. With this background, you will be better able to understand the definitions of the profitability measures employed in the cash flow forecasting and analysis template.

The internal rate of return, another term used in the template, is the discount rate that equates all the future cash flows to the initial cash investment. In other words, given a stated initial cash investment and a set of stated cash flows, the internal rate of return calculates the assumed interest rate delivered by the investment.

The internal rate of return adjusted for reinvestment of the interim cash flows, sometimes called the adjusted rate of return, is like the internal rate of return measure except that it assumes cash flows occurring between the beginning and the end of the forecasting horizon are reinvested until the end of the forecasting horizon at some stated reinvestment rate and then are paid out at the end of the forecasting horizon with the final cash flow.

Although the internal rate of return and adjusted rate of return measures calculate the assumed interest rate based on the stated initial investment and the stated future cash flows, the net present value measure calculates an assumed initial investment based on the stated future cash flows and a stated interest rate. By comparing the actual investment with the assumed investment, you discover whether the investment is falling short of, meeting, or exceeding your stated interest rate. When the assumed initial investment falls short of the actual initial investment, the internal rate of return that the asset delivers falls short of the discount rate. When the assumed initial investment equals the actual initial investment, the internal rate of return that the asset delivers equals the discount rate. When the assumed initial investment exceeds the actual initial investment, the internal rate of return delivered by the asset exceeds the discount rate.

The template also incorporates a common liquidity, or closeness to cash, measure: the payback period. The payback period measure indicates how many periods are required to pay back or return the initial cash investment. Although liquidity is generally less important than profitability, in some situations businesses prefer more-liquid investments to less-liquid investments.

CASH FLOW FORECAST AND ANALYSIS TEMPLATE (CASHFLOW.XLS)

You can use the cash flow forecast and analysis template (CASHFLOW.XLS), shown in Figure 8-1, to construct cash flow forecasts and analysis summaries for assets or investments for which you want to measure profitability and liquidity. To complete it for an asset or investment, develop and then enter information on the initial cash outlay needed to acquire the asset or investment, information on the cash inflows and outflows resulting from holding the asset or investment, and information on any residual cash flows from disposing of the asset or investment.

Given a set of data that includes your initial cash investment, sales and cost of sales, operating expenses, interest expenses, marginal income tax rates, depreciation and other noncash expenses, and debt principal payments and other cash nonexpenses, this template calculates the operating profit (or loss) and cash flows stemming from holding an investment. (Noncash expenses are those expenses, such as depreciation, that do not require any cash outflow. Other noncash expenses include the depletion expense of using up natural resources and the amortization expense of using up an intangible asset. Cash nonexpenses are those cash payments, such as debt principal payments, that represent a cash outflow but that are not considered an expense when calculating profit.) Given a set of data that includes gross residuals, transaction/disposal costs, outstanding debt, nontaxable portions of the residual, and marginal capital gains tax rates, this template calculates the capital gain (or loss) and cash flows stemming from disposing of an asset or investment. (The gross residual is the amount you can sell the asset or investment for. The marginal capital gains tax rate is the percentage that, when multiplied by the capital gains, correctly calculates the capital gains tax.) Given all of this data and your reinvestment and discount rates, the template calculates pretax and after-tax internal rates of return, pretax and after-tax adjusted rates of return, pretax and after-tax net present values, and the asset or investment payback period. You need some or all of this information to evaluate the economics of alternative investments and assets and to calculate overall profits (or losses), overall capital gains (or losses), and overall cash flows.

Forecasting Inputs	Period 0	Period 1	Period 2	Period 3	Period 4	Period 5	Period 6	Period 7	Period 8	Period 9	Period 10
Initial Cash Investment	$15,000										
Pretax Reinvestment Rate	12.00%										
After-Tax Reinvestment Rate	8.00%										
Pretax Discount Rate	12.00%										
After-Tax Discount Rate	8.00%										
Gross Sales		$10,000	$10,000	$10,000	$10,000	$10,000	$10,000	$10,000	$10,000	$10,000	$10,000
Cost of Sales		2,500	2,500	2,500	2,500	2,500	2,500	2,500	2,500	2,500	2,500
Cost Center 1 Costs		3,000	3,000	3,000	3,000	3,000	3,000	3,000	3,000	3,000	3,000
Cost Center 2 Costs		1,000	1,000	1,000	1,000	1,000	1,000	1,000	1,000	1,000	1,000
Cost Center 3 Costs		1,000	1,000	1,000	1,000	1,000	1,000	1,000	1,000	1,000	1,000
Interest Expense		1,000	1,000	1,000	1,000	1,000	1,000	1,000	1,000	1,000	1,000
Marginal Income Tax Rate		33%	33%	33%	33%	33%	33%	33%	33%	33%	33%
Depreciation		$2,500	$2,500	$2,500	$2,500	$2,500	$2,500	$2,500	$2,500	$2,500	$2,500
Other Noncash Expenses		0	0	0	0	0	0	0	0	0	0
Debt Principal Payments		0	0	0	0	0	0	0	0	0	0
Other Cash Nonexpenses		0	0	0	0	0	0	0	0	0	0
Gross Residual		25,000	25,000	25,000	25,000	25,000	25,000	25,000	25,000	25,000	25,000
Transaction/Disposal Costs		1,250	1,250	1,250	1,250	1,250	1,250	1,250	1,250	1,250	1,250
Outstanding Debt on Asset(s)		10,000	10,000	10,000	10,000	10,000	10,000	10,000	10,000	10,000	10,000
Nontaxable Portion of Residual		22,500	20,000	17,500	15,000	12,500	10,000	7,500	5,000	2,500	0
Marginal Tax Rate on Residual		28%	28%	28%	28%	28%	28%	28%	28%	28%	28%

Profit and Loss Statement		Period 1	Period 2	Period 3	Period 4	Period 5	Period 6	Period 7	Period 8	Period 9	Period 10
Gross Sales		$10,000	$10,000	$10,000	$10,000	$10,000	$10,000	$10,000	$10,000	$10,000	$10,000
Less: Cost of Sales		(2,500)	(2,500)	(2,500)	(2,500)	(2,500)	(2,500)	(2,500)	(2,500)	(2,500)	(2,500)
Gross Margin		7,500	7,500	7,500	7,500	7,500	7,500	7,500	7,500	7,500	7,500
Operating Expenses											
Cost Center 1		3,000	3,000	3,000	3,000	3,000	3,000	3,000	3,000	3,000	3,000
Cost Center 2		1,000	1,000	1,000	1,000	1,000	1,000	1,000	1,000	1,000	1,000
Cost Center 3		1,000	1,000	1,000	1,000	1,000	1,000	1,000	1,000	1,000	1,000
Total Operating Expenses		5,000	5,000	5,000	5,000	5,000	5,000	5,000	5,000	5,000	5,000
Operating Income		2,500	2,500	2,500	2,500	2,500	2,500	2,500	2,500	2,500	2,500
Interest Expense		1,000	1,000	1,000	1,000	1,000	1,000	1,000	1,000	1,000	1,000
Net Income (Loss) Before Taxes		1,500	1,500	1,500	1,500	1,500	1,500	1,500	1,500	1,500	1,500
Income Tax Expenses (Savings)		495	495	495	495	495	495	495	495	495	495
Net Income (Loss) After Taxes		$1,005	$1,005	$1,005	$1,005	$1,005	$1,005	$1,005	$1,005	$1,005	$1,005

Figure 8-1. *The cash flow forecast and analysis template, with example data.*

(continued)

Figure 8-1. *continued*

Gain and Loss Statement											
Gross Residual		$25,000	$25,000	$25,000	$25,000	$25,000	$25,000	$25,000	$25,000	$25,000	$25,000
Less: Transaction/Disposal Costs		(1,250)	(1,250)	(1,250)	(1,250)	(1,250)	(1,250)	(1,250)	(1,250)	(1,250)	(1,250)
Net Residual		23,750	23,750	23,750	23,750	23,750	23,750	23,750	23,750	23,750	23,750
Nontaxable Portion of Residual		22,500	20,000	17,500	15,000	12,500	10,000	7,500	5,000	2,500	0
Pretax Gain (Loss) on Disposal		1,250	3,750	6,250	8,750	11,250	13,750	16,250	18,750	21,250	23,750
Income Tax Expenses (Savings)		350	1,050	1,750	2,450	3,150	3,850	4,550	5,250	5,950	6,650
After-Tax Gain (Loss) on Disposal		$900	$2,700	$4,500	$6,300	$8,100	$9,900	$11,700	$13,500	$15,300	$17,100

Operating Cash Flow Statement	Period 0	Period 1	Period 2	Period 3	Period 4	Period 5	Period 6	Period 7	Period 8	Period 9	Period 10
Net Income Before Taxes		$1,500	$1,500	$1,500	$1,500	$1,500	$1,500	$1,500	$1,500	$1,500	$1,500
Addbacks of Noncash Expenses											
Depreciation		2,500	2,500	2,500	2,500	2,500	2,500	2,500	2,500	2,500	2,500
Other		0	0	0	0	0	0	0	0	0	0
Deducts of Cash Nonexpenses											
Debt Principal Payments		0	0	0	0	0	0	0	0	0	0
Other		0	0	0	0	0	0	0	0	0	0
Pretax Operating Cash Flow	($15,000)	4,000	4,000	4,000	4,000	4,000	4,000	4,000	4,000	4,000	4,000
Income Tax Expenses (Savings)		495	495	495	495	495	495	495	495	495	495
After-Tax Operating Cash Flow	($15,000)	$3,505	$3,505	$3,505	$3,505	$3,505	$3,505	$3,505	$3,505	$3,505	$3,505

Liquidation Cash Flow Statement											
Gross Residual		$25,000	$25,000	$25,000	$25,000	$25,000	$25,000	$25,000	$25,000	$25,000	$25,000
Less: Transaction/Sales Costs		(1,250)	(1,250)	(1,250)	(1,250)	(1,250)	(1,250)	(1,250)	(1,250)	(1,250)	(1,250)
Less: Outstanding Debt		(10,000)	(10,000)	(10,000)	(10,000)	(10,000)	(10,000)	(10,000)	(10,000)	(10,000)	(10,000)
Pretax Liquidation Cash Flow		13,750	13,750	13,750	13,750	13,750	13,750	13,750	13,750	13,750	13,750
Income Tax Expenses (Savings)		350	1,050	1,750	2,450	3,150	3,850	4,550	5,250	5,950	6,650
After-Tax Liquidation Cash Flow		$13,400	$12,700	$12,000	$11,300	$10,600	$9,900	$9,200	$8,500	$7,800	$7,100

Figure 8-1. *continued*

Cash Flow Analysis											
Pretax IRR		18.33%	22.93%	24.47%	25.23%	25.66%	25.94%	26.13%	26.27%	26.36%	26.43%
After-Tax IRR		12.70%	16.28%	17.76%	18.68%	19.38%	19.94%	20.41%	20.82%	21.17%	21.48%
Pretax Adjusted IRR		18.33%	21.74%	22.01%	21.67%	21.16%	20.63%	20.11%	19.64%	19.20%	18.79%
After-Tax Adjusted IRR		12.70%	15.44%	15.94%	15.93%	15.75%	15.50%	15.23%	14.97%	14.71%	14.46%
Pretax Net Present Value		$848	$2,722	$4,394	$5,888	$7,221	$8,412	$9,475	$10,424	$11,271	$12,028
After-Tax Net Present Value		653	2,139	3,559	4,915	6,209	7,442	8,616	9,734	10,797	11,808
Pretax Cumulative Cash Flows	($15,000)	($11,000)	($7,000)	($3,000)	$1,000	$5,000	$9,000	$13,000	$17,000	$21,000	$38,750
Pretax Payback Period					Payback						
After-Tax Cumulative Cash Flows	($15,000)	($11,495)	($7,990)	($4,485)	($980)	$2,525	$6,030	$9,535	$13,040	$16,545	$27,150
After-Tax Payback Period						Payback					

Pretax Cash Flow Scenarios	Period 0	Period 1	Period 2	Period 3	Period 4	Period 5	Period 6	Period 7	Period 8	Period 9	Period 10
Number of Periods Held:											
1	($15,000)	$17,750	$0	$0	$0	$0	$0	$0	$0	$0	$0
2	(15,000)	4,000	17,750	0	0	0	0	0	0	0	0
3	(15,000)	4,000	4,000	17,750	0	0	0	0	0	0	0
4	(15,000)	4,000	4,000	4,000	17,750	0	0	0	0	0	0
5	(15,000)	4,000	4,000	4,000	4,000	17,750	0	0	0	0	0
6	(15,000)	4,000	4,000	4,000	4,000	4,000	17,750	0	0	0	0
7	(15,000)	4,000	4,000	4,000	4,000	4,000	4,000	17,750	0	0	0
8	(15,000)	4,000	4,000	4,000	4,000	4,000	4,000	4,000	17,750	0	0
9	(15,000)	4,000	4,000	4,000	4,000	4,000	4,000	4,000	4,000	17,750	0
10	(15,000)	4,000	4,000	4,000	4,000	4,000	4,000	4,000	4,000	4,000	17,750

After-Tax Cash Flow Scenarios	Period 0	Period 1	Period 2	Period 3	Period 4	Period 5	Period 6	Period 7	Period 8	Period 9	Period 10
Number of Periods Held:											
1	($15,000)	$16,905	$0	$0	$0	$0	$0	$0	$0	$0	$0
2	(15,000)	3,505	16,205	0	0	0	0	0	0	0	0
3	(15,000)	3,505	3,505	15,505	0	0	0	0	0	0	0
4	(15,000)	3,505	3,505	3,505	14,805	0	0	0	0	0	0
5	(15,000)	3,505	3,505	3,505	3,505	14,105	0	0	0	0	0
6	(15,000)	3,505	3,505	3,505	3,505	3,505	13,405	0	0	0	0
7	(15,000)	3,505	3,505	3,505	3,505	3,505	3,505	12,705	0	0	0
8	(15,000)	3,505	3,505	3,505	3,505	3,505	3,505	3,505	12,005	0	0
9	(15,000)	3,505	3,505	3,505	3,505	3,505	3,505	3,505	3,505	11,305	0
10	(15,000)	3,505	3,505	3,505	3,505	3,505	3,505	3,505	3,505	3,505	10,605

What the Template Contains and Does

The eight parts of the cash flow forecasting and analysis template are the Forecasting Inputs schedule, the Profit and Loss Statement, the Gain and Loss Statement, the Operating Cash Flow Statement, the Liquidation Cash Flow Statement, the Cash Flow Analysis, the Pretax Cash Flow Scenarios, and the After-Tax Cash Flow Scenarios.

Cash Flow Forecasting Inputs

Only one set of formulas exists in the cash flow Forecasting Inputs schedule: the one in the second row that identifies the period for which the results are calculated. The rest of the rows contain input cells where you can enter your own data. Unless you turn off cell protection, these are the only cells into which you can enter data.

Period. The period identifier simply numbers the periods forecasted. You'll probably want the number of periods in your cash flow forecasting and analysis summary to correspond to the asset or investment with the longest holding period.

The start of the first period is stored as the integer 0. (Using 0 as the starting balance is the traditional way to identify those cash flows that are not discounted because they occur at the beginning of the forecasting horizon.) Periods that follow are stored as the previous period plus 1. For example, the formula for the first period is:

```
=B2+1
```

The formula for the end of the second period is:

```
=C2+1
```

and so on.

Initial Cash Investment. The value you enter for Initial Cash Investment is the amount you outlaid to acquire the asset or investment. If you use debt to fund a portion of the purchase, the initial cash investment is probably the gross sales price of the asset less the amount of the debt.

Pretax Reinvestment Rate and After-Tax Reinvestment Rate. The Pretax and After-Tax Reinvestment Rate figures apply to the adjusted rate of return calculations. The rates represent the forecasted returns at which interim cash flows will be reinvested over the holding period. Generally, pretax rates approximate the yields delivered by intermediate-term taxable bonds, and the after-tax rates approximate the yields delivered by intermediate-term tax-exempt bonds. You don't want to commingle returns with different tax treatment. Both the pretax return and the interest income from a taxable bond are taxable. Both the after-tax return and the interest income from a tax-exempt bond are nontaxable. You pick bonds with intermediate maturities because the maturity of the asset or investment is typically intermediate.

Pretax Discount Rate and After-Tax Discount Rate. The Pretax and After-Tax Discount Rate figures apply to the net present value calculations. Generally, the pretax discount rate approximates the pretax internal rate of return delivered on assets and investments with a similar level of risk, and the after-tax discount rate approximates the after-tax internal rate of return delivered by similarly risky assets and investments. However, wide diversity continues to exist in both the theory and practice of developing and using appropriate discount rates for net present value analysis.

Gross Sales. The Gross Sales values represent the forecasted sales generated by the asset or investment over each of the periods of the forecasting horizon. You use these forecasts to estimate the income tax expense and the cash flows. Accordingly, implicit in the construction of the template is the assumption that you use cash basis accounting for income tax purposes and for development of the sales forecasts.

Cost of Sales. The Cost of Sales values represent the forecasted costs that are tied to sales generated over the forecasting horizon. These values might include cost of goods sold, selling costs, and perhaps other variable sales costs, such as commissions owed salespeople. You use these forecasts to estimate the taxable income and the cash flows.

Operating Expenses—Cost Center 1, 2 and 3 Costs. The operating expenses for cost centers 1, 2 and 3 represent the cash basis operating expenses for the forecasting horizon. These values might be three expense classifications related to holding the asset or investment, or they might be the total expenses for three groups of expenses. You use these forecasts to estimate the taxable income and the cash flows.

Interest Expense. The Interest Expense values represent the period interest expense of carrying any debt related to the asset purchase. The interest expense equals 0 when you use no debt in the asset or investment purchase. You use these forecasts to estimate the taxable income and the cash flows.

Marginal Income Tax Rate. The Marginal Income Tax Rate value is the percentage that, when multiplied by the operating profit (or loss), calculates the income tax expense (or savings).

Depreciation. The Depreciation expenses represent the amounts of depreciation included in operating expenses for cost centers 1, 2, and 3 for the forecasting horizon. When no depreciation is included in the operating expenses for cost centers 1, 2, and 3, this amount equals 0. You use these forecasts to estimate the cash flows.

Other Noncash Expenses. The Other Noncash Expenses values represent the amounts of noncash expenses other than depreciation, included in operating expenses for cost centers 1, 2, and 3 for the forecasting horizon. Examples of such noncash expenses include the depletion of natural resource assets and the amortization of intangible assets. When no other noncash expenses exist in the operating expenses for cost centers 1, 2, and 3, these amounts equal 0. You use these forecasts to estimate the cash flows.

Debt Principal Payments. The Debt Principal Payments values represent the cash paid out to reduce any debt used to fund any portions of the asset or investment purchase. If you use no debt in the asset or investment purchase or you use debt for which the payments you made include only interest, these amounts equal 0. You use these forecasts to estimate the cash flows.

Other Cash Nonexpenses. The Other Cash Nonexpenses values represent the amounts of cash nonexpenses, other than debt principal payments, that affect cash flows but not profits. Examples of such noncash expenses include the expenses that are not deductible for calculation of taxable profits, such as life insurance on key employees, and expenditures that are not expenses, such as deposits paid to vendors and suppliers. You use these forecasts to estimate the cash flows.

Gross Residual. The Gross Residual values represent the figures at which you can dispose of the asset or investment on the forecasting horizon. You use these amounts to calculate the capital gains (or losses) and the liquidation cash flows.

Transaction/Disposal Costs. The Transaction/Disposal Costs values represent any incidental expenses or costs of disposing of the asset or investment. Examples include removal costs and brokerage fees. You use these amounts to calculate the capital gains (or losses) and the liquidation cash flows.

Outstanding Debt on Asset(s). The Outstanding Debt on Asset(s) values represent the debt that you will pay off as a result of disposing of the asset. You use these amounts to calculate the liquidation cash flows.

Nontaxable Portion of Residual. The Nontaxable Portion of Residual values represent those amounts of the cash received upon disposal that are not subject to capital gains taxes. You use these amounts to calculate the capital gains (or losses) and the liquidation cash flows. Typically, the nontaxable portion of the residual is the net book value of the asset or investment. If no depreciation has been charged, this means the nontaxable portion equals the original cost.

Marginal Tax Rate on Residual. The Marginal Tax Rate on Residual, or capital gains rate, represents the percentage that, when multiplied by the net gain or loss stemming from the disposal of the asset, calculates the capital gains tax expense (or savings).

Profit and Loss Statement   The Profit and Loss Statement schedule has 12 rows that contain calculated data.

Gross Sales. The Gross Sales figures show the sales estimates. You enter this amount in the Forecasting Inputs schedule.

Cost of Sales. The Cost of Sales figures show the cost of sales estimates. You enter this amount in the Forecasting Inputs schedule.

Gross Margin. The Gross Margin figures show the amounts left over from the sales proceeds after paying for the cost of sales. The Gross Margin figures represent the amount of cash that goes toward paying your other expenses and your profits.

The Gross Margin value for each period is the Gross Sales figure for the period less the Cost of Sales figure. But because the Cost of Sales figures are pulled into the Profit and Loss Statement as negative amounts, the Gross Margin formula simply adds the positive Gross Sales figure to the negative Cost of Sales figure. For example, the formula for the first period is:

```
=C26+C27
```

The formula for the second period is:

```
=D26+D27
```

and so on.

Operating Expenses—Cost Center 1, 2, and 3. The figures in these three rows show the amounts of the operating expenses for the three categories entered in the Forecasting Inputs schedule.

Total Operating Expenses. The Total Operating Expenses figures show the sums of the operating expenses entered in the Forecasting Inputs schedule for the three expense categories. For example, the formula for the first period is:

```
=SUM(C31:C33)
```

The formula for the second period is:

=SUM(D31:D33)

and so on.

Operating Income. The Operating Income figures show the amounts of sales dollars left after paying the cost of sales and the operating expenses. The Operating Income figures represent the amounts that go toward paying your financing expenses, income taxes, and profits.

The Operating Income value for each period is the Gross Margin figure for the period minus the Total Operating Expenses figure. For example, the formula for the first period is:

=C28–C34

The formula for the second period is:

=D28–D34

and so on.

Interest Expense. The Interest Expense figures show the amounts required to carry any debt used to fund portions of your asset or investment purchase. If you used no debt to fund the purchase, these amounts are 0.

The Interest Expense value for each period is the value you enter in the Forecasting Inputs schedule.

Net Income (Loss) Before Taxes. The Net Income (Loss) Before Taxes figures represent the amounts of operating income left after paying any interest expense. These amounts represent your taxable operating profits.

The Net Income (Loss) Before Taxes figure for each period is the Operating Income figure minus the Interest Expense figure. For example, the formula for the first period is:

=C35–C37

The formula for the second period is:

=D35–D37

and so on.

Income Tax Expenses (Savings). The Income Tax Expenses (Savings) figures show the forecasted income tax expenses (or savings) using the pretax operating profits calculated and the marginal income tax rates entered in the Forecasting Inputs schedule.

The Income Tax Expenses (Savings) figure for each period is the Net Income (Loss) Before Taxes figure multiplied by the Marginal Income Tax Rate figure. For example, the formula for the first period is:

=C14*C38

The formula for the second period is:

=D14*D38

and so on.

Net Income (Loss) After Taxes. The Net Income (Loss) After Taxes figures show the after-tax profits of holding the asset or investment.

The Net Income (Loss) After Taxes value for each period is the net income (or loss) before taxes minus the income tax expenses (or savings). For example, the formula for the first period is:

=C38–C40

The formula for the second period is:

=D38–D40

and so on.

8: Cash Flow Forecast and Analysis Template

Gain and Loss Statement

The Gain and Loss Statement has seven rows of calculated data.

Gross Residual. The Gross Residual figures show the total amounts for which the asset or investment can be liquidated for each period of the forecasting horizon. You enter these figures in the Forecasting Inputs schedule.

Transaction/Disposal Costs. The Transaction/Disposal Costs figures show the costs associated with liquidating the asset or investment for each period of the forecasting horizon. You enter these figures in the Forecasting Inputs schedule.

Net Residual. The Net Residual figures are the amounts left over from liquidating an asset or investment after paying any transaction or disposal costs, using the Gross Residual figures and the Transaction/Disposal Costs figures.

The Net Residual figure for each period is the Gross Residual figure minus the Transaction/Disposal Costs figure. But because the Transaction/Disposal Costs figure is pulled into the Gain and Loss Statement schedule as a negative amount, the Net Residual formula simply adds the positive Gross Residual figure to the negative Transaction/Disposal Costs figure. For example, the formula for the first period is:

   =C45+C46

The formula for the second period is:

   =D45+D46

and so on.

Nontaxable Portion of Residual. The Nontaxable Portion of Residual figures show the amounts of the residuals that are not included in capital gains or losses calculations. You enter these figures in the Forecasting Inputs schedule.

Pretax Gain (Loss) on Disposal. The Pretax Gain (Loss) on Disposal figures are the capital gains or losses that must be included in capital gains tax calculations.

213

The Pretax Gain (Loss) on Disposal figure for each period is the Net Residual figure minus the Nontaxable Portion of Residual figure. For example, the formula for the first period is:

=C47–C49

The formula for the second period is:

=D47–D49

and so on.

Income Tax Expenses (Savings). The Income Tax Expenses (Savings) figures represent the tax effect of the liquidation of the asset or investment, calculated by using the Pretax Gain (Loss) on Disposal figures and the Marginal Income Tax Rate figures entered in the Forecasting Inputs schedule.

The Income Tax Expenses (Savings) value for each period is calculated by multiplying the Marginal Tax Rate on Residual figure by the Pretax Gain (Loss) on Disposal figure. For example, the formula for the first period is:

=C50*C23

The formula for the second period is:

=D50*D23

and so on.

After-Tax Gain (Loss) on Disposal. The After-Tax Gain (Loss) on Disposal figures show the after-tax profit (or loss) from liquidating the asset or investment.

The After-Tax Gain (Loss) on Disposal value for each period is the Pretax Gain (Loss) on Disposal figure minus the Income Tax Expenses (Savings) figure stemming from the disposal. For example, the formula for the first period is:

=C50–C52

The formula for the second period is:

=D50–D52

and so on.

Operating Cash Flow Statement The Operating Cash Flow Statement schedule has eight rows with calculated data.

Net Income Before Taxes. The Net Income Before Taxes figure shows the pretax profits calculated on the Profit and Loss Statement.

Addbacks of Noncash Expenses—Depreciation. The Depreciation figures show the depreciation expenses included in the three operating expense classifications or categories. You enter these amounts in the Forecasting Inputs schedule.

Addbacks of Noncash Expenses—Other. The Other noncash expense figures show the other noncash expenses included in the three operating expense categories. You enter these amounts in the Forecasting Inputs schedule.

Deducts of Cash Nonexpenses—Debt Principal Payments. The Debt Principal Payments figures show the debt principal payments made to reduce the debt used to fund a portion of the asset or investment purchase. You enter these amounts in the Forecasting Inputs schedule.

Deducts of Cash Nonexpenses—Other. The Other cash nonexpense figures show the other cash payments you made that were not expenses and, therefore, were not included in the three operating expense categories. You enter these amounts in the Forecasting Inputs schedule.

Pretax Operating Cash Flow. The Pretax Operating Cash Flow figures are the pretax cash expended or received as a result of holding the asset or investment. The first cash flow figure shows the initial cash outlay needed to acquire the asset or investment. The second and subsequent cash flow figures show the pretax operating cash flow figures. The Cash Flow Analysis schedule uses these pretax cash flows to calculate the pretax profitability and liquidity measures.

The Pretax Operating Cash Flow value for Period 0, the initial cash investment required to acquire the investment, is the value you enter in the Forecasting Inputs schedule. Notice that this amount is pulled into the Operating Cash Flow Statement schedule as a negative amount because it is an outflow. The Pretax Operating Cash Flow values for subsequent periods are calculated by adding noncash expenses to the Net Income (Loss) Before Taxes figure and subtracting the Other Cash Nonexpenses figure from the Net Income (Loss) Before Taxes figure. For example, the formula for the first period is:

```
=C58+C60+C61-C63-C64
```

The formula for the second is:

```
=D58+D60+D61-D63-D64
```

and so on.

Income Tax Expenses (Savings). The Income Tax Expenses (Savings) figures show the income tax expenses (or savings) calculated in the Profit and Loss Statement schedule.

After-Tax Operating Cash Flow. The After-Tax Operating Cash Flow figures are calculated by using the Pretax Operating Cash Flow figures and the Income Tax Expenses (Savings) figures. The Cash Flow Analysis schedule uses these after-tax cash flows to calculate the after-tax profitability and liquidity measures.

The After-Tax Operating Cash Flow value for Period 0, the initial cash investment, is pulled from the cell containing the pretax operating cash flow (B65). The figures for subsequent periods are calculated as the Pretax Operating Cash Flow figure minus the Income Tax Expenses (Savings) figure. For example, the first-period formula is:

```
=C65-C67
```

The formula for the second period is:

=D65–D67

and so on.

Liquidation Cash Flow Statement

The Liquidation Cash Flow Statement schedule has six rows with calculated data.

Gross Residual. The Gross Residual figures show the amounts for which the asset or investment can be sold. You enter these amounts in the Forecasting Inputs schedule.

Transaction/Sales Costs. The Transaction/Sales Costs figures show the expenses of liquidating the asset or investment. You enter these amounts in the Forecasting Inputs schedule.

Outstanding Debt. The Outstanding Debt figures show the principal balances of any debt used to fund portions of the asset or investment purchase. You enter these amounts in the Forecasting Inputs schedule.

Pretax Liquidation Cash Flow. The Pretax Liquidation Cash Flow figures show the pretax cash expended or received for each period as a result of liquidating the asset or investment at the end of the period.

The Pretax Liquidation Cash Flow figure is calculated as the Gross Residual figure minus the Transaction/Sales Costs figure and minus the Outstanding Debt figure. But because the Transaction/Sales Costs figure and the Outstanding Debt figure are pulled into the Liquidation Cash Flow Statement schedule as negative amounts, the Pretax Liquidation Cash Flow formula simply adds the Gross Residual figure to the negative Transaction/Sales Costs figure and the negative Outstanding Debt figure. For example, the first-period formula is:

=C72+C73+C74

The formula for the second period is:

=D72+D73+D74

and so on.

Income Tax Expenses (Savings). The Income Tax Expenses (Savings) figures show any capital gains taxes associated with liquidating the asset or investment.

The figure for each period is the value calculated in the Gain and Loss Statement schedule.

After-Tax Liquidation Cash Flow. The After-Tax Liquidation Cash Flow figures are the after-tax cash received as a result of liquidating an asset or investment at the end of the period.

The After-Tax Liquidation Cash Flow value for each period is the Pretax Liquidation Cash Flow figure minus the Income Tax Expenses (Savings) figure. For example, the formula for the first period is:

=C75–C77

The formula for the second period is:

=D75–D77

and so on.

Cash Flow Analysis The Cash Flow Analysis schedule calculates the profitability and liquidity measures for each of the alternative holding periods. The schedule has 10 rows with calculated data. The values for Pretax IRR, After-Tax IRR, Pretax Adjusted IRR, After-Tax Adjusted IRR, Pretax Net Present Value, and After-Tax Net Present Value are similar in that the value shown in the Period 1 column assumes that the asset or investment is purchased at the beginning of the first period (Period 0), is held for one period, and then is sold at the end of the first period. Similarly, the values shown in the subsequent Period columns assume that the asset or investment is purchased at the beginning of the first period and then is sold at the end of the indicated period. These values often fluctuate, depending on the holding period. By developing and examining the values delivered by the asset or investment under alternative holding periods, you can choose holding periods that enhance profits. For example, a 10 percent pretax internal rate of return of an asset or investment held for 3 years means you get back not only all your initial investment but a dime a year for every dollar invested. An 8 percent pretax internal rate of return for the same asset or investment held for 4 years means you get back all your initial investment but only eight cents for every dollar invested a year.

Pretax IRR. The Pretax IRR figures are the pretax internal rates of return, which are calculated by using the pretax operating and liquidation cash flows that are generated by the asset or investment, assuming the asset or investment is held through the end of the period.

The specific Pretax IRR (internal rate of return) figure for each period is calculated by using the figures in the Pretax Cash Flow Scenarios schedule. The formula for the first period is:

=IRR($B$99:$C$99)

The formula for the second period is:

=IRR($B$100:$D$100)

and so on. The values in the IRR function represent the pretax cash flows forecasted if the asset or investment is held through the period.

After-Tax IRR. The After-Tax IRR figures are the after-tax internal rates of return, which are calculated by using the after-tax operating and liquidation cash flows that are generated by the asset or investment, assuming the asset or investment is held through the end of the period.

The specific After-Tax IRR (internal rate of return) figure for each period is calculated by using the figures in the After-Tax Cash Flow Scenarios schedule. The formula for the first period is:

=IRR($B$112:$C$112)

The formula for the second period is:

=IRR($B$113:$D$113)

and so on. The values in the IRR function represent the after-tax cash flows forecasted if the asset or investment is held through the period.

> **HINT:** The equation that calculates the internal rates of return for an asset or investment held 10 periods is, by definition, a tenth root polynomial equation with up to 10 correct solutions. Accordingly, several internal rates of return can be correct for any investment you analyze. Be particularly careful in applying the internal rate of return measure to those assets or investments for which cash flows fluctuate between positive and negative amounts. Generally, an asset or investment has as many correct IRRs as sign changes in the cash flows. If there is only one sign change—for example, if the initial investment is negative and all the cash flows that follow are positive—you have only one IRR. However, if the first cash flow and fourth cash flows are negative, there are three sign changes and up to three correct IRRs. (The first sign change is the initial negative cash flow changing to positive, the second is the third-period changing to the fourth-period negative, and the third is the fourth-period negative changing to the fifth-period positive cash flow.) For this reason, you might want to use the adjusted rate of return or the net present value profit measures instead of the internal rate of return measure.

Pretax Adjusted IRR. The Pretax Adjusted IRR figures are the pretax internal rates of return, which are calculated by using the pretax operating and liquidation cash flows that are generated by the asset or investment, assuming that the asset or investment is held through the end of the period and assuming that any interim cash flows are reinvested at the pretax reinvestment rate specified in the Forecasting Inputs schedule. (Notice that in Period 1, because there would be no interim cash flows—both the operating and liquidation cash flows occur at the end of the first period—the pretax adjusted

IRR equals the pretax IRR.) This schedule assumes that when you buy an asset or make an investment at the beginning of the first period and sell at the end of the second period, you reinvest the operating cash flow generated by the investment in the first period at the pretax reinvestment rate specified in the Forecasting Inputs schedule until the end of the second period.

The figure for each period's Pretax Adjusted IRR (internal rate of return adjusted for reinvestment of the interim cash flows) is calculated by using the figures in the Pretax Cash Flow Scenarios schedule and the Pretax Reinvestment Rate figure specified in the Forecasting Inputs schedule. The formula for the first period is:

=MIRR($B$99:$C$99,,$B$4)

The formula for the second period is:

=MIRR($B$100:$D$100,,$B$4)

and so on. The values used in the MIRR function represent the pretax cash flows forecasted if the asset or investment is held through the period. The contents of the cell referenced by $B$4 is the pretax reinvestment rate.

After-Tax Adjusted IRR. The After-Tax Adjusted IRR figures are the after-tax internal rates of return, which are calculated by using the after-tax operating and liquidation cash flows that are generated by the asset or investment, assuming the asset or investment is held through the end of the period and assuming that any interim cash flows are reinvested at the after-tax reinvestment rate specified in the Forecasting Inputs schedule. (Notice that in Period 1, because there would be no interim cash flows—both the operating and liquidation cash flows occur at the end of the first period—the after-tax adjusted IRR equals the after-tax IRR.) This schedule assumes that when you buy an asset or make an investment at the beginning of the first period and sell at the end of the second period, you reinvest the operating cash flow generated by the investment in the first period at the after-tax reinvestment rate specified in the Forecasting Inputs schedule until the end of the second period.

The figure for each period's After-Tax Adjusted IRR (internal rate of return adjusted for reinvestment of the interim cash flows) is calculated by using the figures in the After-Tax Cash Flow Scenarios schedule and the After-Tax Reinvestment Rate figure specified in the Forecasting Inputs schedule. The formula for the first period is:

=MIRR($B$112:$C$112,,$B$5)

The formula for the second period is:

=MIRR($B$113:$D$113,,$B$5)

and so on. The values in the MIRR function represent the after-tax cash flows forecasted if the asset or investment is held through the period. The contents of the cell referenced by $B$5 is the after-tax reinvestment rate.

Pretax Net Present Value. The Pretax Net Present Value figures are calculated by using the pretax operating and liquidation cash flows generated by the asset or investment, assuming the asset or investment is held through the end of the period, and by using the pretax discount rate specified in the Forecasting Inputs schedule. Pretax net present values are significant in that they express in current cash the amount by which the investment falls short of or exceeds the time value of money specified by the pretax discount rate. For example, a $1,000 net present value of an asset or investment held for three years means that holding the investment for three years returns $1,000 more (in the current dollar value) than the pretax discount rate specifies. A negative $500 net present value for the same asset or investment held four years means that holding the asset or investment for four years returns $500 less (in current dollar value) than the pretax discount rate specifies. The pretax net present values often fluctuate, depending on the holding period. By developing and examining the pretax net present values delivered by the asset or investment under alternative holding periods, you can choose holding periods to enhance pretax profits.

For instance, in the example introduced in the preceding sentences, you lose $1,500 ($1000 − a negative $500) by holding the investment an additional (fourth) year.

The Pretax Net Present Value figure for each period is calculated by using the figures in the Pretax Cash Flow Scenarios schedule and the Pretax Discount Rate figure specified in the Forecasting Inputs schedule. The formula for the first period is:

```
=NPV($B$6,$C$99:$C$99)+$B$99
```

The formula for the second period is:

```
=NPV($B$6,$C$100:$D$100)+$B$100
```

and so on. The values in the NPV function represent the pretax cash flows forecasted if the asset or investment is held through the period. The contents of the cell referenced by $B$6 is the pretax discount rate. The amount added to the NPV function is the initial investment.

After-Tax Net Present Value. The After-Tax Net Present Value figures are calculated by using the after-tax operating and liquidation cash flows generated by the asset or investment, assuming the asset or investment is held through the end of the period, and by using the after-tax discount rate specified in the Forecasting Inputs schedule. After-tax net present values are significant in that they express in current cash the amount by which the investment falls short of or exceeds the time value of money specified by the after-tax discount rate. For example, a $1,000 net present value of an asset or investment held for three years means that holding the investment for three years returns $1,000 more (in current dollar value) than the after-tax discount rate specifies. A negative $500 net present value for the same asset or investment held four years means that holding the asset or investment for four years returns $500 less (in current dollar value) than the after-tax discount rate specifies. The after-tax net present values often fluctuate, depending on the holding period. By developing and examining the after-tax net present values delivered by the asset or investment under alternative holding periods, you can choose holding periods to enhance after-tax profits. For example, in the example introduced in the preceding sentences, you lose $1,500 ($1,000 − a negative $500) by holding the investment an additional (fourth) year.

The After-Tax Net Present Value figure for each period is calculated by using the figures in the After-Tax Cash Flow Scenarios schedule and the After-Tax Discount Rate figure specified in the Forecasting Inputs schedule. The formula for the first period is:

=NPV($B$7,$C$112:$C$112)+$B$112

The formula for the second period is:

=NPV($B$7,$C$113:$D$113)+$B$113

and so on. The values in the NPV function represent the after-tax cash flows forecasted if the asset or investment is held through the period. The contents of the cell referenced by $B$7 is the after-tax reinvestment rate. The amount added to the NPV function is the initial investment.

Pretax Cumulative Cash Flows. The Pretax Cumulative Cash Flows figures represent the cumulative cash flows that result from holding the asset or investment, which are calculated by using the pretax cash flows from the Pretax Cash Flows Scenarios schedule, assuming the investment is held for 10 periods. The period during which the cumulative cash flow figure turns from a negative amount to a positive amount indicates the period in which the investment pays back the original cash invested—a common measure of liquidity.

The Pretax Cumulative Cash Flows figure for each period is calculated by using the 10-period holding scenario in the Pretax Cash Flow Scenarios schedule. The formula in the Period 0 column for the initial investment is:

=SUM($B$108:B108)

The formula for the first period is:

=SUM($B$108:C108)

The formula for the second period is:

=SUM($B$108:D108)

and so on. The results represent the cumulative pretax cash flows through the period.

Pretax Payback Period. The Pretax Payback Period is a text flag (the word Payback) that identifies the period during which the initial investment and any negative operating cash flows are finally paid back. The text flag appears in the column for the period in which the cumulative cash flow changes from negative to positive.

The Pretax Payback Period formulas determine whether the cumulative pretax cash flow has turned from a negative amount, indicating that the initial investment has not been fully paid back, to a positive amount, indicating that the initial investment has been paid back. The formula for the first period is:

=IF((AND(B91<0,C91>=0))=TRUE(),"Payback"," ")

The formula for the second period is:

=IF((AND(C91<0,D91>=0))=TRUE(),"Payback"," ")

and so on. For the period during which the initial investment is finally paid back, the text flag *Payback* appears in the column.

After-Tax Cumulative Cash Flows. The After-Tax Cumulative Cash Flows figures represent the cumulative cash flows that result from holding the asset or investment calculated by using the after-tax cash flows as calculated in the After-Tax Cash Flow Scenarios schedule, assuming the investment is held for 10 periods. The period during which the cumulative cash flow figure turns from a negative amount to a positive amount indicates the period in which the investment pays back the original cash invested—a common measure of liquidity.

The After-Tax Cumulative Cash Flows figure for each period is calculated by using the 10-year holding period scenario in the After-Tax Cash Flow Scenarios schedule. The formula for the initial investment is:

=SUM($B$121:B121)

The formula for the first period is:

=SUM($B$121:C121)

The formula for the second period is:

=SUM($B$121:D121)

and so on. The results represent the cumulative after-tax cash flows through the period.

After-Tax Payback Period. The After-Tax Payback Period is a text flag (the word Payback) that identifies the period during which the initial investment and any negative operating cash flows are finally paid back. The text flag appears in the column for the period in which the cumulative cash flow moves from a negative amount to a positive amount.

The After-Tax Payback Period formulas determine whether the cumulative after-tax cash flow has turned from a negative amount, indicating that the initial investment has not been fully paid back, to a positive amount, indicating that the initial investment has been paid back. The formula for the first period is:

=IF((AND(B93<0,C93>=0))=TRUE(),"Payback"," ")

The formula for the second period is:

=IF((AND(C93<0,D93>=0))=TRUE(),"Payback"," ")

and so on. For the period during which the initial investment is finally paid back, the text flag *Payback* appears in the column.

Pretax Cash Flow Scenarios

The Pretax Cash Flow Scenarios schedule has 12 rows. These are the forecasted cash flows for the alternative holding periods and are used to calculate the profitability and liquidity measures in the Cash Flow Analysis schedule. You will probably use this schedule only indirectly because it provides the raw data used to calculate the profitability measures. However, to read the schedule, you simply look down column A, which describes the various lengths of time you can hold the asset or investment, until you come to the number of periods held that you want to examine—that row then shows the cash flows occurring each period for the number-of-periods-held scenario. For example, suppose you want to view the pretax cash flows if the investment is held for 5 periods. You first look down the first column of the Pretax Cash Flow Scenarios column. When you come to 5, you're at the row that shows the cash flows that assume you hold the asset or investment for 5 periods. The negative amount in column B shows the period 0 cash flow ($15,000 in Figure 8-1). The positive amounts in columns C through F in Figure 8-1 show the operating cash flow $3,505. The positive cash flow in column G shows the combined operating and liquidation cash flows as $14,105. Notice that in columns H and beyond, representing periods 6 and beyond, the amounts appear as 0 because the asset or investment has been disposed of and, therefore, no longer results in cash flows.

Period 0. The values in the Period 0 cash flows column show the initial cash outlay to acquire the asset or investment and are the same for each of the alternative holding periods.

The Period 0 cash flow, which is the initial cash outlay to acquire the asset or investment, is the same for each of the holding periods in the Pretax Cash Flow Scenarios schedule. The formula for a holding period of 1 is:

```
=-$B$3
```

The formula for a holding period of 2 is:

```
=-$B$3
```

and so on.

Period 1 through 10. The period cash flows show the forecasted pretax cash flow stemming from holding and perhaps disposing of an asset or investment for each of 10 periods. For example, the Period 1 pretax cash flow for holding period 1 equals the sum of both the pretax operating cash flow and the pretax liquidation cash flow for the first period; cash flows beyond the first period equal 0, signifying that asset or investment has been liquidated. Similarly, the Period 2 pretax cash flow for holding period 2 equals the sum of the pretax operating cash flow and the pretax liquidation cash flow for the second period; cash flows for Period 3 and beyond for holding Period 2 equal 0. The Period 1 pretax cash flow for holding period 2 equals the pretax operating cash flow for the first period. This schedule provides the alternative pretax cash flows used in the pretax profitability and liquidity measures shown in the Cash Flow Analysis schedule.

The same basic formula calculates the period cash flows for any of the periods in each of the alternative holding period scenarios. The basic formula uses a nested IF statement with the following structure:

> IF the period is before the period the asset or investment is liquidated, THEN assume that the period cash flow equals the pretax operating cash flow for the period, ELSE IF the period is the same as the period the asset or investment is liquidated, THEN assume the period cash flow equals the sum of the pretax operating cash flow and the pretax liquidation cash flow, ELSE assume the period cash flow is 0 because the period is after the period the asset or investment was liquidated.

For example, the formula to calculate the first-period cash flow when you hold the asset or investment for one period is:

> =IF(C$98<$A99,C$65,IF(C$98=$A99,C$65+C$75,0))

The formula to calculate the second-period cash flow when you hold the asset or investment for one period is:

> =IF(D$98<$A99,D$65,IF(D$98=$A99,D$65+D$75,0))

The formula to calculate the first-period cash flow when you hold the asset or investment for two periods is:

=IF(C$98<$A100,C$65,IF(C$98=$A100,C$65+C$75,0))

The formula to calculate the second-period cash flow when you hold the asset or investment for two periods is:

=IF(D$98<$A100,D$65,IF(D$98=$A100,D$65+D$75,0))

and so on.

After-Tax Cash Flow Scenarios

The After-Tax Cash Flow Scenarios schedule has 12 rows. These are the forecasted cash flows for the alternative holding periods and are used to calculate the profitability and liquidity measures in the Cash Flow Analysis schedule.

Period 0. The values in the Period 0 cash flow column show the initial cash outlay to acquire the asset or investment and are the same for each of the alternative holding periods.

The Period 0 cash flow, which is the initial cash outlay to acquire the asset or investment, is the same for each of the holding periods in the After-Tax Cash Flow Scenarios schedule. The formula for a holding period of 1 is:

=–$B$3

The formula for a holding period of 2 is:

=–$B$3

and so on.

Period 1 through 10. The period cash flows show the forecasted after-tax cash flow stemming from holding and perhaps disposing of an asset or investment for each of 10 periods. For example, the Period 1 after-tax cash flow for holding period 1 equals the sum of both the after-tax operating cash flow and the after-tax liquidation cash flow for the first period; cash flows beyond the first period equal 0, signifying that the asset or investment has been liquidated. Similarly, the Period 2 after-tax cash flow for holding period 2 equals the sum of the after-tax operating cash flow and the after-tax liquidation cash flow for the second period; cash flows for Period 3 and beyond for holding period 2 equal 0. The Period 1 after-tax cash flow for holding period 2 equals the after-tax operating cash flow for the first period. This schedule provides the alternative after-tax cash flows used in the after-tax profitability and liquidity measures shown in the Cash Flow Analysis schedule.

The same basic formula calculates the period cash flows for any of the periods in each of the alternative holding period scenarios. The basic formula uses a compound IF function statement with the following structure:

> IF the period is before the period the asset or investment is liquidated, THEN assume that the period cash flow equals the after-tax operating cash flow for the period, ELSE IF the period is the same as the period the asset or investment is liquidated, THEN assume the period cash flow equals the sum of the after-tax operating cash flow and the after-tax liquidation cash flow, ELSE assume the period cash flow is 0 because the period is after the period the asset or investment was liquidated.

For example, the formula to calculate the first-period cash flow when you hold the asset or investment for one period is:

=IF(C$111<$A112,C$68,IF(C$111=$A112,C$68+C$78,0))

The formula to calculate the second-period cash flow when you hold the asset or investment for one period is:

=IF(D$111<$A112,D$68,IF(D$111=$A112,D$68+D$78,0))

The formula to calculate the first-period cash flow when you hold the asset or investment for two periods is:

=IF(C$111<$A113,C$68,IF(C$111=$A113,C$68+C$78,0))

8: Cash Flow Forecast and Analysis Template

The formula to calculate the second-period cash flow when you hold the asset or investment for two periods is:

=IF(D$111<$A113,D$68,IF(D$111=$A113,D$68+D$78,0))

and so on.

Entering Your Own Data

To enter your own data in the cash flow forecasting and analysis template, use the following steps:

1. Load CASHFLOW.XLS from the templates disk. (The template initially contains the default inputs shown in Figure 8-1.)

2. Enter the Initial Cash Investment value, the amount required to acquire the investment. Enter a cash outflow as a positive amount and a cash inflow as a negative amount.

3. Enter the Pretax Reinvestment Rate value. (You use this value to calculate pretax adjusted rates of return. If you do not want to calculate pretax adjusted rates of return, you do not need to enter this value.)

4. Enter the After-Tax Reinvestment Rate value. (You use this value to calculate after-tax adjusted rates of return. If you do not want to calculate after-tax adjusted rates of return, you do not need to enter this value.)

5. Enter the Pretax Discount Rate value. (You use this value to calculate pretax net present values. If you do not want to calculate pretax net present values, you do not need to enter this value.)

6. Enter the After-Tax Discount Rate value. (You use this value to calculate after-tax net present values. If you do not want to calculate after-tax net present values, you do not need to enter this value.)

7. Enter the Gross Sales value forecasted for each period of the forecasting horizon. Enter cash inflows as positive amounts and cash outflows as negative amounts. (If you are analyzing the cash

flows from financial assets, this amount might be the investment revenue forecasted for each period. If you are analyzing the cash flows from assets that deliver productivity or efficiency gains, this amount might be the cost savings forecasted for each period.)

8. Enter the Cost of Sales values forecasted for each period of the forecasting horizon. Enter cash outflows as positive amounts and cash inflows as negative amounts. (If you are analyzing the cash flows from a financial asset or an asset that delivers productivity gains, this amount might be 0 for each period.)

9. In the Cost Center 1 Costs row, enter those costs that fall into the first classification or category. Enter cash outflows as positive amounts and cash inflows as negative amounts.

10. In the Cost Center 2 Costs row, enter those costs that fall into the second classification or category. Enter cash outflows as positive amounts and cash inflows as negative amounts.

11. In the Cost Center 3 Costs row, enter those costs that fall into the third classification or category. Enter cash outflows as positive amounts and cash inflows as negative amounts.

12. Enter the Interest Expense value, the cost of carrying any debt used to fund a portion of the asset or investment purchase.

13. Enter the Marginal Income Tax Rate values—those that, when multiplied against the profit or loss for the period, calculate the income tax expense (or savings). (If you are interested only in calculating pretax profit measures, enter 0 as this amount.)

14. Enter the Depreciation expenses included in the expense categories 1, 2, or 3 of the forecasting horizon. (If there is no depreciation expense included in the three expense classifications or categories, enter 0 as this amount.) You might use these three categories for three additional cost centers—for example, marketing, administration, and research. Or, you might use these three categories for three specific expense classifications—for example, labor, materials, and overhead.

15. Enter the Other Noncash Expenses values for the forecasting horizon. (If there are no other noncash expenses included in the three expense classifications or categories, enter 0 as this amount.)

16. Enter the Debt Principal Payments values—the payments made each period over the forecasting horizon. Enter cash outflows as positive amounts and cash inflows as negative amounts. (If there is no debt or the debt contains no principal amortization feature, enter 0 as this amount.)

17. Enter the Other Cash Nonexpenses values—those other cash outflows, such as debt principal payments, that are cash payments but that are not expenses and are incurred each period of the forecasting horizon. Enter cash outflows as positive amounts and cash inflows as negative amounts.

18. Enter the Gross Residual value forecasted for each period of the forecasting horizon. Enter cash inflows as positive amounts and cash outflows as negative amounts. (If the asset or investment cannot be liquidated except at the end of the holding period, you need to enter only the final residual forecast.)

19. Enter the Transaction/Disposal Costs values—the costs of liquidating the asset or investment. Enter cash outflows as positive amounts and cash inflows as negative amounts. (You need only enter Transaction/Disposal Costs figures for those periods for which you forecast a gross residual.)

20. Enter the Outstanding Debt on Asset(s) values—the debt that must be paid off when the asset or investment is liquidated. Enter cash outflows as positive amounts and cash inflows as negative amounts. (You need to enter outstanding debt figures only for those periods for which you forecast a gross residual.)

21. Enter the Nontaxable Portion of Residual values. (You need to enter the Nontaxable Portion of Residual figures only for those periods for which you forecast a gross residual.)

22. Enter the Marginal Tax Rate on Residual value—the rate that, when multiplied by the capital gain or loss on the liquidation, calculates the capital gains tax expenses (or savings). (You need to enter Marginal Tax Rate on Residual figures only for those periods for which you forecast a gross residual.)

23. Calculate the template. (Calculation for the template is set to manual because of the time required to calculate the internal and adjusted rates of return.)

24. Save your changes by creating a new file on the disk on which you plan to store any of the subsidiary spreadsheets that support the financial model you're constructing.

25. Print the spreadsheet.

Customizing the Template

You can use the cash flow forecasting and analysis template without modification for many cash flow forecasts and analyses. However, you might want to change the template so that it more closely matches your requirements. For example, you can add text that describes the asset or investment for which cash flows are forecasted and analyzed. You can increase or decrease the number of periods. For example, you can increase the number of periods to 12 if your periods are months and you want to forecast an entire year. You might also want to remove either the pretax or the after-tax profitability and liquidity measures if you don't consider one or the other in your decision making. Before you change anything on the template other than the forecasting inputs, unprotect the document.

Increasing the number of periods

To increase the number of periods, follow these steps:

1. Remove the border from the last column of the cash flow forecasting and analysis schedules.

2. Copy the current last column of the cash flow forecast and analysis schedules to the right as needed.

3. Replace the border on the right of the cash flow forecast and analysis schedules.

4. Insert the same number of rows below the Pretax Cash Flow Scenarios matrix in the same way that you added columns to the cash flow forecasting and analysis summary.

5. Remove the bottom borders of the Pretax Cash Flow Scenarios and After-Tax Cash Flow Scenarios schedules.

6. Copy the last row of both the Pretax Cash Flow Scenarios and After-Tax Cash Flow Scenarios into the same number of rows in the same way that you added columns to the cash flow forecasting and analysis summary.

7. Replace the bottom borders on both the Pretax Cash Flow Scenarios and the After-Tax Cash Flow Scenarios schedules.

8. Adjust the pretax and after-tax internal rate of return, adjusted rate of return, and net present value formulas for the new columns so that the cash flow value arguments in the IRR, MIRR, and NPV functions use the correct row of the Pretax Cash Flow Scenarios or After-Tax Cash Flow Scenarios.

9. Reinstate cell protection as needed.

Decreasing the number of periods

To decrease the number of periods, follow these steps:

1. Delete any unneeded columns from the right side of the schedule.

2. In the Pretax Cash Flow Scenarios and After-Tax Cash Flow Scenarios schedules, delete the rows that correspond to the columns you deleted.

3. Reinstate cell protection as needed.

Removing the pretax profitability and liquidity measures

To remove the pretax profitability and liquidity measures from the spreadsheet, follow these steps:

1. Delete the Pretax Cash Flow Scenarios schedule.

2. From the Cash Flow Analysis schedule, delete the Pretax IRR, the Pretax Adjusted IRR, the Pretax Net Present Value, the Pretax Cumulative Cash Flows, and the Pretax Payback Period rows.

3. Reinstate cell protection as needed.

Removing the after-tax profitability and liquidity measures

To remove the after-tax profitability and liquidity measures from the spreadsheet, follow these steps:

1. Delete the After-Tax Cash Flow Scenarios schedule.

2. From the Cash Flow Analysis schedule, delete the After-Tax IRR, the After-Tax Adjusted IRR, the After-Tax Net Present Value, the After-Tax Cumulative Cash Flows, and the After-Tax Payback Period rows.

3. Reinstate cell protection as needed.

Linking this Template to Others in the Toolkit

Other templates in this toolkit are specifically designed to provide data to the cash flow forecasting and analysis template. In fact, each of the templates described in previous chapters provides data that can be used as input to the Forecasting Inputs schedule: one of the asset depreciation templates can provide the depreciation expenses and the net book value (representing the nontaxable portion of the residual), one of the debt amortization templates can provide the interest expense and debt principal payments for each period and the outstanding debt amount, the cost center template can be used to construct detailed forecasts of various categories of expenses, and the sales forecasting template can be used to develop the sales and cost of sales figures.

For example, assume that you construct a straight-line asset depreciation schedule for a $25,000 asset. For income tax accounting purposes, suppose that the asset will be depreciated over 10 years and that the salvage value is $5,000. Figure 8-2 shows the example depreciation spreadsheet (DEPRECTN.XLS) constructed for this scenario. Also suppose that you used a bank loan to fund a portion of the asset purchase—a $10,000 note with a debt term of 10 years, an amortization term of 20 years, and an annual interest rate of 10 percent. Figure 8-3 on page 238 shows the example spreadsheet (AMORTIZE.XLS) containing the annual payments, the interest and principal components of the payments, and the outstanding principal balances over the term of the debt.

Straight-Line Depreciation Calculation Inputs	
Original Cost	$25,000
Salvage Value	$5,000
Estimated Life	10

Straight-Line Depreciation Schedule			
Period	Period Depreciation	Accumulated Depreciation	Net Book Value
1	$2,000	$2,000	$23,000
2	$2,000	4,000	21,000
3	$2,000	6,000	19,000
4	$2,000	8,000	17,000
5	$2,000	10,000	15,000
6	$2,000	12,000	13,000
7	$2,000	14,000	11,000
8	$2,000	16,000	9,000
9	$2,000	18,000	7,000
10	$2,000	20,000	5,000
11	$0	20,000	5,000
12	$0	20,000	5,000
13	$0	20,000	5,000
14	$0	20,000	5,000
15	$0	20,000	5,000
16	$0	20,000	5,000
17	$0	20,000	5,000
18	$0	20,000	5,000
19	$0	20,000	5,000
20	$0	20,000	5,000

Figure 8-2. *The straight-line depreciation template, calculating the investments depreciation and net book values for input to the cash flow analysis template.*

Microsoft Excel Small Business Consultant

Fixed Interest Rate Amortization Inputs

Principal	$10,000
Debt Term	10
Amortize Term	20
Interest Rate	10.00%

Fixed Interest Rate Amortization Schedule

Period	Total Payment	Interest Component	Principal Component	Principal Balance
1	$1,175	$1,000	$175	$9,825
2	1,175	983	192	9,633
3	1,175	963	211	9,422
4	1,175	942	232	9,190
5	1,175	919	256	8,934
6	1,175	893	281	8,653
7	1,175	865	309	8,344
8	1,175	834	340	8,003
9	1,175	800	374	7,629
10	1,175	763	412	7,217
11	0	0	0	0
12	0	0	0	0
13	0	0	0	0
14	0	0	0	0
15	0	0	0	0
16	0	0	0	0
17	0	0	0	0
18	0	0	0	0
19	0	0	0	0
20	0	0	0	0

Balloon Payment Schedule

Balloon Payment	Full Principal Payment	True Balance
$0	$175	$9,825
0	192	9,633
0	211	9,422
0	232	9,190
0	256	8,934
0	281	8,653
0	309	8,344
0	340	8,003
0	374	7,629
7,217	7,629	0
0	0	0
0	0	0
0	0	0
0	0	0
0	0	0
0	0	0
0	0	0
0	0	0
0	0	0
0	0	0

Figure 8-3. *The fixed interest rate debt amortization template, calculating the payments interest, balances, and balloon payment for the debt used to fund a portion of the investment purchase.*

Rather than simply entering the forecasted depreciation, interest expense, outstanding debt, and nontaxable portions of the residual into the Forecasting Inputs schedule shown in Figure 8-4 on pages 241–43, you can link the cells that contain these variables to the subsidiary templates. To construct such a link, assuming DEPRECTN.XLS and AMORTIZE.XLS are stored in the WINDOWS directory on your hard disk, you do the following:

1. Load CASHFLOW.XLS from the templates disk. (The template initially contains the inputs shown in Figure 8-1.)

2. Enter the amount of asset depreciation for the first period by entering the following formula into cell C15:

    ='C:\WINDOWS\DEPRECTN.XLS'!$C$11

    DEPRECTN.XLS supplies the period depreciation expense, which is the amount you're forecasting as the period asset depreciation. Cell C11 in that file is the cell that contains the first-period depreciation expense. In the same way, you can enter the depreciation expense for periods 2 through 10.

3. Enter the amount of nontaxable residual (assuming it is the same as the net book value in C22), by entering the following formula:

    ='C:\WINDOWS\DEPRECTN.XLS'!$E$11

    Cell E11 in DEPRECTN.XLS is the cell that contains the first-period depreciation expense. In the same way, you can enter the forecasted net book values as the nontaxable portion of the residual for periods 2 through 10.

4. In cell C13, enter the amount of interest expense for the first period by entering the following formula:

    ='C:\WINDOWS\AMORTIZE.XLS'!$D$12

AMORTIZE.XLS supplies the interest component of the first payment, which is the amount you're forecasting as the interest expense. Cell D12 in that file is the cell that contains the interest component of the first-period payment. In the same way, you can enter the interest expense for periods 2 through 10.

5. In cell C21, enter the principal balance from the debt amortization template as the outstanding debt amount by entering the following formula:

   ='C:\WINDOWS\AMORTIZE.XLS'!$F$12

   Cell F12 in AMORTIZE.XLS is the cell that contains the principal balance at the end of the period. In the same way, you can enter the forecasted principal balances as of the end of periods 2 through 10.

Forecasting Inputs	Period 0	Period 1	Period 2	Period 3	Period 4	Period 5	Period 6	Period 7	Period 8	Period 9	Period 10
Initial Cash Investment	$15,000										
Pretax Reinvestment Rate	12.00%										
After-Tax Reinvestment Rate	8.00%										
Pretax Discount Rate	12.00%										
After-Tax Discount Rate	8.00%										
Gross Sales		$10,000	$10,000	$10,000	$10,000	$10,000	$10,000	$10,000	$10,000	$10,000	$10,000
Cost of Sales		2,500	2,500	2,500	2,500	2,500	2,500	2,500	2,500	2,500	2,500
Cost Center 1 Costs		3,000	3,000	3,000	3,000	3,000	3,000	3,000	3,000	3,000	3,000
Cost Center 2 Costs		1,000	1,000	1,000	1,000	1,000	1,000	1,000	1,000	1,000	1,000
Cost Center 3 Costs		1,000	1,000	1,000	1,000	1,000	1,000	1,000	1,000	1,000	1,000
Interest Expense		1,000	983	963	942	919	893	865	834	800	763
Marginal Income Tax Rate		33%	33%	33%	33%	33%	33%	33%	33%	33%	33%
Depreciation		$2,000	$2,000	$2,000	$2,000	$2,000	$2,000	$2,000	$2,000	$2,000	$2,000
Other Noncash Expenses		0	0	0	0	0	0	0	0	0	0
Debt Principal Payments		175	192	211	232	256	281	309	340	374	412
Other Cash Nonexpenses		0	0	0	0	0	0	0	0	0	0
Gross Residual		25,000	25,000	25,000	25,000	25,000	25,000	25,000	25,000	25,000	25,000
Transaction/Disposal Costs		1,250	1,250	1,250	1,250	1,250	1,250	1,250	1,250	1,250	1,250
Outstanding Debt on Asset(s)		9,825	9,633	9,422	9,190	8,934	8,653	8,344	8,003	7,629	7,217
Nontaxable Portion of Residual		23,000	21,000	19,000	17,000	15,000	13,000	11,000	9,000	7,000	5,000
Marginal Tax Rate on Residual		28%	28%	28%	28%	28%	28%	28%	28%	28%	28%

Profit and Loss Statement											
Gross Sales		$10,000	$10,000	$10,000	$10,000	$10,000	$10,000	$10,000	$10,000	$10,000	$10,000
Less: Cost of Sales		(2,500)	(2,500)	(2,500)	(2,500)	(2,500)	(2,500)	(2,500)	(2,500)	(2,500)	(2,500)
Gross Margin		7,500	7,500	7,500	7,500	7,500	7,500	7,500	7,500	7,500	7,500
Operating Expenses											
Cost Center 1		3,000	3,000	3,000	3,000	3,000	3,000	3,000	3,000	3,000	3,000
Cost Center 2		1,000	1,000	1,000	1,000	1,000	1,000	1,000	1,000	1,000	1,000
Cost Center 3		1,000	1,000	1,000	1,000	1,000	1,000	1,000	1,000	1,000	1,000
Total Operating Expenses		5,000	5,000	5,000	5,000	5,000	5,000	5,000	5,000	5,000	5,000
Operating Income		2,500	2,500	2,500	2,500	2,500	2,500	2,500	2,500	2,500	2,500
Interest Expense		1,000	983	963	942	919	893	865	834	800	763
Net Income (Loss) Before Taxes		1,500	1,517	1,537	1,558	1,581	1,607	1,635	1,666	1,700	1,737
Income Tax Expenses (Savings)		495	501	507	514	522	530	539	550	561	573
Net Income (Loss) After Taxes		$1,005	$1,017	$1,030	$1,044	$1,059	$1,076	$1,095	$1,116	$1,139	$1,164

(continued)

Figure 8-4. *The cash flow forecasting and analysis template, with depreciation, nontaxable portions of residual, debt principal payments, interest expense, and outstanding balances pulled from the spreadsheet, shown in Figures 8-2 and 8-3.*

Figure 8-4. *continued*

Gain and Loss Statement											
Gross Residual		$25,000	$25,000	$25,000	$25,000	$25,000	$25,000	$25,000	$25,000	$25,000	$25,000
Less: Transaction/Disposal Costs		(1,250)	(1,250)	(1,250)	(1,250)	(1,250)	(1,250)	(1,250)	(1,250)	(1,250)	(1,250)
Net Residual		23,750	23,750	23,750	23,750	23,750	23,750	23,750	23,750	23,750	23,750
Nontaxable Portion of Residual		23,000	21,000	19,000	17,000	15,000	13,000	11,000	9,000	7,000	5,000
Pretax Gain (Loss) on Disposal		750	2,750	4,750	6,750	8,750	10,750	12,750	14,750	16,750	18,750
Income Tax Expenses (Savings)		210	770	1,330	1,890	2,450	3,010	3,570	4,130	4,690	5,250
After-Tax Gain (Loss) on Disposal		$540	$1,980	$3,420	$4,860	$6,300	$7,740	$9,180	$10,620	$12,060	$13,500

Operating Cash Flow Statement	Period 0	Period 1	Period 2	Period 3	Period 4	Period 5	Period 6	Period 7	Period 8	Period 9	Period 10
Net Income Before Taxes		$1,500	$1,517	$1,537	$1,558	$1,581	$1,607	$1,635	$1,666	$1,700	$1,737
Addbacks of Noncash Expenses											
Depreciation		2,000	2,000	2,000	2,000	2,000	2,000	2,000	2,000	2,000	2,000
Other		0	0	0	0	0	0	0	0	0	0
Deducts of Cash Nonexpenses											
Debt Principal Payments		(175)	(192)	(211)	(232)	(256)	(281)	(309)	(340)	(374)	(412)
Other		0	0	0	0	0	0	0	0	0	0
Pretax Operating Cash Flow	($15,000)	3,325	3,325	3,325	3,325	3,325	3,325	3,325	3,325	3,325	3,325
Income Tax Expenses (Savings)		495	501	507	514	522	530	539	550	561	573
After-Tax Operating Cash Flow	($15,000)	$2,830	$2,825	$2,818	$2,811	$2,804	$2,795	$2,786	$2,776	$2,765	$2,752

Liquidation Cash Flow Statement											
Gross Residual		$25,000	$25,000	$25,000	$25,000	$25,000	$25,000	$25,000	$25,000	$25,000	$25,000
Less: Transaction/Sales Costs		(1,250)	(1,250)	(1,250)	(1,250)	(1,250)	(1,250)	(1,250)	(1,250)	(1,250)	(1,250)
Less: Outstanding Debt		(9,825)	(9,633)	(9,422)	(9,190)	(8,934)	(8,653)	(8,344)	(8,003)	(7,629)	(7,217)
Pretax Liquidation Cash Flow		13,925	14,117	14,328	14,560	14,816	15,097	15,406	15,747	16,121	16,533
Income Tax Expenses (Savings)		210	770	1,330	1,890	2,450	3,010	3,570	4,130	4,690	5,250
After-Tax Liquidation Cash Flow		$13,715	$13,347	$12,998	$12,670	$12,366	$12,087	$11,836	$11,617	$11,431	$11,283

Figure 8-4. *continued*

Cash Flow Analysis											
Pretax IRR		15.00%	19.49%	20.95%	21.64%	22.01%	22.23%	22.36%	22.45%	22.49%	22.52%
After-Tax IRR		10.30%	13.69%	14.99%	15.74%	16.26%	16.65%	16.97%	17.23%	17.45%	17.64%
Pretax Adjusted IRR		15.00%	18.79%	16.48%	15.34%	14.67%	14.22%	13.90%	13.66%	13.47%	13.33%
After-Tax Adjusted IRR		10.30%	13.22%	11.45%	10.58%	10.06%	9.71%	9.47%	9.28%	9.14%	9.02%
Pretax Net Present Value		$359	$1,673	$2,844	$3,887	$4,816	$5,644	$6,380	$7,035	$7,618	$8,136
After-Tax Net Present Value		296	1,375	2,405	3,388	4,324	5,215	6,063	6,868	7,632	8,356
Pretax Cumulative Cash Flows	($15,000)	($11,675)	($8,349)	($5,024)	($1,698)	$1,627	$4,952	$8,278	$11,603	$14,929	$34,787
Pretax Payback Period						Payback					
After-Tax Cumulative Cash Flows	($15,000)	($12,170)	($9,345)	($6,527)	($3,715)	($912)	$1,884	$4,670	$7,445	$10,210	$24,245
After-Tax Payback Period							Payback				

Pretax Cash Flow Scenarios	Period 0	Period 1	Period 2	Period 3	Period 4	Period 5	Period 6	Period 7	Period 8	Period 9	Period 10
Number of Periods Held:											
1	($15,000)	$17,250	$0	$0	$0	$0	$0	$0	$0	$0	$0
2	(15,000)	3,325	17,442	0	0	0	0	0	0	0	0
3	(15,000)	3,325	3,325	17,653	0	0	0	0	0	0	0
4	(15,000)	3,325	3,325	3,325	17,886	0	0	0	0	0	0
5	(15,000)	3,325	3,325	3,325	3,325	18,141	0	0	0	0	0
6	(15,000)	3,325	3,325	3,325	3,325	3,325	18,423	0	0	0	0
7	(15,000)	3,325	3,325	3,325	3,325	3,325	3,325	18,732	0	0	0
8	(15,000)	3,325	3,325	3,325	3,325	3,325	3,325	3,325	19,072	0	0
9	(15,000)	3,325	3,325	3,325	3,325	3,325	3,325	3,325	3,325	19,446	0
10	(15,000)	3,325	3,325	3,325	3,325	3,325	3,325	3,325	3,325	3,325	19,858

After-Tax Cash Flow Scenarios	Period 0	Period 1	Period 2	Period 3	Period 4	Period 5	Period 6	Period 7	Period 8	Period 9	Period 10
Number of Periods Held:											
1	($15,000)	$16,545	$0	$0	$0	$0	$0	$0	$0	$0	$0
2	(15,000)	2,830	16,171	0	0	0	0	0	0	0	0
3	(15,000)	2,830	2,825	15,816	0	0	0	0	0	0	0
4	(15,000)	2,830	2,825	2,818	15,482	0	0	0	0	0	0
5	(15,000)	2,830	2,825	2,818	2,811	15,170	0	0	0	0	0
6	(15,000)	2,830	2,825	2,818	2,811	2,804	14,882	0	0	0	0
7	(15,000)	2,830	2,825	2,818	2,811	2,804	2,795	14,622	0	0	0
8	(15,000)	2,830	2,825	2,818	2,811	2,804	2,795	2,786	14,392	0	0
9	(15,000)	2,830	2,825	2,818	2,811	2,804	2,795	2,786	2,776	14,195	0
10	(15,000)	2,830	2,825	2,818	2,811	2,804	2,795	2,786	2,776	2,765	14,035

9

Financial Statements with Ratios Template

Pro forma financial statements—income statements, balance sheets, and cash flow statements—usually constitute an integral part of business planning and the overall budgeting process. Financial ratios are usually applied to these statements to assist both the builder and the user of the pro forma financial statements in assessing the strengths, weaknesses, and performance of the business and the reasonableness of the model.

The financial statements with ratios template (FINANCLS.XLS), described in this chapter, provides a framework to use in constructing pro forma financial statements and in applying ratio analysis to the pro forma statements. This template, with minor modifications, lets you apply ratio analysis to a set of existing financial statements. This chapter shows how to use the financial statements with ratios template, print it, modify it, and link it with subsidiary spreadsheets.

FINANCIAL STATEMENTS AND FINANCIAL RATIOS: A SHORT PRIMER

Financial statements describe either the past or the future financial condition and performance of a business. The term "financial statement" can refer to one of several types of schedules and summaries of economic information. Typically, however, the term describes a set of documents that includes an income statement (also called a statement of operations), a balance sheet (also called a statement of financial condition), and a cash flow statement. An income statement details the profits and losses of a business for a specific period. For example, you might want to know the profits or losses of your business over the past month. Therefore, you would prepare an income statement that lists your revenues and expenses and calculates the profits or losses for the month. A balance sheet identifies and lists the assets and liabilities of a business as of a specific time. It paints a clear picture of what the business owns, what the business owes, and the difference between the two (often called the net worth or owner equity). Typically, you prepare a balance sheet as of the end of the period for which an income statement is prepared. For example, if you prepare an income statement for a month, you might also want to prepare a balance sheet as of the last day of the month. A cash flow statement outlines the cash inflows and outflows of a business for a specific period. Generally, you prepare a cash flow statement for the same period for which you prepare an income statement.

Financial ratios express relationships among the amounts reported in the financial statements. The ratios can offer insights into the economic health of a business. The ratios can also indicate the reasonableness of the assumptions implicit in a forecast. For example, by comparing the ratios of your business with the ratios of similar businesses, you can compare the financial characteristics of your business with those of other businesses. By comparing the ratios in your pro forma model with industry averages and standards, you also test your modeling assumptions for reasonableness. Two general categories of financial ratios exist: common size ratios and intrastatement or interstatement ratios. Common size ratios convert a financial statement—usually a balance sheet or an income statement—from dollars to percentages. Common size ratios allow for comparisons of the assets, liabilities, revenues, owner equity, and expenses of businesses of various sizes. The comparison can be either at a point in time or as a trend over time. Intrastatement or interstatement ratios quantify relationships among amounts from different financial statements or from different parts of the same financial statement. Intrastatement and interstatement ratios are an attempt to account for the fact that amounts usually cannot be interpreted alone, but must be viewed in the context of other key financial factors and events. In general, both categories of ratios are most valuable when compared to industry averages and trends.

FINANCIAL STATEMENTS WITH RATIOS TEMPLATE (FINANCLS.XLS)

You can use the financial statements template (FINANCLS.XLS), shown in Figure 9-1 on the next five pages, to construct pro forma financial statements that let you forecast profits and losses, financial condition, and cash flows for a business or organization. To complete the template, you develop and then enter information on the assets; the creditor and owner equities at the start of the forecasting horizon; the expected changes in the assets and equities over the forecasting horizon; and the revenues and expenses for each period on the forecasting horizon.

Given data that includes your starting asset, liability, owner equity balances, and expected changes in these amounts for the forecasting horizon, this template constructs a balance sheet. Given data that includes sales and costs of sales, operating expenses, interest income and expenses, and marginal income tax rates, this template constructs an income statement. From the balance sheet and income statement, this template constructs a cash flow statement.

What the Template Contains and Does

The seven parts of the financial statements with ratios template are Forecasting Inputs, Balance Sheet, Common Size Balance Sheet, Income Statement, Common Size Income Statement, Cash Flow Statement, and Financial Ratios Table.

Forecasting Inputs

In the Forecasting Inputs schedule, there is one set of formulas. The second row identifies the period for which the results are calculated.

Period. The Period identifier numbers the periods for which values are entered.

Forecasting Inputs	Period 0	Period 1	Period 2	Period 3	Period 4	Period 5	Period 6	Period 7	Period 8	Period 9	Period 10
Balance Sheet Forecasting Inputs:											
Cash & Equivalents	15,000										
Yield on Cash & Equivalents		10.00%	10.00%	10.00%	10.00%	10.00%	10.00%	10.00%	10.00%	10.00%	10.00%
Accounts Receivable	10,000										
# Periods of Sales in A/R		0.08	0.08	0.08	0.08	0.08	0.08	0.08	0.08	0.08	0.08
Inventory	10,000										
Inventory Purchased/Produced		55,000	65,000	55,000	65,000	55,000	65,000	55,000	65,000	55,000	65,000
Other Current Assets	5,000										
Chgs in Other Current Assets		100	-100	100	-100	100	-100	100	-100	100	-100
Plant, Property, & Equipment	75,000										
Chgs in P,P,& E		0	0	0	0	15,000	0	0	0	0	-10,000
Accumulated Depreciation	15,000										
Chgs in Accum. Depreciation		3,750	3,750	3,750	3,750	3,750	3,750	3,750	3,750	3,750	-6,250
Other Noncurrent Assets	5,000										
Chgs in Other Noncurrent Assets		100	-100	100	-100	100	-100	100	-100	100	-100
Accounts Payable	10,000										
# Periods Cost of Sales in A/P		0.08	0.08	0.08	0.08	0.08	0.08	0.08	0.08	0.08	0.08
Accrued Expenses	7,500										
# Periods Operating Expenses in A/E		0.04	0.04	0.04	0.04	0.04	0.04	0.04	0.04	0.04	0.04
Other Current Liabilities	7,500										
Chgs in Other Current Liabilities		100	-100	100	-100	100	-100	100	-100	100	-100
Long-Term Liabilities	35,000										
Chgs in Long-Term Liabilities		0	0	0	0	0	0	0	0	0	0
Other Noncurrent Liabilities	4,000										
Chgs in Other Noncurrent Liabilities		100	-100	100	-100	100	-100	100	-100	100	-100
Owner Equity	41,000										
Chgs in Owner Equity		-25,000	-25,000	-25,000	-25,000	-25,000	-25,000	-25,000	-25,000	-25,000	-25,000
Profit and Loss Statement Inputs:											
Sales Revenue		120,000	120,000	120,000	120,000	120,000	120,000	120,000	120,000	120,000	120,000
Cost of Sales		60,000	60,000	60,000	60,000	60,000	60,000	60,000	60,000	60,000	60,000
Cost Center 1 Costs		5,000	5,000	5,000	5,000	5,000	5,000	5,000	5,000	5,000	5,000
Cost Center 2 Costs		5,000	5,000	5,000	5,000	5,000	5,000	5,000	5,000	5,000	5,000
Cost Center 3 Costs		5,000	5,000	5,000	5,000	5,000	5,000	5,000	5,000	5,000	5,000
Interest Expense		3,500	3,500	3,500	3,500	3,500	3,500	3,500	3,500	3,500	3,500
Marginal Income Tax Rate		33%	33%	33%	33%	33%	33%	33%	33%	33%	33%

Figure 9-1. *The financial statements with ratios template with sample data.*

Balance Sheet	Period 0	Period 1	Period 2	Period 3	Period 4	Period 5	Period 6	Period 7	Period 8	Period 9	Period 10
Assets											
Current Assets											
Cash & Equivalents	$15,000	$15,685	$18,291	$31,071	$34,708	$33,589	$37,394	$51,454	$56,457	$71,795	$78,160
Accounts Receivable	10,000	10,000	10,000	10,000	10,000	10,000	10,000	10,000	10,000	10,000	10,000
Inventory	10,000	5,000	10,000	5,000	10,000	5,000	10,000	5,000	10,000	5,000	10,000
Other Current Assets	5,000	5,100	5,000	5,100	5,000	5,100	5,000	5,100	5,000	5,100	5,000
Total Current Assets	40,000	35,785	43,291	51,171	59,708	53,689	62,394	71,554	81,457	91,895	103,160
Plant, Property, & Equipment	75,000	75,000	75,000	75,000	75,000	90,000	90,000	90,000	90,000	90,000	80,000
Less: Accumulated Depreciation	(15,000)	(18,750)	(22,500)	(26,250)	(30,000)	(33,750)	(37,500)	(41,250)	(45,000)	(48,750)	(42,500)
Net Plant, Property, & Equipment	60,000	56,250	52,500	48,750	45,000	56,250	52,500	48,750	45,000	41,250	37,500
Other Noncurrent Assets	5,000	5,100	5,000	5,100	5,000	5,100	5,000	5,100	5,000	5,100	5,000
Total Assets	$105,000	$97,135	$100,791	$105,021	$109,708	$115,039	$119,894	$125,404	$131,457	$138,245	$145,660
Liabilities											
Current Liabilities											
Accounts Payable	$10,000	$5,000	$5,000	$5,000	$5,000	$5,000	$5,000	$5,000	$5,000	$5,000	$5,000
Accrued Expenses	7,500	625	625	625	625	625	625	625	625	625	625
Other Current Liabilities	7,500	7,600	7,500	7,600	7,500	7,600	7,500	7,600	7,500	7,600	7,500
Total Current Liabilities	25,000	13,225	13,125	13,225	13,125	13,225	13,125	13,225	13,125	13,225	13,125
Noncurrent Liabilities											
Long-Term Liabilities	35,000	35,000	35,000	35,000	35,000	35,000	35,000	35,000	35,000	35,000	35,000
Other Noncurrent Liabilities	4,000	4,100	4,000	4,100	4,000	4,100	4,000	4,100	4,000	4,100	4,000
Total Noncurrent Liabilities	39,000	39,100	39,000	39,100	39,000	39,100	39,000	39,100	39,000	39,100	39,000
Owner Equity	41,000	44,810	48,666	52,696	57,583	62,714	67,769	73,079	79,332	85,920	93,535
Total Liabilities and Owner Equity	$105,000	$97,135	$100,791	$105,021	$109,708	$115,039	$119,894	$125,404	$131,457	$138,245	$145,660

(continued)

Figure 9-1. *continued*

Common Size Balance Sheet	Period 0	Period 1	Period 2	Period 3	Period 4	Period 5	Period 6	Period 7	Period 8	Period 9	Period 10
Assets											
Current Assets											
Cash & Equivalents	14.29%	16.15%	18.15%	29.59%	31.64%	29.20%	31.19%	41.03%	42.95%	51.93%	53.66%
Accounts Receivable	9.52%	10.29%	9.92%	9.52%	9.12%	8.69%	8.34%	7.97%	7.61%	7.23%	6.87%
Inventory	9.52%	5.15%	9.92%	4.76%	9.12%	4.35%	8.34%	3.99%	7.61%	3.62%	6.87%
Other Current Assets	4.76%	5.25%	4.95%	4.86%	4.56%	4.43%	4.17%	4.07%	3.80%	3.69%	3.43%
Total Current Assets	38.10%	36.84%	42.95%	48.72%	54.42%	46.67%	52.04%	57.06%	61.96%	66.47%	70.82%
Plant, Property, & Equipment	71.43%	77.21%	74.41%	71.41%	68.36%	78.23%	75.07%	71.77%	68.46%	65.10%	54.92%
Less: Accumulated Depreciation	-14.29%	-19.30%	-22.32%	-24.99%	-27.35%	-29.34%	-31.28%	-32.89%	-34.23%	-35.26%	-29.18%
Net Plant, Property, & Equipment	57.14%	57.91%	52.09%	46.42%	41.02%	48.90%	43.79%	38.87%	34.23%	29.84%	25.74%
Other Noncurrent Assets	4.76%	5.25%	4.95%	4.86%	4.56%	4.43%	4.17%	4.07%	3.80%	3.69%	3.43%
Total Assets	100.00%	100.00%	100.00%	100.00%	100.00%	100.00%	100.00%	100.00%	100.00%	100.00%	100.00%
Liabilities											
Current Liabilities											
Accounts Payable	9.52%	5.15%	4.96%	4.76%	4.56%	4.35%	4.17%	3.99%	3.80%	3.62%	3.43%
Accrued Expenses	7.14%	0.64%	0.62%	0.60%	0.57%	0.54%	0.52%	0.50%	0.48%	0.45%	0.43%
Other Current Liabilities	7.14%	7.82%	7.44%	7.24%	6.84%	6.61%	6.26%	6.06%	5.71%	5.50%	5.15%
Total Current Liabilities	23.81%	13.62%	13.02%	12.59%	11.96%	11.50%	10.95%	10.55%	9.98%	9.57%	9.01%
Noncurrent Liabilities											
Long-Term Liabilities	33.33%	36.03%	34.73%	33.33%	31.90%	30.42%	29.19%	27.91%	26.62%	25.32%	24.03%
Other Noncurrent Liabilities	3.81%	4.22%	3.97%	3.90%	3.65%	3.56%	3.34%	3.27%	3.04%	2.97%	2.75%
Total Noncurrent Liabilities	37.14%	40.25%	38.69%	37.23%	35.55%	33.99%	32.53%	31.18%	29.67%	28.28%	26.77%
Owner Equity	39.05%	46.13%	48.28%	50.18%	52.49%	54.52%	56.52%	58.28%	60.35%	62.15%	64.21%
Total Liabilities and Owner Equity	100.00%	100.00%	100.00%	100.00%	100.00%	100.00%	100.00%	100.00%	100.00%	100.00%	100.00%

Income Statement	Period 1	Period 2	Period 3	Period 4	Period 5	Period 6	Period 7	Period 8	Period 9	Period 10
Sales Revenue	$120,000	$120,000	$120,000	$120,000	$120,000	$120,000	$120,000	$120,000	$120,000	$120,000
Less: Cost of Sales	(60,000)	(60,000)	(60,000)	(60,000)	(60,000)	(60,000)	(60,000)	(60,000)	(60,000)	(60,000)
Gross Margin	60,000	60,000	60,000	60,000	60,000	60,000	60,000	60,000	60,000	60,000
Operating Expenses										
Cost Center 1	5,000	5,000	5,000	5,000	5,000	5,000	5,000	5,000	5,000	5,000
Cost Center 2	5,000	5,000	5,000	5,000	5,000	5,000	5,000	5,000	5,000	5,000
Cost Center 3	5,000	5,000	5,000	5,000	5,000	5,000	5,000	5,000	5,000	5,000
Total Operating Expenses	15,000	15,000	15,000	15,000	15,000	15,000	15,000	15,000	15,000	15,000
Operating Income	45,000	45,000	45,000	45,000	45,000	45,000	45,000	45,000	45,000	45,000
Interest Income	1,500	1,569	1,829	3,107	3,471	3,359	3,739	5,145	5,646	7,179
Interest Expense	3,500	3,500	3,500	3,500	3,500	3,500	3,500	3,500	3,500	3,500
Net Income (Loss) Before Taxes	43,000	43,069	43,329	44,607	44,971	44,859	45,239	46,645	47,146	48,679
Income Tax Expenses (Savings)	14,190	14,213	14,299	14,720	14,840	14,803	14,929	15,393	15,558	16,064
Net Income (Loss) After Taxes	$28,810	$28,856	$29,030	$29,887	$30,130	$30,055	$30,310	$31,252	$31,588	$32,615

Common Size Income Statement	Period 1	Period 2	Period 3	Period 4	Period 5	Period 6	Period 7	Period 8	Period 9	Period 10
Sales Revenue	100.00%	100.00%	100.00%	100.00%	100.00%	100.00%	100.00%	100.00%	100.00%	100.00%
Less: Cost of Sales	-50.00%	-50.00%	-50.00%	-50.00%	-50.00%	-50.00%	-50.00%	-50.00%	-50.00%	-50.00%
Gross Margin	50.00%	50.00%	50.00%	50.00%	50.00%	50.00%	50.00%	50.00%	50.00%	50.00%
Operating Expenses										
Cost Center 1	4.17%	4.17%	4.17%	4.17%	4.17%	4.17%	4.17%	4.17%	4.17%	4.17%
Cost Center 2	4.17%	4.17%	4.17%	4.17%	4.17%	4.17%	4.17%	4.17%	4.17%	4.17%
Cost Center 3	4.17%	4.17%	4.17%	4.17%	4.17%	4.17%	4.17%	4.17%	4.17%	4.17%
Total Operating Expenses	12.50%	12.50%	12.50%	12.50%	12.50%	12.50%	12.50%	12.50%	12.50%	12.50%
Operating Income	37.50%	37.50%	37.50%	37.50%	37.50%	37.50%	37.50%	37.50%	37.50%	37.50%
Interest Income	1.25%	1.31%	1.52%	2.59%	2.89%	2.80%	3.12%	4.29%	4.70%	5.98%
Interest Expense	2.92%	2.92%	2.92%	2.92%	2.92%	2.92%	2.92%	2.92%	2.92%	2.92%
Net income (Loss) Before Taxes	35.83%	35.89%	36.11%	37.17%	37.48%	37.38%	37.70%	38.87%	39.29%	40.57%
Income Tax Expenses (Savings)	11.83%	11.84%	11.92%	12.27%	12.37%	12.34%	12.44%	12.83%	12.97%	13.39%
Net Income (Loss) After Taxes	24.01%	24.05%	24.19%	24.91%	25.11%	25.05%	25.26%	26.04%	26.32%	27.18%

(continued)

Figure 9-1. *continued*

Cash Flow Statement	Period 1	Period 2	Period 3	Period 4	Period 5	Period 6	Period 7	Period 8	Period 9	Period 10
Beginning Cash Balance	$15,000	$15,685	$18,291	$31,071	$34,708	$33,589	$37,394	$51,454	$56,457	$71,795
Sources of Cash										
Net Income After Taxes	$28,810	$28,856	$29,030	$29,887	$30,130	$30,055	$30,310	$31,252	$31,588	$32,615
Addback of Depreciation	3,750	3,750	3,750	3,750	3,750	3,750	3,750	3,750	3,750	(6,250)
Accounts Payable Financing	(5,000)	0	0	0	0	0	0	0	0	0
Accrued Expenses Financing	(6,875)	0	0	0	0	0	0	0	0	0
Other Current Liabilities Financing	100	(100)	100	(100)	100	(100)	100	(100)	100	(100)
Long-Term Liabilities Financing	0	0	0	0	0	0	0	0	0	0
Other Noncurrent Liabilities Financing	100	(100)	100	(100)	100	(100)	100	(100)	100	(100)
Uses of Cash										
Accounts Receivable Investments	0	0	0	0	0	0	0	0	0	0
Inventory Investments	(5,000)	5,000	(5,000)	5,000	(5,000)	5,000	(5,000)	5,000	(5,000)	5,000
Other Current Assets Investments	100	(100)	100	(100)	100	(100)	100	(100)	100	(100)
Plant, Property, & Equip Investments	0	0	0	0	15,000	0	0	0	0	(10,000)
Other Noncurrent Assets Investments	100	(100)	100	(100)	100	(100)	100	(100)	100	(100)
Other Owner Equity Changes	25,000	25,000	25,000	25,000	25,000	25,000	25,000	25,000	25,000	25,000
Net Cash Generated (Used)	685	2,606	12,780	3,637	(1,120)	3,805	14,060	5,002	15,338	6,365
Ending Cash Balance	$15,685	$18,291	$31,071	$34,708	$33,589	$37,394	$51,454	$56,457	$71,795	$78,160

Financial Ratios Table	Period 1	Period 2	Period 3	Period 4	Period 5	Period 6	Period 7	Period 8	Period 9	Period 10
Working Capital Ratios:										
Current Ratio	2.71	3.30	3.87	4.55	4.06	4.75	5.41	6.21	6.95	7.86
Quick Ratio	1.94	2.16	3.11	3.41	3.30	3.61	4.65	5.06	6.18	6.72
Working Capital to Total Assets	0.23	0.30	0.36	0.42	0.35	0.41	0.47	0.52	0.57	0.62
Receivables Turnover	12.00	12.00	12.00	12.00	12.00	12.00	12.00	12.00	12.00	12.00
Inventory Turnover	12.00	6.00	12.00	6.00	12.00	6.00	12.00	6.00	12.00	6.00
Operating Ratios:										
Times Interest Earned	13.29	13.31	13.38	13.74	13.85	13.82	13.93	14.33	14.47	14.91
Sales to Operational Assets	2.13	2.29	2.46	2.67	2.13	2.29	2.46	2.67	2.91	3.20
Return on Total Assets	33.26%	32.10%	30.98%	30.43%	29.23%	27.99%	26.96%	26.44%	25.38%	24.79%
Return on Equity	64.29%	59.29%	55.09%	51.90%	48.04%	44.35%	41.48%	39.39%	36.76%	34.87%
Investment Turnover	1.24	1.19	1.14	1.09	1.04	1.00	0.96	0.91	0.87	0.82
Financial Leverage	31.03%	27.19%	24.11%	21.47%	18.81%	16.36%	14.51%	12.96%	11.38%	10.08%

The start of the first period is stored in cell B2 as the integer 0. Periods that follow are stored as the previous period plus 1. For example, the formula for Period 1 is:

=B2+1

The formula for Period 2 is:

=C2+1

and so on.

The Period identifiers in the Balance Sheet, Common Size Balance Sheet, Income Statement, Cash Flow Statement, and Financial Ratios Table schedules use similar formulas.

You enter the following variables in the Forecasting Inputs schedule for the balance sheet and cash flow statement:

Cash & Equivalents. The value you enter for Cash & Equivalents is the starting cash and cash equivalents, the dollar total of all the cash held at the beginning of the forecasting period.

Yield on Cash & Equivalents. The Yield on Cash & Equivalents value is the period interest rate you anticipate earning on the cash and equivalents held at the beginning of the period. The model estimates the period interest income by multiplying the cash and equivalents balance by the yield on cash and equivalents.

Accounts Receivable. The value you enter for Accounts Receivable is the starting accounts receivable balance, the balance at the beginning of the forecasting horizon, excluding any allowance for uncollectible amounts.

# of Periods of Sales in A/R. The value you enter for # of Periods of Sales in A/R, or number of periods of sales in accounts receivable, is the number of periods or the fraction of a period for which sales are held in accounts receivable. If accounts receivable typically amount to about 30 days of sales and you use months as your forecasting periods, you hold one period of sales in accounts receivable. Alternatively, if accounts receivable typically amount to about 30 days of sales and you use years as your forecasting periods, you hold one-twelfth of a period of sales in accounts receivable.

Inventory. The Inventory value is the starting inventory balance, the total dollar amount of the inventory purchased for resale or manufactured for resale and held at the beginning of the forecasting horizon.

Inventory Purchased/Produced. The Inventory Purchased/Produced value is the dollar total of items purchased or produced over the period.

Other Current Assets. The Other Current Assets starting balance is the dollar total of any other current assets with which you begin the forecasting horizon. These other current assets might include prepaid expenses, short-term investments, and deposits made with vendors.

Chgs in Other Current Assets. The value for Chgs in Other Current Assets, or changes in other current assets for the period, is the dollar total of increases or decreases in the accounts included in the starting Other Current Assets balance.

Plant, Property, & Equipment. The starting Plant, Property, & Equipment balance is the dollar total of the fixed assets. This amount includes such items as realty, manufacturing equipment, and furniture.

Chgs in P, P, & E. The Chgs in P, P, & E value is the dollar total of decreases or increases in the plant, property, and equipment accounts for the period. Increases in these accounts probably stem from purchases of additional fixed assets. Decreases in these accounts probably stem from disposal of assets.

Accumulated Depreciation. The starting Accumulated Depreciation balance represents the depreciation expenses charged to date on the assets identified in the starting Plant, Property, & Equipment balance.

Chgs in Accum. Depreciation. The Chgs in Accum. Depreciation value is the dollar total of increases and decreases in the accumulated depreciation account for the period. Increases in the accumulated depreciation balance probably stem from the current period depreciation expense. Decreases in the accumulated depreciation balance probably stem from removing the accumulated depreciation attributed to a fixed asset that you disposed of.

Other Noncurrent Assets. The starting Other Noncurrent Assets balance is the dollar total of all other noncurrent assets held at the start of the forecasting period. Other noncurrent assets might include copyrights, patents, and goodwill.

Chgs in Other Noncurrent Assets. The Chgs in Other Noncurrent Assets value is the dollar total increase or decrease for the period in the accounts included in the starting Other Noncurrent Assets balance.

Accounts Payable. The starting Accounts Payable balance is the dollar total of amounts owed vendors for inventory at the start of the forecasting horizon. This template calculates future Accounts Payable balances, based on the cost of sales volumes.

 # Periods Cost of Sales in A/P. The # Periods Cost of Sales in A/P is the number of periods or the fraction of a period for which the cost of sales is held in accounts payable. If accounts payable typically amount to about 30 days of cost of sales and you use months as your forecasting periods, you hold one period of cost of sales in accounts payable. Alternatively, if accounts payable typically amount to about 30 days of cost of sales and you use years as your forecasting periods, you hold one-twelfth of a period of cost of sales in accounts payable.

Accrued Expenses. The starting Accrued Expenses balance is the dollar total of amounts owed vendors for operating expenses at the start of the forecasting horizon. This template calculates future Accrued Expenses balances, based on the operating expenses levels.

 # Periods Operating Expenses in A/E. The # Periods Operating Expenses in A/E value is the number of periods or the fraction of a period for which operating expenses are held in accrued expenses. If accrued expenses typically amount to about 30 days of operating expenses and you use months as your forecasting periods, you hold one period of operating expenses in accrued expenses. Alternatively, if accrued expenses typically amount to about 30 days of operating expenses and you use years as your forecasting periods, you hold one-twelfth of a period of operating expenses in accrued expenses.

Other Current Liabilities. The Other Current Liabilities starting balance is the dollar total of all other current liabilities held at the start of the forecasting period. Other current liabilities might include income tax payable, product warranty liability, and the current portion of a long-term liability.

Chgs in Other Current Liabilities. The Chgs in Other Current Liabilities value is the dollar total of increases or decreases for the period in the accounts included in the starting Other Current Liabilities balance.

Long-Term Liabilities. The starting Long-Term Liabilities balance is the dollar total of debt that will be paid back sometime after the next year.

Chgs in Long-Term Liabilities. The Chgs in Long-Term Liabilities value is the increase or decrease for the period in the outstanding long-term debt. You need to include the principal component of debt service payments as negative amounts because they decrease the amount of long-term liability.

Other Noncurrent Liabilities. The Other Noncurrent Liabilities starting balance is the dollar total of all other noncurrent liabilities held at the start of the forecasting period. These might include deferred income tax, employee pension plan liabilities, and capitalized lease obligations.

Chgs in Other Noncurrent Liabilities. The Chgs in Other Noncurrent Liabilities value is the dollar total of increases or decreases for the period in the accounts included in the starting Other Noncurrent Liabilities balance.

Owner Equity. The Owner Equity starting balance is the dollar total of the capital originally contributed by owners and the earnings retained by the business at the start of the forecasting horizon.

Chgs in Owner Equity. The Chgs in Owner Equity value is the dollar total of increases for the period in Owner Equity, other than those stemming from the profits of a business and all decreases in Owner Equity. For example, increases in the Owner Equity balance might result from additional offerings of common or preferred stock and treasury stock transactions; decreases in the Owner Equity balance might result from dividends and other distributions to stockholders.

For the Income Statement and Cash Flow Statement, you need to enter the following variables.

Sales Revenue. The Sales Revenue values represent the forecasted sales revenues generated by the business over each period of the forecasting horizon.

Cost of Sales. The Cost of Sales values represent the forecasted costs of the inventory sold for the forecasting horizon.

Cost Center 1, 2, and 3 Costs. The operating expenses for cost centers 1, 2, and 3 represent the operating expenses for the forecasting horizon. These figures might be three expense classifications related to operating the business, or they might be the total expenses for three groups of expenses.

Interest Expense. The Interest Expense values represent the period interest expenses of carrying any debt related to the business.

Marginal Income Tax Rate. The Marginal Income Tax Rate value is the percentage that, when multiplied by the operating profit (or loss), calculates the income tax expense (or savings).

Unless you turn off cell protection, input cells in the Forecasting Inputs schedule are the only cells into which you can enter data.

Balance Sheet   The Balance Sheet schedule has 20 rows with calculated data. The first row contains the text label Period.

Period. As in the Forecasting Inputs schedule, the Period identifier numbers the periods for which values are forecasted.

The identifier representing the start of the first period is stored in B40 as the integer 0. Periods that follow are stored as the previous period plus 1. For example, the formula for Period 1 is:

=B40+1

The formula for Period 2 is:

=C40+1

and so on.

Cash & Equivalents. The Cash & Equivalents figures show the projected cash on hand at the end of each of the forecasting periods.

The starting balance is the value you enter in the Forecasting Inputs schedule. The balance for the first and subsequent periods is pulled from the Cash Flow Statement schedule, where it is calculated.

Accounts Receivable. The Accounts Receivable figures show the net receivables held as of the end of each forecasting period.

The starting balance is the value you enter in the Forecasting Inputs schedule. The balance for the first and subsequent periods is based on the Sales Revenue and the # Periods of Sales in A/R values you enter in the Forecasting Inputs schedule. For example, the formula for the first period is:

=C7*C31

The formula for the second period is:

=D7*D31

and so on.

Inventory. The Inventory values show the dollar total of the inventory held at the end of each forecasting period.

The starting balance is the value you enter in the Forecasting Inputs schedule. The balance for the first and subsequent periods is the previous period balance plus any inventory purchases or production costs minus any cost of sales. For example, the first-period formula is:

=B45+C9–C32

The formula for the second period is:

=C45+D9–D32

and so on.

Other Current Assets. The Other Current Assets figures show the dollar total of the other current assets held at the end of each forecasting period.

The starting balance for Other Current Assets is the value you enter in the Forecasting Inputs schedule. The balance for the first and subsequent periods is the previous balance plus the change in the balance. For example, the formula for the first period is:

=B46+C11

The formula for the second period is:

=C46+D11

and so on.

Total Current Assets. The Total Current Assets figures show the dollar total of the current assets at the end of each of the forecasting horizons.

The balance at any time is the sum of Cash & Equivalents, Accounts Receivable, Inventory, and Other Current Assets. For example, the formula for the starting Total Current Assets balance is:

=SUM(B43:B46)

The formula for the first period is:

=SUM(C43:C46)

and so on.

Plant, Property, & Equipment. The Plant, Property, & Equipment figures show the original dollar cost of the plant, property, and equipment at the end of each forecasting horizon.

The starting Plant, Property, & Equipment balance is the value you enter in the Forecasting Inputs schedule. The balance for the first and subsequent periods is the previous balance plus any additions to the plant, property, and equipment accounts. For example, the formula for the first period is:

=B48+C13

The formula for the second period is:

=C48+D13

and so on.

Accumulated Depreciation. The Accumulated Depreciation figures show the cumulative depreciation expenses charged through the current period for the plant, property, and equipment.

The starting balance is the value you enter in the Forecasting Inputs schedule. The balance for the first and subsequent periods is the previous balance minus the current period's changes in accumulated depreciation. For example, the formula for the first period is:

=B49–C15

The formula for the second period is:

=C49–D15

and so on. Because the accumulated depreciation is shown as a negative amount, you need to subtract the positive number pulled from the forecasting inputs.

Net Plant, Property, & Equipment. The Net Plant, Property, & Equipment figures show the difference between Plant, Property, & Equipment and Accumulated Depreciation at the end of each of the forecasting horizons.

For example, the formula for the starting balance is:

=B48+B49

The formula for the first period is:

=C48+C49

and so on. Because the Accumulated Depreciation balance is shown as a negative amount, you simply add these two amounts in the formula for the Net Plant, Property, & Equipment amount.

Other Noncurrent Assets. The Other Noncurrent Assets figures show the dollar total of any other noncurrent assets held at the end of each of the forecasting periods.

The starting balance is the value you enter in the Forecasting Inputs schedule. The balance for the first and subsequent periods is the previous period balance plus the change in the account in the current period. For example, the formula for the first period is:

=B51+C17

The formula for the second period is:

=C51+D17

and so on.

Total Assets. The Total Assets figures show the dollar total of all the assets held at the end of the forecasting periods.

The balance at any time is the sum of Current Assets; Net Plant, Property, & Equipment; and Other Noncurrent Assets. For example, the formula for the starting balance is:

=B47+B50+B51

The formula for the second period is:

=C47+C50+C51

and so on.

Accounts Payable. The Accounts Payable figures show the debt that is related to the cost of sales outstanding at the end of each forecasting period.

The starting balance is the value you enter in the Forecasting Inputs schedule. The balance for the first and subsequent periods is Cost of Sales for the period times # of Periods of Cost of Sales in A/P. For example, the formula for the first period is:

=C19*C32

The formula for the second period is:

=D19*D32

and so on.

Accrued Expenses. The Accrued Expenses figures show the debt that is related to the operating expenses outstanding at the end of each forecasting period.

The starting balance is the value you enter in the Forecasting Inputs schedule. The balance for the first and subsequent periods is the operating expenses times # of Periods Operating Expenses in A/E. For example, the formula for the first period is:

=C21*SUM(C33:C35)

The formula for the second period is:

=D21*SUM(D33:D35)

and so on.

Other Current Liabilities. The Other Current Liabilities figures show the dollar total of other debts outstanding at the end of the forecasting periods that will be paid within the current year or business cycle.

The starting balance is the value you enter in the Forecasting Inputs schedule. The balance for the first and subsequent periods is the previous balance plus the change in the current period. For example, the formula for the first period is:

=B59+C23

The formula for the second period is:

=C59+D23

and so on.

Total Current Liabilities. The Total Current Liabilities figures show the dollar total of all the current liabilities at the end of each of the forecasting periods.

The balance at any time is the sum of Accounts Payable, Accrued Expenses, and Other Current Liabilities. For example, the formula for the starting balance is:

=SUM(B57:B59)

The formula for the first period is:

=SUM(C57:C59)

and so on.

Long-Term Liabilities. The Long-Term Liabilities figures show the dollar total of the long-term outstanding debt at the end of each forecasting period.

The starting balance is the value you enter in the Forecasting Inputs schedule. The balance for the first and subsequent periods is the previous balance plus any changes in the Long-Term Liabilities balance in the current period. For example, the formula for the first period is:

=B62+C25

The formula for the second period is:

=C62+D25

and so on.

Other Noncurrent Liabilities. The Other Noncurrent Liabilities figures show the dollar total of any other noncurrent outstanding debt at the end of each forecasting period.

The starting balance is the value you enter in the Forecasting Inputs schedule. The balance for the first and subsequent periods is the previous period balance plus the change in the current period. For example, the formula for the first period is:

=B63+C27

The formula for the second period is:

=C63+D27

and so on.

Total Noncurrent Liabilities. The Total Noncurrent Liabilities figures show the dollar totals of the long-term debt and the other noncurrent outstanding debt at the end of each of the forecasting periods.

The balance at any time is the sum of Long-Term Liabilities and Other Noncurrent Liabilities. For example, the formula for the starting balance is:

=B62+B63

The formula for the first period is:

=C62+C63

and so on.

Owner Equity. The Owner Equity figures show the dollar totals of the owner equity accounts at the end of each forecasting period.

The starting balance is the value you enter in the Forecasting Inputs schedule. The balance for the first and subsequent periods is the previous period balance plus Net Income After Taxes for the period plus other adjustments, such as additional capital contributions and dividends. For example, the formula for the first period is:

=B65+C29+C116

The formula for the second period is:

=C65+D29+D116

and so on.

Total Liabilities and Owner Equity. The Total Liabilities and Owner Equity figures show the dollar totals of Current Liabilities, Noncurrent Liabilities, and Owner Equity at the end of each forecasting period.

For example, the formula for the starting balance is:

=B60+B64+B65

The formula for the first period is:

=C60+C64+C65

and so on.

> **HINT:** The Total Assets value should equal the Total Liabilities and Owner Equity value. If they differ, your model contains an error.

Common Size Balance Sheet

The Common Size Balance Sheet schedule lists, in the balance sheet format, what percentage of the total assets each individual asset represents and what percentage of the total liabilities and owner equity each individual liability and the owner equity represents. When you compare these percentages with those of business peers, you can see the relative financial strength or weakness of your business. Trends in the percentages over time can indicate improvement or deterioration in the overall financial condition of your business.

The Common Size Balance Sheet schedule has 19 rows with calculated data that express line-item amounts as percentages of the total. For the asset side of the balance sheet, assets are expressed as a percentage of the total assets. For the creditor and owner equity side of the balance sheet, equities are expressed as a percentage of the total liabilities and owner equity. The formulas for all rows except Total Assets and Total Liabilities and Owner Equity simply convert the Balance Sheet values to percentages. For example, the Cash & Equivalents formula for the first period is:

    =B43/B$52

The formula for the second period is:

    =C43/C$52

and so on. All asset percentages are derived from dividing by total assets, which explains why the absolute reference to row $52 is used in all asset formulas. Similarly, the absolute reference to row $66 appears in all formulas in the liabilities and equity formulas.

Total Assets. The formula for the Total Assets percentage at any time is the sum of the Current Assets; the Net Plant, Property, & Equipment; and the Other Noncurrent Assets percentages. The result always equals 100 percent. For example, the formula for the starting Total Assets percentage is:

=B76+B79+B80

The formula for the first period is:

=C76+C79+C80

and so on.

Total Liabilities and Owner Equity. The formula for the Total Liabilities and Owner Equity percentage at any time is the sum of the Current Liabilities, the Noncurrent Liabilities, and Owner Equity percentages. The result always is 100 percent. For example, the formula for the starting Total Liabilities and Owner Equity percentage is:

=B89+B93+B94

The formula for the first period is:

=C89+C93+C94

and so on.

Income Statement The Income Statement schedule has 14 rows of calculated data. The first row contains the text label Period.

Period. As in other schedules, the Period identifier numbers the periods for which values are calculated. The first period is stored in cell C99 as the integer 1. Periods that follow are stored as the previous period plus 1. For example, the formula for Period 2 is:

=C99+1

The formula for Period 3 is:

=D99+1

and so on.

267

Sales Revenue. The Sales Revenue figures are the estimates you enter in the Forecasting Inputs schedule. The amount for the period is the value you enter in the Forecasting Inputs schedule.

Cost of Sales. The Cost of Sales figures are the Cost of Sales estimates you enter in the Forecasting Inputs schedule.

Gross Margin. The Gross Margin figures show the amounts left over from the sales proceeds after subtracting Cost of Sales. Subtracting your other expenses from the Gross Margin amount gives you your profit figure.

The Gross Margin formula is Sales Revenue for the period minus Cost of Sales. For example, the formula for the first period is:

```
=C100+C101
```

The formula for the second period is:

```
=D100+D101
```

and so on. Notice that because the Cost of Sales figures are pulled into the Income Statement schedule as negative amounts, the Gross Margin formula simply adds the Sales Revenue figure to the negative Cost of Sales figure.

Operating Expenses—Cost Centers 1, 2, and 3. The Operating Expenses figures for Cost Centers 1, 2, and 3 show the amount for each operating expense classification or category that you enter in the Forecasting Inputs schedule.

Total Operating Expenses. The Total Operating Expenses figures show the sums of the operating expenses you enter in the Forecasting Inputs schedule for the three operating expense categories or classifications.

The total for each period is the sum of the operating expenses for Cost Centers 1, 2, and 3. For example, the formula for the first period is:

```
=SUM(C105:C107)
```

The formula for the second period is:

=SUM(D105:D107)

and so on.

Operating Income. The Operating Income figures show the sales dollar amounts left after paying the cost of sales and the operating expenses. The Operating Income figures represent the amounts that go toward paying your financing expenses and income tax, and the amount that constitutes your profits.

The amount for each period is the Gross Margin figure for the period minus the Total Operating Expenses figure. For example, the formula for the first period is:

=C102−C108

The formula for the second period is:

=D102−D108

and so on.

Interest Income. The Interest Income figures show the earnings from investing the cash of the business.

The amount for each period is the beginning Cash & Equivalents balance from the Forecasting Inputs times the period Yield on Cash & Equivalents. For example, the formula for the first period is:

=B43*C5

The formula for the second period is:

=C43*D5

and so on.

Interest Expense. The Interest Expense figures show the costs of using borrowed funds for operations and asset purchases.

The amount for each period is the value you enter in the Forecasting Inputs schedule.

Net Income (Loss) Before Taxes. The Net Income (Loss) Before Taxes figures show the amount of operating income left after receiving any interest income and paying any interest expense.

The amount for each period is the Operating Income figure for the period plus the Interest Income figure for the period minus the Interest Expense figure for the period. For example, the formula for the first period is:

=C109+C111−C112

The formula for the second period is:

=D109+D111−D112

and so on.

Income Tax Expenses (Savings). The Income Tax Expenses (Savings) figures show the income tax expenses (or savings) that use the calculated Net Income (Loss) Before Taxes figures and the Marginal Income Tax Rate figures you forecasted in the Forecasting Inputs schedule. Notice that the model calculates a current period savings in income taxes when there is a net loss before taxes. This might be the case when a current period loss is carried back to a prior period or when the current period loss is consolidated with the current period income of related businesses. Basically, then, the model assumes that a net loss before income taxes results in a current period tax refund—that is, an overall tax savings—because you can deduct a loss in one business from the profits of another business. However, if a current period loss does not result in a current period income tax savings, you need to modify the formula, as described in the section of this chapter titled "Customizing the Template."

The amount for each period is the Net Income (Loss) Before Taxes multiplied by the Marginal Income Tax Rate figure. For example, the formula for the first period is:

    =C37*C113

The formula for the second period is:

    =D37*D113

and so on.

Net Income (Loss) After Taxes. The Net Income (Loss) After Taxes figures calculate the after-tax profits of operating the business.

The amount for each period is the Net Income (Loss) Before Taxes figure minus the Income Tax Expenses (Savings) figure. For example, the formula for the first period is:

    =C113–C115

The formula for the second period is:

    =D113–D115

and so on.

Common Size Income Statement

The Common Size Income Statement schedule lists, in income statement format, what percentage of the total sales revenue each income statement line item represents. When you compare these percentages against those of business peers, you can see the relative financial performance of your business. Trends in the percentages over the forecasting horizon can indicate improvement or deterioration in the financial performance of your business.

The Common Size Income Statement schedule has 13 rows of calculated data that express the component line-item amount for each period as a percentage of the sales revenue figure for the period. The formulas for all rows except Sales Revenue simply convert the Income Statement values to percentages.

Sales Revenue. The Sales Revenue figures add the Cost of Sales, Total Operating Expenses, Interest Income, Interest Expense, Income Tax Expenses (Savings), and Net Income (Loss) After Taxes percentages. The results always equal 100 percent.

The Sales Revenue percentage adds the expense and profit percentages. Those expenses shown as negative amounts, therefore, are subtracted. The formula for the first period is:

    =–C121+C125+C126+C127–C131+C132+C133

The formula for the second period is:

    =–D121+D125+D126+D127–D131+D132+D133

and so on.

Cash Flow Statement

The Cash Flow Statement schedule has 18 rows of calculated data.

Period. As in other schedules, the Period identifier numbers the periods for which values are calculated. The first period is stored in cell C141 as the integer 1. Periods that follow are stored as the previous period plus 1. For example, the formula for Period 2 is:

    =C141+1

The formula for Period 3 is:

    =D141+1

and so on.

Beginning Cash Balance. The Beginning Cash Balance figures show the forecasted cash and equivalents balance at the start of each forecasting period.

The starting balance is the value you enter in the Forecasting Inputs schedule. For subsequent periods, the Beginning Cash Balance is the previous period's Ending Cash Balance.

Net Income After Taxes. The Net Income After Taxes figures show the amounts calculated in the Income Statement schedule as the business profits for each forecasting period.

Addback of Depreciation. The Addback of Depreciation figures show the change in the accumulated depreciation balance for each forecasting period. Normally, this change stems from the period depreciation expense; it must be added back into the Net Income After Taxes figure because the depreciation expense uses no cash.

The depreciation added back for each period is the value you enter in the Forecasting Inputs schedule as the change in accumulated depreciation.

Accounts Payable Financing. The Accounts Payable Financing figures show the change in the Accounts Payable balance for the period. Increases in this balance result when the cost of sales expense paid during the period is lower than the expense incurred. Decreases in this balance result when the cost of sales expense paid is higher than the expense incurred. By recognizing the changes in this account balance, the model adjusts for differences between the income statement's accrual-based accounting of cost of sales expenses and the actual cash disbursements for costs of sales expenses.

The Accounts Payable Financing figure for each period is the difference between the Accounts Payable balance at the end of the previous period and the balance at the end of the current period. For example, the formula for the first period is:

    =C57–B57

The formula for the second period is:

    =D57–C57

and so on.

Accrued Expenses Financing. The Accrued Expenses Financing figures show the change in the accrued expenses balance for the period. Increases in this balance result when the operating expense paid during the period is lower than the expense incurred. Decreases in this balance result when the operating expense paid during the period is higher than the expense incurred. By recognizing the changes in this account balance, the model adjusts for differences between the Income Statement's accrual-based accounting of operating expenses and the actual cash disbursements for operating expenses.

The Accrued Expenses Financing figure for each period is the difference between the Accrued Expenses balance at the end of the previous period and the balance at the end of the current period. For example, the formula for the first period is:

=C58–B58

The formula for the second period is:

=D58–C58

and so on.

Other Current Liabilities Financing. The Other Current Liabilities Financing figures show the change in the Other Current Liabilities balance for the period. This amount increases when, either directly or indirectly, cash is generated by borrowing. This amount decreases when, either directly or indirectly, cash is used to pay off short-term borrowing.

The Other Current Liabilities Financing figure for each period is the difference between the Other Current Liabilities balance at the end of the previous period and the balance at the end of the current period. For example, the formula for the first period is:

=C59–B59

The formula for the second period is:

    =D59–C59

and so on.

Long-Term Liabilities Financing. The Long-Term Liabilities Financing figures show the changes in the long-term liabilities amount for the period. This balance increases when, either directly or indirectly, cash is generated by long-term borrowing. This amount decreases when, either directly or indirectly, cash is used to pay off long-term borrowing.

The Long-Term Liabilities Financing figure for each period is the difference between the Long-Term Liabilities balance at the end of the previous period and the balance at the end of the current period. For example, the formula for the first period is:

    =C62–B62

The formula for the second period is:

    =D62–C62

and so on.

Other Noncurrent Liabilities Financing. The Other Noncurrent Liabilities Financing figures show the changes in the Other Noncurrent Liabilities balance for the period. This amount increases when, either directly or indirectly, cash is generated by other long-term borrowing. This amount decreases when, either directly or indirectly, cash is used to pay off other long-term borrowing.

The Other Noncurrent Liabilities Financing figure for each period is the difference between the Other Noncurrent Liabilities balance at the end of the previous period and the balance at the end of the current period. For example, the formula for the first period is:

    =C63–B63

The formula for the second period is:

=D63–C63

and so on.

Accounts Receivable Investments. The Accounts Receivable Investments figures show the change in the Accounts Receivable balance for each forecasting period. This amount increases when the sales revenue collected during the period is less than the revenue recorded. This amount decreases when the sales revenue collected during the period is more than recorded. By recognizing the changes in this account balance, the model adjusts for differences between the income statement's accrual-based accounting of sales revenues and the actual cash collections for sales.

The Accounts Receivable Investments figure for each period is the difference between the Accounts Receivable balance at the end of the previous period and the balance at the end of the current period. For example, the formula for the first period is:

=C44–B44

The formula for the second period is:

=D44–C44

and so on.

Inventory Investments. The Inventory Investments figures show the change in the inventory balance for each forecasting period. This amount increases when the inventory sold is less than the inventory acquired. This amount decreases when the inventory sold is more than the inventory acquired. By recognizing the changes in this account balance, the model recognizes the cash effects of changing inventory balances.

The Inventory Investments figure for each period is the difference between the Inventory balance at the end of the previous period and the balance at the end of the current period. For example, the formula for the first period is:

    =C45–B45

The formula for the second period is:

    =D45–C45

and so on.

Other Current Assets Investments. The Other Current Assets Investments figures show the changes in the Other Current Assets balance for the period. This amount increases when, either directly or indirectly, cash is used to acquire current assets. This amount decreases when indirectly or directly cash is generated by converting current assets to cash.

The Other Current Assets Investments figure for each period is the difference between the Other Current Assets balance at the end of the previous period and the balance at the end of the current period. For example, the formula for the first period is:

    =C46–B46

The formula for the second period is:

    =D46–C46

and so on.

Plant, Property, & Equip Investments. The Plant, Property, & Equip Investments figures show the change in the Plant, Property, & Equipment balance for the period. This amount increases when, either directly or indirectly, cash is used to acquire plants, property, and equipment. This amount decreases when, either directly or indirectly, cash is generated by converting plants, property, and equipment to cash.

The Plant, Property, & Equip Investments figure for each period is the difference between the Plant, Property, & Equipment balance at the end of the previous period and the balance at the end of the current period. For example, the formula for the first period is:

=C48–B48

The formula for the second period is:

=D48–C48

and so on.

Other Noncurrent Assets Investments. The Other Noncurrent Assets Investments figures show the changes in the Other Noncurrent Assets balance for the period. This amount increases when, either directly or indirectly, cash is used to acquire other noncurrent assets. This amount decreases when, either directly or indirectly, cash is generated by converting other noncurrent assets to cash.

The Other Noncurrent Assets Investments figure for each period is the difference between the Other Noncurrent Assets balance at the end of the previous period and the balance at the end of the current period. For example, the formula for the first period is:

=C51–B51

The formula for the second period is:

=D51–C51

and so on.

Other Owner Equity Changes. The Other Owner Equity Changes figures show the cash flows stemming from any additional capital contributions made by the owners to the business or from dividends and other distributions made by the business to the owners.

The Other Owner Equity Changes figure is the value you enter in the Forecasting Inputs schedule. The Other Owner Equity Changes

9: Financial Statements with Ratios Template

figures are pulled into the Uses of Cash section as negative values because a positive change in the owner equity, such as an additional capital contribution, doesn't use cash but provides cash; and a negative change in the owner equity, such as a dividend, does use cash.

Net Cash Generated (Used). The Net Cash Generated (Used) figures show the total cash flow for each period of the forecasting horizon, based on the listed sources and uses of cash.

The amount for each period is the sources of cash for the period less the uses of cash for the period. For example, the formula for the first period is:

=SUM(C145:C151)−SUM(C154:C159)

The formula for the second period is:

=SUM(D145:D151)−SUM(D154:D159)

and so on.

Ending Cash Balance. The Ending Cash Balance figures show the forecasted cash and equivalents balance at the end of each period.

The balance is the Beginning Cash Balance figure for the period plus the Net Cash Generated (Used) figure for the period. For example, the formula for the first period is:

=C142+C160

The formula for the second period is:

=D142+D160

and so on.

Financial Ratios Table

The Financial Ratios Table has 12 rows of calculated data.

Period. As in other schedules, the Period identifier numbers the periods for which values are calculated. The first period is stored in cell

279

C165 as the integer 1. Periods that follow are stored as the previous period plus 1. For example, the formula for Period 2 is:

    =C165+1

The formula for Period 3 is:

    =D165+1

and so on.

Current Ratio. The Current Ratio figures show the ratio of current assets to current liabilities. The current ratio provides one measure of a business's ability to meet its short-term obligations. Generally, a current ratio of 2 or higher indicates an ability to meet financial commitments.

The Current Ratio figure for each period is the Total Current Assets figure from the Balance Sheet schedule divided by the Total Current Liabilities figure. For example, the formula for the first period is:

    =C47/C60

The formula for the second period is:

    =D47/D60

and so on.

Quick Ratio. The Quick Ratio figures show the ratio of the sum of the cash and equivalents plus the accounts receivable to the current liabilities. The quick ratio provides a more stringent measure of a business's ability to meet its short-term financial obligations than other ratios. Generally, a quick ratio of 1 or higher indicates an ability to meet financial commitments.

The Quick Ratio figure for each period is the sum of the Cash & Equivalents figure and the Accounts Receivable figure divided by the Total Current Liabilities figure. For example, the formula for the first period is:

    =(C43+C44)/C60

The formula for the second period is:

=(D43+D44)/D60

and so on.

Working Capital to Total Assets. The Working Capital to Total Assets figures show the ratio of working capital (the current assets minus the current liabilities) to the total assets. The Working Capital to Total Assets ratio is another measure of a firm's ability to meet its financial obligations and gives an indication as to the distribution of a business's assets into liquid and nonliquid resources.

The Working Capital to Total Assets ratio for each period is calculated by dividing the difference between the Current Assets and Current Liabilities figures by the Total Assets figure. For example, the formula for the first period is:

=(C47−C60)/C52

The formula for the second period is:

=(D47−D60)/D52

and so on.

Receivables Turnover. The Receivables Turnover figures show the ratio of sales to the accounts receivable balance. The Receivables Turnover ratio indicates the efficiency of sales collections. One problem with the measure as it's usually applied is that both credit and cash sales might be included in the ratio denominator. Two potential shortcomings exist with this approach. First, the presence of the cash sales might make the receivables collections appear more efficient than is the case. Also, mere changes in the mix of credit and cash sales might affect the ratio, even though the efficiency of the receivables collections process has not changed.

The Receivables Turnover figure for each period is calculated by dividing the Sales Revenue figure for the period by the Accounts Receivable balance outstanding at the end of the period. For example, the formula for the first period is:

=C100/C44

The formula for the second period is:

=D100/D44

and so on.

Inventory Turnover. The Inventory Turnover row shows the ratio of the cost of sales to the inventory balance. The Inventory Turnover ratio calculates how long inventory is held. It can indicate depleted or excessive inventory balances.

The Inventory Turnover ratio for each period is calculated by dividing the Cost of Sales figure for the period by the inventory held at the end of the period. For example, the formula for the first period is:

=−C101/C45

The formula for the second period is:

=−D101/D45

and so on.

Times Interest Earned. The Times Interest Earned row shows the ratio of the sum of the net income after taxes plus the interest income to the interest expense. The ratio indicates the relative ease with which the business is paying its financing costs.

The Times Interest Earned ratio for each period is calculated by dividing the sum of the Operating Income and Interest Income figures from the Income Statement schedule by the Interest Expense figure. For example, the formula for the first period is:

=(C109+C111)/C112

The formula for the second period is:

=(D109+D111)/D112

and so on.

Sales to Operational Assets. The Sales to Operational Assets row shows the ratio of sales revenue to net plant, property, and equipment. The ratio indicates the efficiency with which a business uses its operational assets to generate sales revenue.

The Sales to Operational Assets ratio for each period is the Sales Revenue figure you enter in the Forecasting Inputs schedule divided by the Net Plant, Property, & Equipment figure from the Balance Sheet schedule. For example, the formula for the first period is:

=C100/C50

The formula for the second period is:

=D100/D50

and so on.

Return on Total Assets. The Return on Total Assets row shows the ratio of the sum of the net income after taxes plus the interest expense to the total assets for each period. The ratio indicates the overall operating profitability of the business, expressed as a rate of return on the business assets.

The formula for the first period is:

=(C116+C112)/C52

The formula for the second period is:

=(D116+D112)/D52

and so on.

Return on Equity. The Return on Equity row shows the ratio of the net income after taxes to the owner equity for each period. The ratio indicates the profitability of the business as an investment of the owners.

The Return on Equity ratio for each period is the Net Income (Loss) After Taxes figure from the Income Statement schedule divided by the Owner Equity figure from the Balance Sheet schedule. For example, the formula for the first period is:

=C116/C65

The formula for the second period is:

=D116/D65

and so on.

Investment Turnover. The Investment Turnover row shows the ratio of the sales revenue to the total assets. The ratio, like the Sales to Operational Assets ratio, indicates the efficiency with which a business uses its assets (in this case, its total assets) to generate sales.

The Investment Turnover ratio for each period is the Sales Revenue figure you enter in the Forecasting Inputs schedule divided by the Total Assets figure from the Balance Sheet schedule. For example, the formula for the first period is:

=C100/C52

The formula for the second period is:

=D100/D52

and so on.

Financial Leverage. The Financial Leverage row shows the difference between the return on the owners equity and the return on the total assets. The ratio indicates the increase or decrease in an equity return as a result of borrowing. A positive value indicates an improvement in the return on owner equity by using financial leverage; a negative value indicates a deterioration in the return on owner equity.

The Financial Leverage figure for each period is the Return on Total Assets figure minus the Return on Equity figure. For example, the formula for the first period is:

=C176–C175

The formula for the second period is:

=D176–D175

and so on.

Entering Your Own Data

To enter your own data in the financial statements with ratios template, use the following steps. Enter positive balances or increases as positive amounts, and enter negative balances or decreases as negative amounts.

1. Load FINANCLS.XLS from the templates disk. (The template initially contains the default inputs shown in Figure 9-1.)

2. Enter the Cash & Equivalents balance for the start of the forecasting horizon.

3. Enter the forecasted period yield that you expect the cash and equivalents to deliver. (You use this value to estimate interest income. If you do not want to include interest income in your model, you can enter the forecasted period yield as 0.)

4. Enter the accounts receivable balance for the start of the forecasting horizon.

5. Enter the number of periods of sales in accounts receivable. (For example, if you forecast in months and you estimate that your accounts receivable balance typically amounts to about one month of sales, enter 1.)

6. Enter the dollar amount of the inventory held at the start of the forecasting horizon.

7. Enter the forecasted dollar amount of inventory purchased or produced for each period of the forecasting horizon.

8. Enter the amount of the other current assets held at the start of the forecasting horizon. This might include such items as prepaid expenses and vendor deposits.

9. Enter the amount of the change in the other current assets for each period of the forecasting horizon.

10. Enter the amount of the plant, property, and equipment at the start of the forecasting horizon.

11. Enter the amount of the change in the plant, property, and equipment for each period of the forecasting horizon.

12. Enter the amount of the accumulated depreciation on the plant, property, and equipment at the start of the forecasting horizon.

13. Enter the amount of the change in the accumulated depreciation for each period of the forecasting horizon. Increases in, or credits to, the accumulated depreciation balance probably stem from the period depreciation expenses. Decreases in, or debits to, the accumulated depreciation balance probably stem from removing the accumulated depreciation related to an asset being retired.

14. Enter the amount of the other noncurrent assets at the start of the period. This might include such items as copyrights, patents, and goodwill.

15. Enter the amount of the change in the other noncurrent assets for each period of the forecasting horizon.

16. Enter the amount of the accounts payable balance at the start of the forecasting horizon. (Remember that to add precision to the forecasts of accounts payable, the model assumes that accounts payable represent debt incurred for the cost of sales.)

17. Enter the number of periods of the cost of sales in accounts payable. (If you use large forecasting periods, such as quarters or years, you will probably want to enter this value as a fraction. For example, if you use years as your forecasting horizons and you usually have about one month of cost of sales as the accounts payable balance, you enter this input as =1/12, or 0.0833.)

18. Enter the amount of the accrued expenses balance at the start of the forecasting horizon. (Remember that to add precision to the forecasts of accrued expenses, the model assumes that accrued expenses represent debt incurred for operating expenses.)

19. Enter the number of periods of operating expenses in accrued expenses. (If you use large forecasting periods, such as quarters or years, you will probably want to enter this value as a fraction. For example, if you use years as your forecasting horizons and you usually have about half a month of operating expenses of sales as the accounts payable balance, you enter this input as =1/24, or 0.04166.)

20. Enter the amount of the other current liabilities at the start of the forecasting period. This might include such items as income tax payable and product warrant liability.

21. Enter the amount of the change in the other current liabilities for each period of the forecasting horizon.

22. Enter the amount of the long-term liabilities balance at the start of the forecasting horizon.

23. Enter the amount of the change in the long-term liabilities for each period of the forecasting horizon. These changes might include decreases stemming from the amortization of principal through debt service payments and increases stemming from additional funds provided by creditors.

24. Enter the amount of the other noncurrent liabilities at the start of the forecasting horizon.

25. Enter the amount of the change in the other noncurrent liabilities for each period of the forecasting horizon. These changes might include decreases stemming from the amortization of principal through debt service payments and increases stemming from additional funds provided by creditors.

26. Enter the amount of the owner equity balance at the start of the forecasting horizon.

27. Enter the amount of the change in the owner equity balance for each period of the forecasting horizon stemming from additional capital contributions, dividends, and other special distributions to owners. (Notice that changes to the owner equity balance resulting from the profit or loss for the period are calculated in the income statement; they are not entered.)

28. Enter the sales revenue forecasted for each period of the forecasting horizon.

29. Enter the cost of sales forecasted for each period of the forecasting horizon.

30. Enter those costs that fall into the first operating expense classification or category for each period of the forecasting horizon.

31. Enter those costs that fall into the second operating expense classification or category for each period of the forecasting horizon.

32. Enter those costs that fall into the third operating expense classification or category for each period of the forecasting horizon.

33. Enter the interest expense of carrying any debt used to fund operations or asset purchases.

34. Enter the marginal income tax rate that, when multiplied against the profit or loss for the period, calculates the income tax expense (or savings). (If you are interested only in calculating pretax profits and losses, enter this amount as 0.)

35. Calculate the template. (By default, the template calculation is set to manual because of the time required to calculate the model.)

36. Save your changes by saving them as a new file on the disk on which you plan to store any of the subsidiary worksheets that support this financial model.

37. Print the spreadsheet.

Customizing the Template

You can use the financial statements with ratios template for many business projections. However, you might want to change the template so that it more closely matches your requirements. For example, you can add text that describes the business and the forecasting horizon. You can increase or decrease the number of periods. For example, you can increase the number of periods to 12 if your periods are months and you want to forecast an entire year. Before you change anything on the template other than the forecasting inputs, unprotect the document.

Increasing the number of periods

To increase the number of periods, follow these steps:

1. Remove the borders from the last column.
2. Copy the current last column to the right as needed.
3. Replace the borders on the right.
4. Reinstate cell protection as needed.

Decreasing the number of periods

To decrease the number of periods, follow these steps:

1. Delete any unneeded column from the right side of the schedule.
2. Replace the borders on the right.
3. Reinstate cell protection as needed.

Microsoft Excel Small Business Consultant

Customizing the template for existing financial statements

If you want to perform financial ratio analysis on a set of existing financial statements, follow these steps:

1. Copy the contents of column C, from the row in the Forecasting Inputs schedule that contains the sales revenue forecast (row 31) through the last row of the ratios table, into column B.

2. Remove the columns for periods 1 through 10 (columns C through L), following the steps described above.

3. Delete the cash flow statement.

4. Add appropriate column headings as needed.

5. Reinstate cell protection as needed.

To use the modified template, enter the necessary balance sheet and income statement data into each of the unshaded cells in column B of the Forecasting Inputs schedule. (Typically, the "as of" date of the balance sheet and the ending date of the income statement period are the same.)

Calculating taxes for a current net loss before taxes

To calculate the income tax expense as 0 when there is a current period net loss before income taxes, follow these steps:

1. Edit the formula in the cell that calculates the income tax expense (or savings) for the first period (cell C115) so that it takes the maximum of the calculated expense amount or 0 by using the MAX function:

    =MAX(C37*C113,0)

2. Copy the formula into the rest of the cells in the forecasting horizon that calculate the income tax expense (or savings).

3. Edit the income statement line-item descriptions as needed.

4. Reinstate cell protection as needed.

9: Financial Statements with Ratios Template

Linking This Template to Others in the Toolkit

Other templates in this toolkit are specifically designed to provide data to the financial statements with ratios template. For example, you might construct an asset depreciation schedule that uses the straight-line depreciation convention for a $25,000 asset representing your entire plant, property, and equipment investment. Suppose that the asset will be depreciated over 10 years and that the salvage value is $5,000. Figure 9-2 shows the depreciation schedule constructed using the straight-line depreciation template. Also suppose that you use a bank loan to fund a portion of the asset purchase—a $10,000 note with a

Straight-Line Depreciation Calculation Inputs	
Original Cost	$25,000
Salvage Value	$5,000
Estimated Life	10

Straight-Line Depreciation Schedule			
Period	Period Depreciation	Accumulated Depreciation	Net Book Value
1	$2,000	$2,000	$23,000
2	$2,000	4,000	21,000
3	$2,000	6,000	19,000
4	$2,000	8,000	17,000
5	$2,000	10,000	15,000
6	$2,000	12,000	13,000
7	$2,000	14,000	11,000
8	$2,000	16,000	9,000
9	$2,000	18,000	7,000
10	$2,000	20,000	5,000
11	$0	20,000	5,000
12	$0	20,000	5,000
13	$0	20,000	5,000
14	$0	20,000	5,000
15	$0	20,000	5,000
16	$0	20,000	5,000
17	$0	20,000	5,000
18	$0	20,000	5,000
19	$0	20,000	5,000
20	$0	20,000	5,000

Figure 9-2. *The straight-line depreciation template, supplying a depreciation expense for a link.*

debt term of 10 years, an amortization term of 20 years, and an annual interest rate of 10 percent. Figure 9-3 shows the annual payments, the interest, the principal components of the payments, and the outstanding principal balances over the term of the debt.

However, rather than simply enter the forecasted depreciation, interest expense, and outstanding debt into the forecasting inputs schedule shown in Figure 9-4 on pages 295 through 299, you can link the cells that contain these variables to the subsidiary templates. If you wanted to construct such a link (assuming you have the files named DEPRECTN.XLS, which is the depreciation schedule shown in Figure 9-2, and AMORTIZE.XLS, which is the debt amortization schedule shown in Figure 9-3, both stored in the WINDOWS directory on your hard disk), you would do the following:

1. Load FINANCLS.XLS from the templates disk. (The template essentially contains the inputs shown in Figure 9-1, with two exceptions: the changes in the plant, property, and equipment balances.)

2. Enter the amount of asset depreciation for the first period by entering the following formula into cell C15:

    ='C:\WINDOWS\DEPRECTN.XLS'!$C$11

    DEPRECTN.XLS supplies the period depreciation expense, which is the amount you're forecasting as the period asset depreciation. Cell C11 in that file is the cell that contains the first period depreciation expense. In the same way, you can enter the depreciation expense for periods 2 through 10.

3. Enter the amount of interest expense for the first period by entering the following formula into cell C36:

    ='C:\WINDOWS\AMORTIZE.XLS'!$D$12

    AMORTIZE.XLS supplies the interest component of the first payment, which is the amount you're forecasting as the interest expense. Cell D12 in that file is the cell that contains the interest

Fixed Interest Rate Amortization Inputs	
Principal	$10,000
Debt Term	10
Amortize Term	20
Interest Rate	10.00%

Fixed Interest Rate Amortization Schedule			
Period	Total Payment	Interest Component	Principal Component	Principal Balance
1	$1,175	$1,000	$175	$9,825
2	1,175	983	192	9,633
3	1,175	963	211	9,422
4	1,175	942	232	9,190
5	1,175	919	256	8,934
6	1,175	893	281	8,653
7	1,175	865	309	8,344
8	1,175	834	340	8,003
9	1,175	800	374	7,629
10	1,175	763	412	7,217
11	0	0	0	0
12	0	0	0	0
13	0	0	0	0
14	0	0	0	0
15	0	0	0	0
16	0	0	0	0
17	0	0	0	0
18	0	0	0	0
19	0	0	0	0
20	0	0	0	0

Balloon Payment Schedule		
Balloon Payment	Full Principal Payment	True Balance
$0	$175	$9,825
0	192	9,633
0	211	9,422
0	232	9,190
0	256	8,934
0	281	8,653
0	309	8,344
0	340	8,003
0	374	7,629
7,217	7,629	0
0	0	0
0	0	0
0	0	0
0	0	0
0	0	0
0	0	0
0	0	0
0	0	0
0	0	0
0	0	0

Figure 9-3. *The fixed rate amortization template, supplying annual payments, interest, principal components of payments, and outstanding principal balances for a link.*

component of the first period payment. In the same way, you can enter the interest expense for periods 2 through 10.

3. Enter the change in the long-term liabilities balance as the principal component of the debt service payment in cell C25 by entering the following formulas:

   ='C:\WINDOWS\AMORTIZE.XLS'!$E$12

   Cell E12 in AMORTIZE.XLS is the cell that contains the principal component of the first period payment. In the same way, you can enter the forecasted principal components of debt service payments for periods 2 through 10.

Forecasting Inputs	Period 0	Period 1	Period 2	Period 3	Period 4	Period 5	Period 6	Period 7	Period 8	Period 9	Period 10
Balance Sheet Forecasting Inputs:											
Cash & Equivalents	15,000										
Yield on Cash & Equivalents		10.00%	10.00%	10.00%	10.00%	10.00%	10.00%	10.00%	10.00%	10.00%	10.00%
Accounts Receivable	10,000										
# Periods of Sales in A/R		0.08	0.08	0.08	0.08	0.08	0.08	0.08	0.08	0.08	0.08
Inventory	10,000										
Inventory Purchased/Produced		55,000	65,000	55,000	65,000	55,000	65,000	55,000	65,000	55,000	65,000
Other Current Assets	5,000										
Chgs in Other Current Assets		100	-100	100	-100	100	-100	100	-100	100	-100
Plant, Property, & Equipment	75,000										
Chgs in P,P,& E		0	0	0	0	0	0	0	0	0	0
Accumulated Depreciation	15,000										
Chgs in Accum. Depreciation		2,000	2,000	2,000	2,000	2,000	2,000	2,000	2,000	2,000	2,000
Other Noncurrent Assets	5,000										
Chgs in Other Noncurrent Assets		100	-100	100	-100	100	-100	100	-100	100	-100
Accounts Payable	10,000										
# Periods Cost of Sales in A/P		0.08	0.08	0.08	0.08	0.08	0.08	0.08	0.08	0.08	0.08
Accrued Expenses	7,500										
# Periods Operating Expenses in A/E		0.04	0.04	0.04	0.04	0.04	0.04	0.04	0.04	0.04	0.04
Other Current Liabilities	7,500										
Chgs in Other Current Liabilities		100	-100	100	-100	100	-100	100	-100	100	-100
Long-Term Liabilities	35,000										
Chgs in Long-Term Liabilities		175	192	211	232	256	281	309	340	374	412
Other Noncurrent Liabilities	4,000										
Chgs in Other Noncurrent Liabilities		100	-100	100	-100	100	-100	100	-100	100	-100
Owner Equity	41,000										
Chgs in Owner Equity		-25,000	-25,000	-25,000	-25,000	-25,000	-25,000	-25,000	-25,000	-25,000	-25,000
Profit and Loss Statement Inputs:											
Sales Revenue		120,000	120,000	120,000	120,000	120,000	120,000	120,000	120,000	120,000	120,000
Cost of Sales		60,000	60,000	60,000	60,000	60,000	60,000	60,000	60,000	60,000	60,000
Cost Center 1 Costs		5,000	5,000	5,000	5,000	5,000	5,000	5,000	5,000	5,000	5,000
Cost Center 2 Costs		5,000	5,000	5,000	5,000	5,000	5,000	5,000	5,000	5,000	5,000
Cost Center 3 Costs		5,000	5,000	5,000	5,000	5,000	5,000	5,000	5,000	5,000	5,000
Interest Expense		1,000	983	963	942	919	893	865	834	800	763
Marginal Income Tax Rate		33%	33%	33%	33%	33%	33%	33%	33%	33%	33%

Figure 9-4. *The financial statements with ratios template, with inputs supplied by links.*

(continued)

Figure 9-4. *continued*

Balance Sheet	Period 0	Period 1	Period 2	Period 3	Period 4	Period 5	Period 6	Period 7	Period 8	Period 9	Period 10
Assets											
Current Assets											
Cash & Equivalents	$15,000	$15,785	$18,526	$31,483	$35,344	$49,502	$54,651	$70,192	$76,826	$93,962	$102,308
Accounts Receivable	10,000	10,000	10,000	10,000	10,000	10,000	10,000	10,000	10,000	10,000	10,000
Inventory	10,000	5,000	10,000	5,000	10,000	5,000	10,000	5,000	10,000	5,000	10,000
Other Current Assets	5,000	5,100	5,000	5,100	5,000	5,100	5,000	5,100	5,000	5,100	5,000
Total Current Assets	40,000	35,885	43,526	51,583	60,344	69,602	79,651	90,292	101,826	114,062	127,308
Plant, Property, & Equipment	75,000	75,000	75,000	75,000	75,000	75,000	75,000	75,000	75,000	75,000	75,000
Less: Accumulated Depreciation	(15,000)	(17,000)	(19,000)	(21,000)	(23,000)	(25,000)	(27,000)	(29,000)	(31,000)	(33,000)	(35,000)
Net Plant, Property, & Equipment	60,000	58,000	56,000	54,000	52,000	50,000	48,000	46,000	44,000	42,000	40,000
Other Noncurrent Assets	5,000	5,100	5,000	5,100	5,000	5,100	5,000	5,100	5,000	5,100	5,000
Total Assets	$105,000	$98,985	$104,526	$110,683	$117,344	$124,702	$132,651	$141,392	$150,826	$161,162	$172,308
Liabilities											
Current Liabilities											
Accounts Payable	$10,000	$5,000	$5,000	$5,000	$5,000	$5,000	$5,000	$5,000	$5,000	$5,000	$5,000
Accrued Expenses	7,500	625	625	625	625	625	625	625	625	625	625
Other Current Liabilities	7,500	7,600	7,500	7,600	7,500	7,600	7,500	7,600	7,500	7,600	7,500
Total Current Liabilities	25,000	13,225	13,125	13,225	13,125	13,225	13,125	13,225	13,125	13,225	13,125
Noncurrent Liabilities											
Long-Term Liabilities	35,000	35,175	35,367	35,578	35,811	36,066	36,348	36,657	36,997	37,371	37,783
Other Noncurrent Liabilities	4,000	4,100	4,000	4,100	4,000	4,100	4,000	4,100	4,000	4,100	4,000
Total Noncurrent Liabilities	39,000	39,275	39,367	39,678	39,811	40,166	40,348	40,757	40,997	41,471	41,783
Owner Equity	41,000	46,485	52,034	57,780	64,408	71,311	79,179	87,410	96,704	106,466	117,400
Total Liabilities and Owner Equity	$105,000	$98,985	$104,526	$110,683	$117,344	$124,702	$132,651	$141,392	$150,826	$161,162	$172,308

Common Size Balance Sheet	Period 0	Period 1	Period 2	Period 3	Period 4	Period 5	Period 6	Period 7	Period 8	Period 9	Period 10
Assets											
Current Assets											
Cash & Equivalents	14.29%	15.95%	17.72%	28.44%	30.12%	39.70%	41.20%	49.64%	50.94%	58.30%	59.38%
Accounts Receivable	9.52%	10.10%	9.57%	9.03%	8.52%	8.02%	7.54%	7.07%	6.63%	6.20%	5.80%
Inventory	9.52%	5.05%	9.57%	4.52%	8.52%	4.01%	7.54%	3.54%	6.63%	3.10%	5.80%
Other Current Assets	4.76%	5.15%	4.78%	4.61%	4.26%	4.09%	3.77%	3.61%	3.32%	3.16%	2.90%
Total Current Assets	38.10%	36.25%	41.64%	46.60%	51.42%	55.81%	60.05%	63.86%	67.51%	70.77%	73.88%
Plant, Property, & Equipment	71.43%	75.77%	71.75%	67.76%	63.91%	60.14%	56.54%	53.04%	49.73%	46.54%	43.53%
Less: Accumulated Depreciation	-14.29%	-17.17%	-18.18%	-18.97%	-19.60%	-20.05%	-20.35%	-20.51%	-20.55%	-20.48%	-20.31%
Net Plant, Property, & Equipment	57.14%	58.59%	53.58%	48.79%	44.31%	40.10%	36.19%	32.53%	29.17%	26.06%	23.21%
Other Noncurrent Assets	4.76%	5.15%	4.78%	4.61%	4.26%	4.09%	3.77%	3.61%	3.32%	3.16%	2.90%
Total Assets	100.00%	100.00%	100.00%	100.00%	100.00%	100.00%	100.00%	100.00%	100.00%	100.00%	100.00%
Liabilities											
Current Liabilities											
Accounts Payable	9.52%	5.05%	4.78%	4.52%	4.26%	4.01%	3.77%	3.54%	3.32%	3.10%	2.90%
Accrued Expenses	7.14%	0.63%	0.60%	0.56%	0.53%	0.50%	0.47%	0.44%	0.41%	0.39%	0.36%
Other Current Liabilities	7.14%	7.68%	7.18%	6.87%	6.39%	6.09%	5.65%	5.38%	4.97%	4.72%	4.35%
Total Current Liabilities	23.81%	13.36%	12.56%	11.95%	11.19%	10.61%	9.89%	9.35%	8.70%	8.21%	7.62%
Noncurrent Liabilities											
Long-Term Liabilities	33.33%	35.54%	33.84%	32.14%	30.52%	28.92%	27.40%	25.93%	24.53%	23.19%	21.93%
Other Noncurrent Liabilities	3.81%	4.14%	3.83%	3.70%	3.41%	3.29%	3.02%	2.90%	2.65%	2.54%	2.32%
Total Noncurrent Liabilities	37.14%	39.68%	37.66%	35.85%	33.93%	32.21%	30.42%	28.83%	27.18%	25.73%	24.25%
Owner Equity	39.05%	46.96%	49.78%	52.20%	54.89%	57.18%	59.69%	61.82%	64.12%	66.06%	68.13%
Total Liabilities and Owner Equity	100.00%	100.00%	100.00%	100.00%	100.00%	100.00%	100.00%	100.00%	100.00%	100.00%	100.00%

(*continued*)

Figure 9-4. *continued*

Income Statement	Period 1	Period 2	Period 3	Period 4	Period 5	Period 6	Period 7	Period 8	Period 9	Period 10
Sales Revenue	$120,000	$120,000	$120,000	$120,000	$120,000	$120,000	$120,000	$120,000	$120,000	$120,000
Less: Cost of Sales	(60,000)	(60,000)	(60,000)	(60,000)	(60,000)	(60,000)	(60,000)	(60,000)	(60,000)	(60,000)
Gross Margin	60,000	60,000	60,000	60,000	60,000	60,000	60,000	60,000	60,000	60,000
Operating Expenses										
Cost Center 1	5,000	5,000	5,000	5,000	5,000	5,000	5,000	5,000	5,000	5,000
Cost Center 2	5,000	5,000	5,000	5,000	5,000	5,000	5,000	5,000	5,000	5,000
Cost Center 3	5,000	5,000	5,000	5,000	5,000	5,000	5,000	5,000	5,000	5,000
Total Operating Expenses	15,000	15,000	15,000	15,000	15,000	15,000	15,000	15,000	15,000	15,000
Operating Income	45,000	45,000	45,000	45,000	45,000	45,000	45,000	45,000	45,000	45,000
Interest Income	1,500	1,579	1,853	3,148	3,534	4,950	5,465	7,019	7,683	9,396
Interest Expense	1,000	983	963	942	919	893	865	834	800	763
Net Income (Loss) Before Taxes	45,500	45,596	45,889	47,206	47,615	49,057	49,600	51,185	51,882	53,633
Income Tax Expenses (Savings)	15,015	15,047	15,143	15,578	15,713	16,189	16,368	16,891	17,121	17,699
Net Income (Loss) After Taxes	$30,485	$30,549	$30,746	$31,628	$31,902	$32,868	$33,232	$34,294	$34,761	$35,934

Common Size Income Statement	Period 1	Period 2	Period 3	Period 4	Period 5	Period 6	Period 7	Period 8	Period 9	Period 10
Sales Revenue	100.00%	100.00%	100.00%	100.00%	100.00%	100.00%	100.00%	100.00%	100.00%	100.00%
Less: Cost of Sales	-50.00%	-50.00%	-50.00%	-50.00%	-50.00%	-50.00%	-50.00%	-50.00%	-50.00%	-50.00%
Gross Margin	50.00%	50.00%	50.00%	50.00%	50.00%	50.00%	50.00%	50.00%	50.00%	50.00%
Operating Expenses										
Cost Center 1	4.17%	4.17%	4.17%	4.17%	4.17%	4.17%	4.17%	4.17%	4.17%	4.17%
Cost Center 2	4.17%	4.17%	4.17%	4.17%	4.17%	4.17%	4.17%	4.17%	4.17%	4.17%
Cost Center 3	4.17%	4.17%	4.17%	4.17%	4.17%	4.17%	4.17%	4.17%	4.17%	4.17%
Total Operating Expenses	12.50%	12.50%	12.50%	12.50%	12.50%	12.50%	12.50%	12.50%	12.50%	12.50%
Operating Income	37.50%	37.50%	37.50%	37.50%	37.50%	37.50%	37.50%	37.50%	37.50%	37.50%
Interest Income	1.25%	1.32%	1.54%	2.62%	2.95%	4.13%	4.55%	5.85%	6.40%	7.83%
Interest Expense	0.83%	0.82%	0.80%	0.79%	0.77%	0.74%	0.72%	0.70%	0.67%	0.64%
Net Income (Loss) Before Taxes	37.92%	38.00%	38.24%	39.34%	39.68%	40.88%	41.33%	42.65%	43.24%	44.69%
Income Tax Expenses (Savings)	12.51%	12.54%	12.62%	12.98%	13.09%	13.49%	13.64%	14.08%	14.27%	14.75%
Net Income (Loss) After Taxes	25.40%	25.46%	25.62%	26.36%	26.59%	27.39%	27.69%	28.58%	28.97%	29.95%

Cash Flow Statement	Period 1	Period 2	Period 3	Period 4	Period 5	Period 6	Period 7	Period 8	Period 9	Period 10
Beginning Cash Balance	$15,000	$15,785	$18,526	$31,483	$35,344	$49,502	$54,651	$70,192	$76,826	$93,962
Sources of Cash										
Net Income After Taxes	$30,485	$30,549	$30,746	$31,628	$31,902	$32,868	$33,232	$34,294	$34,761	$35,934
Addback of Depreciation	2,000	2,000	2,000	2,000	2,000	2,000	2,000	2,000	2,000	2,000
Accounts Payable Financing	(5,000)	0	0	0	0	0	0	0	0	0
Accrued Expenses Financing	(6,875)	0	0	0	0	0	0	0	0	0
Other Current Liabilities Financing	100	(100)	100	(100)	100	(100)	100	(100)	100	(100)
Long-Term Liabilities Financing	175	192	211	232	256	281	309	340	374	412
Other Noncurrent Liabilities Financing	100	(100)	100	(100)	100	(100)	100	(100)	100	(100)
Uses of Cash										
Accounts Receivable Investments	0	0	0	0	0	0	0	0	0	0
Inventory Investments	(5,000)	5,000	(5,000)	5,000	(5,000)	5,000	(5,000)	5,000	(5,000)	5,000
Other Current Assets Investments	100	(100)	100	(100)	100	(100)	100	(100)	100	(100)
Plant, Property, & Equip Investments	0	0	0	0	0	0	0	0	0	0
Other Noncurrent Assets Investments	100	(100)	100	(100)	100	(100)	100	(100)	100	(100)
Other Owner Equity Changes	25,000	25,000	25,000	25,000	25,000	25,000	25,000	25,000	25,000	25,000
Net Cash Generated (Used)	785	2,741	12,957	3,860	14,158	5,149	15,541	6,634	17,135	8,346
Ending Cash Balance	$15,785	$18,526	$31,483	$35,344	$49,502	$54,651	$70,192	$76,826	$93,962	$102,308

Financial Ratios Table	Period 1	Period 2	Period 3	Period 4	Period 5	Period 6	Period 7	Period 8	Period 9	Period 10
Working Capital Ratios:										
Current Ratio	2.71	3.32	3.90	4.60	5.26	6.07	6.83	7.76	8.62	9.70
Quick Ratio	1.95	2.17	3.14	3.45	4.50	4.93	6.06	6.62	7.86	8.56
Working Capital to Total Assets	0.23	0.29	0.35	0.40	0.45	0.50	0.55	0.59	0.63	0.66
Receivables Turnover	12.00	12.00	12.00	12.00	12.00	12.00	12.00	12.00	12.00	12.00
Inventory Turnover	12.00	6.00	12.00	6.00	12.00	6.00	12.00	6.00	12.00	6.00
Operating Ratios:										
Times Interest Earned	46.50	47.41	48.64	51.10	52.81	55.91	58.32	62.35	65.83	71.30
Sales to Operational Assets	2.07	2.14	2.22	2.31	2.40	2.50	2.61	2.73	2.86	3.00
Return on Total Assets	31.81%	30.17%	28.65%	27.76%	26.32%	25.45%	24.12%	23.29%	22.07%	21.30%
Return on Equity	65.58%	58.71%	53.21%	49.11%	44.74%	41.51%	38.02%	35.46%	32.65%	30.61%
Investment Turnover	1.21	1.15	1.08	1.02	0.96	0.90	0.85	0.80	0.74	0.70
Financial Leverage	33.77%	28.54%	24.56%	21.35%	18.42%	16.06%	13.90%	12.17%	10.58%	9.31%

Appendix

Auditing and Documenting Your Financial Spreadsheets

If you modify any of the templates on the accompanying disks to make them more closely fit your needs, you will likely find that you've altered the relationships within the spreadsheet and that the documentation in this book no longer reflects these relationships. Fortunately, Microsoft Excel provides four features that give you the ability to audit and document your models. First, Microsoft Excel lets you use names rather than column and row coordinates to reference cells. Second, Microsoft Excel lets you annotate cells with documentation of complex formulas and details about modeling assumptions. Third, Microsoft Excel provides information about precedent and dependent cell relationships, letting you track and understand these relationships. Fourth, Microsoft Excel provides two powerful commands that let you search through your spreadsheet, the charts related to your spreadsheet, and your spreadsheet cell notes for variables, text fragments, and other references for the effects of and the references to a transaction or assumption.

This appendix provides a brief overview of each of these features and its general application to financial modeling. For detailed information and step-by-step instructions on the auditing and documenting features, consult the online Help Feature Guide or the *Microsoft Excel Reference Guide*.

USING REFERENCE NAMES

Microsoft Excel's naming capabilities go beyond those of other spreadsheet products. As with many spreadsheet programs, you can name cells and then use the cell name rather than the cell coordinates when referencing the cell in functions and formulas. (This technique is used in many of the templates in this collection.) However, Microsoft Excel offers two additional naming capabilities you should be aware of. First, you can name constants, even those not included in a spreadsheet cell. Second, by naming columns and rows of a spreadsheet, you can use the column and row names to reference a cell, as you might use column letters and row numbers to reference a cell. By carefully crafting your spreadsheet column and row titles, you can avoid such cryptic formulas as:

=B1–B2

by using names, such as:

=January Revenues–January Expenses

Within the business forecasting and planning templates, these two naming capabilities weren't used for two reasons. First, this book delivers, in more detail, the same documentation for each formula. Second, the generalized row and column titles are appropriate for the templates, but they are neither very descriptive nor unique, fundamental requirements for using Microsoft Excel's powerful reference naming capabilities. However, if you make the column and row titles more unique and descriptive and if this book begins to lose its accuracy because of enhancements, you might want to use this powerful feature. Figure A-1 shows a simple profit and loss spreadsheet, and Figure A-2 shows the same spreadsheet with the Display Formulas option set. Notice that because column B is named January, row 2 is named Revenues, and row 3 is named Expenses, the formula in cell B4, which calculates the profits, is:

=January Revenues–January Expenses

Appendix: Auditing and Documenting Your Financial Spreadsheets

	A	B
1		January
2	Revenues	100000
3	Expenses	45000
4	Profits	55000

Figure A-1. *A simple profit and loss statement.*

	A	B
1		January
2	Revenues	=1*100000
3	Expenses	45000
4	Profits	=January Revenues-January Expenses

Figure A-2. *The profit and loss statement, displaying formulas that use reference names.*

ANNOTATING CELLS

Another useful feature provided by Microsoft Excel is its ability to annotate cells. Simply by choosing the Formula Note command, you can attach notes to cells. As mentioned earlier, you might use these notes for describing complex formulas or for describing the source and logic of a modeling assumption. For example, Figure A-3 shows

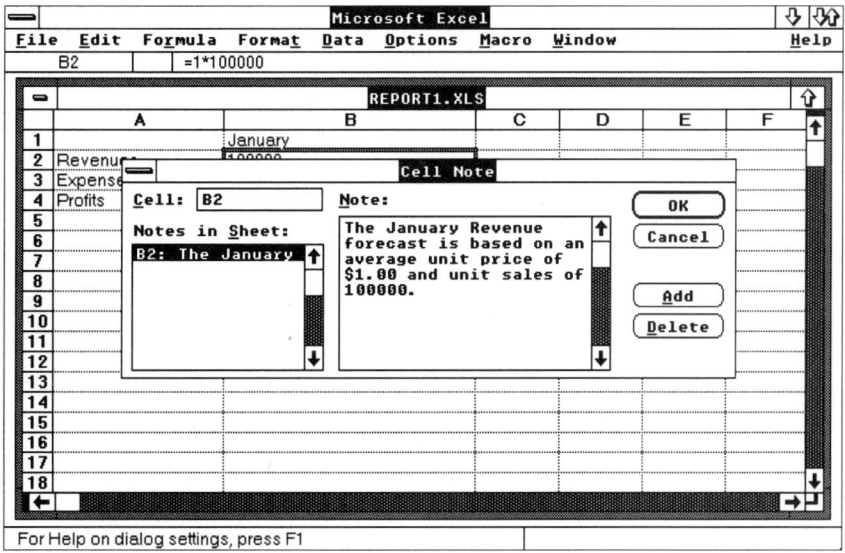

Figure A-3. *Using Microsoft Excel's annotation feature to document formulas.*

303

Microsoft Excel Small Business Consultant

the simple profit and loss statement introduced in Figures A-1 and A-2. Using the built-in annotation feature, documenting the modeling assumptions or complex formulas and logic is easy.

IDENTIFYING CELL PRECEDENTS AND DEPENDENTS

Microsoft Excel also provides a convenient way to explore precedent and dependent cell references. Figure A-4 illustrates the use of the Window Show Info command, which can show not only any note attached to the cell currently selected, but also precedent cells and dependent cells. This feature makes it easier to answer the question: How does this cell relate to others in the spreadsheet?

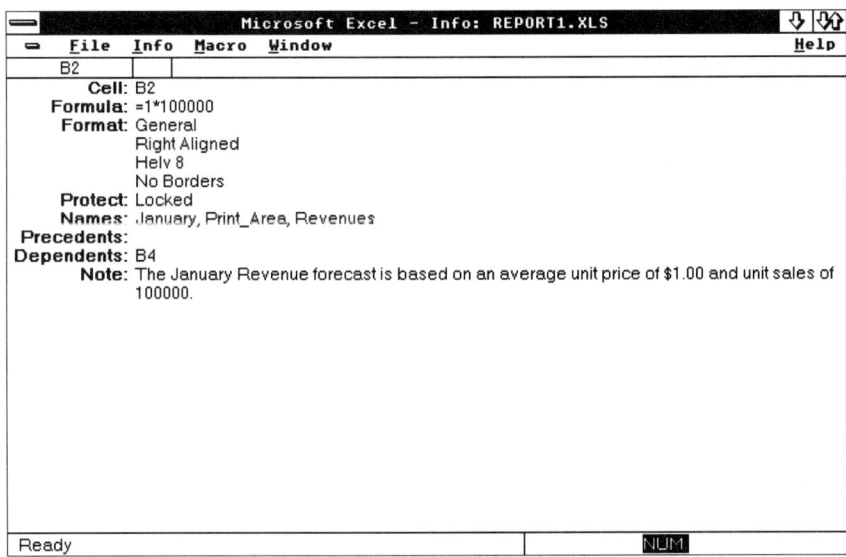

Figure A-4. *Using Excel's Window Show Info command to explore cell references.*

USING THE FORMULA SELECT SPECIAL AND FORMULA FIND COMMANDS

The Formula Select Special and Formula Find commands represent two additional auditing tools with tremendous applicability and usefulness, particularly within large spreadsheet models.

The Formula Select Special command selects cells with certain specified attributes—for example, cells with notes or with certain contents. You can limit the area within which Microsoft Excel conducts its search, you can search for cells that differ from a specified cell, or you can search for a cell that is a precedent or a dependent.

The Formula Find command locates cells that contain the text or number listed as the search argument. For example, you can use the command for searching spreadsheets for possible errors by specifying #REF!, #NAME?, or #DIV/0! as the search argument or for locating a cell or a cell note in which the search argument appears. You also can specify a particular area for the Formula Find command to search, you can specify whether the search argument can be part of a larger text or number, and you can specify search order—by column or by row.

Obviously, both commands ease the burden of auditing and error checking within large spreadsheets. You might, for example, use the Formula Select Special command to search for the internally documented modeling assumptions contained in cell notes. Or you might use Formula Find to search for all references to interest rates in cell notes as part of assessing the effect of changing interest rates.

Index

A

Accelerated Cost Recovery System (ACRS) 20
Accounts Payable 255, 262
Accounts Payable Financing 273
Accounts Receivable 253, 258
Accounts Receivable Investments 276
Accrued Expenses 255, 262–63
Accrued Expenses Financing 274
Accumulated Depreciation
   Activity Depreciation Schedule 55
   Annuity or Sinking Fund Depreciation schedule 49
   Declining-Balance Depreciation Schedule 24–25
   financial statements with ratios template 254, 260–61
   Straight-Line Conversion Depreciation Schedule 32
   Straight-Line Depreciation Schedule 18, 27, 41
   Sum-of-the-Years'-Digits Depreciation Schedule 38
Activity Depreciation Calculation Inputs schedule 53
Activity Depreciation Schedule 53–56
activity depreciation (ACTIVITY.XLS) template 2, 9, 13–14, 51–57
   contents and functions 52–56
   customizing 57
   entering data into 56
   fully depreciating 56
   parameters 51
   sample spreadsheet 52
Addback of Depreciation 273
Addbacks of Noncash Expenses 215
Addbacks of Noncash Expenses — Other 215
After-Tax Adjusted IRR 221–22, 236

After-Tax Cash Flow Scenarios schedule 229–31
   removing 236
After-Tax Cumulative Cash Flows 225–26, 236
After-Tax Gain (Loss) on Disposal 214–15
After-Tax IRR 219–20, 236
After-Tax Net Present Value 223–24, 236
After-Tax Operating Cash Flow 216–17
After-Tax Payback Period 226, 236
amortization templates. *See* debt amortization templates
amortization term 62
   fixed rate, annuity due template 81, 83
   fixed rate, ordinary annuity template 63, 65
   variable rate, annuity due template 90, 92
   variable rate, ordinary annuity template 73
AMORTIZE.XLS
   linked to DEPRECTN.XLS and CASHFLOW.XLS 236–43
   linked to DEPRECTN.XLS and FINANCLS.XLS 291–99
annuity due 62, 105
Annuity or Sinking Fund Depreciation Schedule 46–49
annuity or sinking fund depreciation (ANNUITY.XLS) template 2, 9, 11–13, 44–51
   contents and functions of 45–49
   customizing 50–51
   entering data into 50
   expressing estimated life in integer format 50
   parameters 45, 46
   sample spreadsheet 44
annuity variable 104

asset depreciation templates 2, 9–59
   activity depreciation 51–57
   annuity and sinking fund depreciation 44–51
   declining balance depreciation 20–34
   linking, to other spreadsheets 57–59
   primer on asset depreciation 10–14
   straight-line depreciation 14–20
   sum-of-the-years' digits 34–43
auditing and documenting features, Microsoft Excel 4, 301–5
   cell annotation 303–4
   cell precedents and dependents, identifying 304
   Formula Find and Formula Select Special commands 304–5
   reference names 302–3

B

balance sheet 245, 246
   variables for 253–57
Balance Sheet schedule 258–66
Balloon Payment column
   fixed rate, annuity due template 88
   fixed rate, ordinary annuity template 69–70
   variable rate, annuity due template 97
   variable rate, ordinary annuity template 78
Balloon Payment Schedule
   fixed rate, annuity due template 87–88
   fixed rate, ordinary annuity template 69–70
   removing 71, 80, 90, 100
   variable rate, annuity due template 97–98

Index

Balloon Payment Schedule, *continued*
   variable rate, ordinary annuity template 78–79
bar charts 193, *194*
Beginning Cash Balance 272
Beginning Dollars on Hand 154
Beginning Inventory–Balance in Dollars variable 146, 149
Beginning Inventory Unit Cost 150
Beginning Inventory–Units on Hand variable 146, 149
Beginning Units on Hand 153
break-even analysis 163, 165, 173–75
Break-Even Analysis Forecast 173–75, 186
Break-Even Analysis Line Chart Data 183
BREAKEVN.XLC chart 3, 168, *191*, 192

C

capital gains tax 202
Cash & Equivalents 253, 258
Cash Flow Analysis schedule 218–26
cash flow forecast and analysis (CASHFLOW.XLS) template 3, 199–243
   contents and functions 206–31
   customizing 234–36
   entering data into 231–34
   input variables 202, 206–9
   linking, to other templates 236–43
   primer on cash flow forecasting and analysis 199–202
   sample spreadsheet *203–5*
Cash Flow Forecasting Inputs schedule 206–9
cash flow statement 245, 246
   variables for balance sheet and 253–57
   variables for income statement and 257

Cash Flow Statement schedule 272–79
cell annotation 303–4
charts 168, 182–83, 189–97
   area (COSTPROF.XLC) *190–92*
   bar and column 193, *194*
   combination *197*
   line (BREAKEVN.XLC) *191*, 192
   pie *195*
   scaling 192
   scatter *196*
Chgs in Accum. Depreciation 254–55
Chgs in Long-Term Liabilities 256
Chgs in Other Current Assets 254
Chgs in Other Current Liabilities 256
Chgs in Other Noncurrent Assets 255
Chgs in Other Noncurrent Liabilities 256
Chgs in Owner Equity 257
Chgs in P, P, & E (plant, property, equipment) 254
column charts 193, *194*
combination charts *197*
Common Size Balance Sheet schedule 266–67
common size financial ratios 246
Common Size Income Statement schedule 271–72
Common Size Profit Volume Forecast 182
   removing 186
contribution margin 165
Contribution Margin–Fixed Costs variable 180
Contribution Margin variable 175, 179–80
Cost Center 1, 2, and 3 Costs 257
cost center (COSTSRPT.XLS) template 2, 133–41
   contents and functions of 136–37

cost center, *continued*
   customizing 138–39
   entering data into 137
   linking, to other templates 139–41
   primer on cost centers 133–34
   sample spreadsheet *135*
cost classifications 136, 144
Cost of Goods Sold 152
Cost of Sales 207, 210, 257, 268
COSTPROF.XLC chart 3, 168, *190–92*
Cost Totals and Statistics schedule 150–51
Current Ratio 280
customizing templates
   activity depreciation template 57
   annuity or sinking fund depreciation template 50
   cash flow forecast and analysis template 234–36
   cost center template 138–39
   declining balance depreciation template 33–34
   financial statements with ratios template 289–90
   fixed interest rate, annuity due template 89–90
   fixed interest rate, ordinary annuity template 70–71
   future value of an annuity due template 128–29
   future value of a onetime deposit template 113
   future value of an ordinary annuity template 120–21
   profit volume and break-even analysis template 185–87
   sales and cost of sales template 157
   straight-line depreciation template 19–20
   sum-of-the-years'-digits depreciation template 43
   variable rate, annuity due template 99
   variable rate, ordinary annuity template 80

D

data entry
  activity depreciation template 56
  annuity or sinking fund depreciation template 50
  cash flow forecast and analysis template 231–34
  cost center template 137
  declining balance depreciation template 32–33
  financial statements with ratios template 285–89
  fixed interest rate, annuity due template 89
  fixed interest rate, ordinary annuity template 70
  future value of an annuity due template 127–28
  future value of a onetime deposit template 112–13
  future value of an ordinary annuity template 119–20
  profit volume and break-even analysis template 183–85
  sales and cost of sales template 155–56
  straight-line depreciation template 19
  sum-of-the-years'-digits depreciation template 42–43
  variable rate, annuity due template 98
  variable rate, ordinary annuity template 79
debt amortization templates 2, 61–102
  fixed rate, annuity due template 81–90
  fixed rate, ordinary annuity template 63–71
  linking to other spreadsheets 100–102
  primer on amortizing debt 61–63
  variable rate, annuity due template 90–99
  variable rate, ordinary annuity template 71–80

Debt Principal Payments 208
debt service payment 62
debt term parameter 62
  fixed rate, annuity due template 81, 83
  fixed rate, ordinary annuity template 63, 65
  variable rate, annuity due template 90, 92
  variable rate, ordinary annuity template 73
Decline Percentage parameter 20, 22–23
Declining Balance Depreciation Calculation Inputs 22–23
Declining Balance Depreciation Schedule 23–25
declining balance depreciation (DECLIN'G.XLS) template 2, 9, 10–11, 20–34
  contents and functions 22–32
  customizing 33–34
  entering data into 32–33
  parameters 20
  sample spreadsheet 22
  using low salvage value 29
Deducts of Cash Nonexpenses — Debt Principal Payments 215
Deducts of Cash Nonexpenses — Other 215
Deposit input 109
Deposit output 110
Deposit variable (present value) 104, 108
depreciation. *See* asset depreciation templates
Depreciation column 208
DEPRECTN.XLS
  linked to AMORTIZE.XLS and CASHFLOW.XLS 236–43
  linked to AMORTIZE.XLS and FINANCLS.XLS 291–99
Direct Labor 171–72, 173, 177
Direct Material 171–72, 174, 177
Dollars Produced/Purchased 154–55
Dollars Sold 155

E

economic life 16, 22, 53
Ending Cash Balance 279
Ending Dollars on Hand 155
Ending Units on Hand 154
Estimated Life parameter
  activity depreciation template 51, 53
  annuity or sinking fund depreciation template 45, 46
  declining-balance depreciation template 20, 22–23
  straight-line depreciation template 14, 15–16
  sum-of-the-years'-digits depreciation template 34, 35
Excess Accelerated Depreciation 28–30, 42
expense categories column, cost centers 137

F

Factory Overhead variable 171–72, 174, 177–78
FACTORY.XLS spreadsheet
  linked to FIXRATE.XLS 100–102
  linked to STRAIGHT.XLS 57–59
Federal Income Tax variable 171, 181
finance and accounting knowledge 5
Financial Accounting Standards Board 12
Financial Leverage 284–85
financial measurement periods, consistency in 14, 63
financial ratios 246–47
Financial Ratios Table 279–85
financial statements 245–47
financial statements with ratios (FINANCLS.XLS) template 3, 245–99
  contents and functions 247–85
  customizing 289–90
  entering data into 285–89

financial statements with ratios, *continued*
  linking, to other templates 291–99
  primer on financial statements and financial ratios 245–47
  sample spreadsheet *248–52*
First-In-First-Out (FIFO) inventory costing 151
FIXCOSTS.XLS linked to PROFTVOL.XLS 187, *188–89*
Fixed Costs variable 175, 180
Fixed Interest Rate, Annuity Due Amortization Inputs 81–83
Fixed Interest Rate, Annuity Due Amortization Schedule 83–87
fixed interest rate, annuity due (FIXDUE.XLS) template 2, 61, 81–90
  balances from beginning or end of payment period 85
  contents and functions of 81–88
  customizing 89–90
  entering data into 89
  parameters 81, 83
  sample spreadsheet *82*
fixed interest rate, ordinary annuity (FIXRATE.XLS) template 2, 61, 63–71
  contents and functions 63–70
  customizing 70–71
  entering data into 70
  linked to COSTSRPT.XLS 139–41
  linked to FACTORY.XLS spreadsheet 100–102
  parameters 63, 65
  sample spreadsheet *64*
Fixed Interest Rate Amortization Inputs 63–65
Fixed Interest Rate Amortization Schedule 65–68

forecast(s). *See* cash flow forecast and analysis (CASHFLOW.XLS) template; cost center (COSTSRPT.XLS) template; future value templates
Forecasting Inputs 247, 253–57
Formula Find command 304–5
Formula Note command *303–4*
Formula Select Special command 304–5
Full Principle Payment
  fixed rate, annuity due template 88
  fixed rate, ordinary annuity template 69
  variable rate, annuity due template 97–98
  variable rate, ordinary annuity template 78
Future Value Annuity Due Inputs & Outputs 123–25
future value of an annuity due (FVANNDUE.XLS) template 2, 103, 121–29
  contents and functions 122–27
  customizing 128–29
  entering data into 127–28
  sample spreadsheet *122*
  variables 121, 122–23
Future Value input column 109, 116, 123
Future Value Onetime Deposit Inputs & Outputs 109–10
future value of a onetime deposit (FVDPOSIT.XLS) template 2, 103, 107–13
  contents and functions 108–11
  customizing 113
  entering data into 112–13
  linked to FVORDANN.XLS 129–32
  sample spreadsheet *107*
  variables 107, 108
Future Value Ordinary Annuity Inputs & Outputs 116–17
future value of an ordinary annuity (FVORDANN.XLS) template 2, 103, 114–21
  contents and functions 115–19

future value of an ordinary annuity, *continued*
  customizing 120–21
  entering data into 119–20
  linked to FVDPOSIT.XLS 129–32
  sample spreadsheet *114*
  variables 115
Future Value output column
  future value of an annuity due template 124
  future value of a onetime deposit template 109
  future value of an ordinary annuity template 116
future value templates 2, 103–32
  future value of an annuity due template 121–29
  future value of a onetime deposit template 107–13
  future value of an ordinary annuity template 114–21
  linking to other templates 129–32
  primer on future value and present value 103–6
Future Value variable 103–4, 108, 115, 121, 122
FV function 104, 116, 124

G–H

Gain and Loss Statement schedule 213–15
Generally Accepted Accounting Principles (GAAP) 12, 44
Gross Margin 210, 268
Gross Residual 202, 209, 213, 217
Gross Sales 207, 210–12
Gross Sales Margin 153
hardware required for Microsoft Excel 6
High Unit Volume Tested variable 171

I

IF statements, nested 228, 230
income statement 245–46, 257

Income Statement schedule 267–71
Income Tax Expenses (Savings) 212, 214, 216, 218, 270
inflation 106
initial cash investment 206
Interest Component
  fixed rate, annuity due template 85–86
  fixed rate, ordinary annuity template 67
  variable rate, annuity due template 94–95
  variable rate, ordinary annuity template 76
Interest Expense 208, 211, 257, 270
Interest Income 111, 118, 126, 269
Interest Income and Principal Balances Schedule 110–11
Interest input column 109, 116, 124
Interest output column 110, 117, 124
interest rate index 93
Interest Rate parameter 62, 63, 65, 81, 83
Interest variable 104, 108, 115, 121, 123
internal rate of return 218–22
  calculating 220
Intrastatement and interstatement financial ratios 246–47
inventory, and sales and costs of sales 143, 146, 149, 153–55
Inventory Forecast schedule 153–55
Inventory Investments 276–77
Inventory Purchased/Produced 254
Inventory Turnover 282
inventory (value) 254, 258
Investment Revenue 48
Investment Turnover 284

L–M

Last-In-First-Out (LIFO) inventory costing 151
linking templates to spreadsheets
  CASHFLOW.XLS to DEPRECTN.XLS and AMORTIZE.XLS 236–40, *241–43*
  COSTSRPT.XLS to STRAIGHT.XLS and FIXRATE.XLS 139–40, *141*
  FINANCLS.XLS to DEPRECTN.XLS and AMORTIZE.XLS 291–94 *295–99*
  FIXRATE.XLS to FACTORY.XLS 100–101, *102*
  future values 129, *130*, 131, *132*
  PROFTVOL.XLS 187, *188, 189*
  SALESRPT.XLS template 157–59, *160–61*
  STRAIGHT.XLS to FACTORY.XLS 57, *58, 59*
Liquidation Cash Flow Statement schedule 217–18
Long-Term Liabilities 256, 264
Long-Term Liabilities Financing 275
Low Unit Volume Tested variable 171
marginal capital gains 202
Marginal Income Tax Rate 208, 257
Marginal Tax Rate on Residual 209
MAX function 187, 290
Microsoft Excel spreadsheet templates product 1–7
MIN statement 17, 55, 186–87
MIRR function 222
Modified Accelerated Cost Recovery System (MACRS) 20

N

Net Book Value
  Activity Depreciation Schedule 55–56

Net Book Value, *continued*
  Annuity or Sinking Fund Depreciation schedule 49
  Declining-Balance Depreciation Schedule 24
  Straight-Line Conversion Depreciation Schedule 32
  Straight-Line Depreciation Schedule 18, 28, 41
  Sum-of-the-Years'-Digits Depreciation Schedule 39
Net Cash Generated (Used) 279
Net Income After Taxes 273
Net Income (Loss) After Taxes 212, 271
Net Income Before Taxes 215
Net Income (Loss) Before Taxes 211–12, 270
Net Plant, Property, & Equipment 261
Net Residual 213
Nontaxable Portion of Residual 209, 213
NPER function 104, 109, 110, 116, 117, 124
NPV function 223, 224
Periods Cost of Sales in A/P 255
Periods Operating Expenses in A/E 255–56
of Periods of Sales in A/R 253–54

O

Operating Cash Flow Statement schedule 215–17
Operating Expenses — Cost Center 1, 2, and 3 210, 268
Operating Expenses — Cost Center 1, 2, and 3 Costs 208
Operating Income 211, 269
ordinary annuity 62, 105
Original Cost parameter
  Activity Depreciation Schedule 51, 53
  Annuity or Sinking Fund Depreciation schedule 45, 46

Original Cost parameter, *continued*
  Declining-Balance Depreciation Schedule 20, 22–23
  Straight-Line Depreciation Schedule 14, 15–16
  Sum-of-the-Years'-Digits Depreciation Schedule 34, 35
Other Cash Nonexpenses 209
Other Current Assets 254, 258
Other Current Assets Investments 277
Other Current Liabilities 256, 263
Other Current Liabilities Financing 274–75
Other Noncash Expenses 208
Other Noncurrent Assets 255, 261
Other Noncurrent Assets Investments 278
Other Noncurrent Liabilities 256, 264
Other Noncurrent Liabilities Financing 275–76
Other Owner Equity Changes 278–79
Other Variable Costs column 152
Other Variable Costs variable 146
Other Vary-with-Profit Costs 171, 181
Other Vary-with-Revenue Costs variable 171, 174–75, 179
Other Vary-with-Unit Costs variable 171, 174, 178
Outstanding Debt 217
Outstanding Debt on Asset(s) 209
OVERHEAD.XLS linked to SALESRPT.XLS 157–61
Owner Equity 257, 265

P

Payment Amount column 118, 126
payment in advance. *See* annuity due
payment in arrears. *See* ordinary annuity
Payment input column 116, 124
Payment output column 117, 125
Payments 117–19, 125–27
Payment variable
  future value of an annuity due template 121, 123
  future value of an ordinary annuity template 115
Period 0 227, 229
Period 1 through 10 228, 229
Period Depreciation
  Activity Depreciation Schedule 54–55
  Annuity or Sinking Fund Depreciation schedule 47
  Declining-Balance Depreciation Schedule 23–24
  Straight-Line Conversion Depreciation Schedule 31–32
  Straight-Line Depreciation Schedule 17, 26–27, 40
  Sum-of-the-Years'-Digits Depreciation Schedule 37–38
Period Expense Total column 137
Period identifier
  activity depreciation template 53–54
  annuity or sinking fund depreciation template 46–47
  cash flow forecast and analysis template 206
  cost center template 136–37
  declining-balance depreciation template 23
  financial statements with ratios template 247, 253, 258, 267, 272, 279–80
  fixed rate, annuity due template 83
  fixed rate, ordinary annuity template 65–66
  future value of an annuity due template 125

Period identifier, *continued*
  future value of a onetime deposit template 107
  future value of an ordinary annuity template 117–18
  sales and cost of sales template 149
  Straight-Line Conversion Depreciation Schedule 30–32
  straight-line depreciation template 16–17, 26, 39–40
  sum-of-the-years'-digits depreciation template 36–37
  variable rate, annuity due template 92–93
  variable rate, ordinary annuity template 74
Period Interest Rate column
  variable rate, annuity due template 93
  variable rate, ordinary annuity template 74
Period Interest Rates parameter
  variable rate, annuity due template 90, 92
  variable rate, ordinary annuity template 73
Periods input column
  future value of an annuity due template 124
  future value of a onetime deposit template 109
  future value of an ordinary annuity template 116
Periods output column
  future value of an annuity due template 124
  future value of a onetime deposit template 109–10
  future value of an ordinary annuity template 116–17
Periods variable 104
  future value of an annuity due template 121, 122
  future value of a onetime deposit template 108
  future value of an ordinary annuity template 115

Period Units of Use 54
pie charts *195*
Plant, Property, & Equip Investments 277–78
Plant, Property, & Equipment 254, 260
PMT function 62, 66, 75, 84, 94, 104, 117
present value variable 104
Pretax Adjusted IRR 220–21, 235
Pretax Cash Flow Scenarios schedule 227–29, 235
Pretax Cumulative Cash Flows 224–25, 235
Pretax Discount Rate and After-Tax Discount Rate 207
Pretax Gain (Loss) on Disposal 213–14
Pretax IRR 219, 235
Pretax Liquidation Cash Flow 217
Pretax Net Present Value 222–23, 235
Pretax Operating Cash Flow 215–16
Pretax Payback Period 225, 235
Pretax Reinvestment Rate and After-Tax Reinvestment Rate 207
Principal Balance column
 fixed rate, annuity due template 86–87
 fixed rate, ordinary annuity template 68
 future value of an annuity due template 126–27
 future value of a onetime deposit template 111
 future value of an ordinary annuity template 119
 variable rate, annuity due template 96–97
 variable rate, ordinary annuity template 77–78
Principal Component
 fixed rate, annuity due template 86
 fixed rate, ordinary annuity template 67–68

Principal Component, *continued*
 variable rate, annuity due template 95–96
 variable rate, ordinary annuity template 76–77
Principal parameter 62
 fixed rate, annuity due template 81, 83
 fixed rate, ordinary annuity template 63, 65
 variable rate, annuity due template 90, 92
 variable rate, ordinary annuity template 73
Produced/Purchased Unit Cost 151
Profit and Loss Statement schedule 210–12
Profit Before Vary-with-Profits Costs (PBVPC) 165–68, 175
Profits variable 182
Profit Volume Area Chart Data 182–83
profit volume and break-even analysis (PROFTVOL.XLS) template 3, 163–97
 charts 168, 189–97
 contents and functions 171–83
 customizing 185–87
 define variables and costs 168
 entering data into 183–85
 linking to other spreadsheets 187–89
 primer on profit volume and break-even analysis 163–68
 sample spreadsheet *169–70*
 variable relationships 165
 variables 171–72
Profit Volume Forecast 176–82, 186–87
Profit Volume Inputs schedule 171–72
public utilities 44–45
PV function 12, 47

Q–R

Quick Ratio 280–81
RATE function 104, 110, 117, 125
Receivables Turnover 281–82

reference names 302–3
Return on Equity 284
Return on Total Assets 283

S

Sales Commissions variable 171, 174, 178
sales and cost of sales (SALESRPT.XLS) template 3, 143–61
 contents and functions of 145–57
 customizing 157
 entering data into 155–56
 linking to other spreadsheets 157–61
 primer on sales and cost of sales forecasting 143–46
 sample spreadsheet *147–48*
 variables 146
Sales Forecast Schedule heading box 149
Sales and Gross Margin Forecast schedule 152–53
Sales Income Tax variable 180
Sales Revenue 257, 268, 272
Sales Tax variable 171, 174, 178–79
Sales to Operational Assets 283
Salvage Value parameter
 activity depreciation 51, 53
 annuity or sinking fund depreciation 45, 46
 declining-balance depreciation 20, 22–23, *29*
 straight-line depreciation 14, 15–16
 sum-of-the-years'-digits depreciation 34, 35
Scatter charts *196*
Specified Return parameter, annuity or sinking fund depreciation 45, 46
State Income Tax variable 171
Straight-Line Conversion Depreciation Schedule 30–32
Straight-Line Depreciation Calculation Inputs schedule 15–16

Straight-Line Depreciation Schedule 16–18, 26–28, 39–42
straight-line depreciation (STRAIGHT.XLS) template 2, 9, 10, 14–20
  contents and functions of 14–18
  customizing 19–20
  entering data into 19
  linked to COSTSRPT.XLS 139–41
  linked to FACTORY.XLS spreadsheet 57–59
  parameters 14
  sample spreadsheet *15*
Sum-of-the-Years'-Digits Calculation Inputs schedule 36
Sum-of-the-Years'-Digits Depreciation schedule 36–39
sum-of-the-years'-digits depreciation (SUMYEARS.XLS) template 2, 9, 11
  contents and functions 34–42
  customizing 43
  entering data into 42–43
  express estimated life in integer format 42
  parameters 34
  sample spreadsheet *35*

T
taxes
  capital gains 202
  declining balance depreciation and 10–11
  profit volume analysis, and federal and state 165–68, 171, 180, 181
Times Interest Earned 282–83
Total Assets 262, 266–67
Total Cost of Sales 152–53
Total Current Assets 259–60
Total Current Liabilities 263

Total Liabilities and Owner Equity 265, 267
Total Noncurrent Liabilities 264–65
Total Operating Expenses 210–11, 268–69
Total Payment column
  fixed rate, annuity due template 83–84
  fixed rate, ordinary annuity template 66
  variable rate, annuity due template 93–94
  variable rate, ordinary annuity template 74–75
Total Production/Purchase Costs 150
Total Sales 152, 173, 176–77
Total Variable Costs variable 175, 179, 183
Total Vary-with-Profit Costs variable 181
Transaction/Disposal Costs 209, 213, 217
True Balance
  fixed rate, annuity due template 88
  fixed rate, ordinary annuity template 69–70
  variable rate, annuity due template 98
  variable rate, ordinary annuity template 79

U–Y
Unit Sales Price variable 146
Unit Sales variable 146, 171
Units Produced/Purchased variable 146, 154
Units Sold 154
U.S. Treasury Internal Revenue Service Schedule C 136
Variable Interest Rate, Annuity Due Amortization Inputs 92
Variable Interest Rate, Annuity Due Amortization Schedule 92–97

variable interest rate, annuity due (VARIDUE.XLS) template 2, 61, 90–99
  balances from beginning or end of payment period 96
  contents and functions 92–98
  customizing 99
  entering data into 98
  parameters 90, 92
  sample spreadsheet *91*
variable interest rate, ordinary annuity (VARIRATE.XLS) template 2, 61, 71–80
  contents and functions 73–79
  customizing 80
  entering data into 79
  sample spreadsheet *72*
Variable Interest Rate Amortization Inputs schedule 73
Variable Interest Rate Amortization Schedule 74–78
Volume in Units 173, 176
Weighted Average Unit Cost 151
Window Show Info command *304*
Working Capital to Total Assets 281
Yield on Cash & Equivalents 253

Stephen L. Nelson

A CPA and former senior consultant to Arthur Andersen & Co., Stephen L. Nelson has written for *Inc.* and *Lotus* magazines and has conducted a series of financial modeling workshops. Nelson holds an MBA from the University of Washington.

The manuscript for this book was prepared and submitted to Microsoft Press in electronic form. Text files were processed and formatted using Microsoft Word.

Cover design by Becker Design Associates
Photography by Studio 3, Inc.
Interior text design by Darcie S. Furlan
Principal typography by Ruth Pettis
Color separations by Wescan Color Corp.

Text composition by Microsoft Press in Times Roman with display in Times Roman Bold, using the Magna composition system and the Linotronic 300 laser imagesetter.